THE PURPLE ONE

American Made
Music Series

THE PURPLE ONE

Prince, Race, Gender, and Everything in Between

Edited by Judson L. Jeffries,
Shannon M. Cochran, and Molly Reinhoudt

University Press of Mississippi / Jackson

The University Press of Mississippi is the scholarly publishing agency of the Mississippi Institutions of Higher Learning: Alcorn State University, Delta State University, Jackson State University, Mississippi State University, Mississippi University for Women, Mississippi Valley State University, University of Mississippi, and University of Southern Mississippi.

www.upress.state.ms.us

The University Press of Mississippi is a member of the Association of University Presses.

"The Prince of Gotham: Prince's Multifaceted Batman Project," by Laurel Westrup and Paul N. Reinsch (chapter 7) was originally published in *Spectrum: A Journal on Black Men* 7, no. 2 (2020): 111–32.

∞

Library of Congress Control Number: 2024944765
Hardback ISBN 978-1-4968-5388-2
Trade paperback ISBN 978-1-4968-5389-9
Epub single ISBN 978-1-4968-5390-5
Epub institutional ISBN 978-1-4968-5391-2
PDF single ISBN 978-1-4968-5392-9
PDF institutional ISBN 978-1-4968-5393-6

British Library Cataloging-in-Publication Data available

CONTENTS

THE PURPLE ONE

INTRODUCTION

While universal agreement exists on the importance of Prince as a music icon, few scholars or other writers have in any substantive and in-depth manner explained or put into context his unique impact or the roots of the ideas expressed in his work. Volume 2 of PrincEnlighTenmenT features two themes. The first theme, "Black Masculinity and Gender Performativity," opens with Zada Johnson's exploration of Black masculinity in Prince's cult classic *Under the Cherry Moon*. This chapter examines the way that Prince's performance challenges typical cinema stereotypes of Black men and reimagines representations of Black masculinity. Johnson argues that Prince's performance as gigolo, Christopher Tracey, rescripts Black masculinity through representations of Black vernacular idioms and visual representation. Chapter 2 then moves into a discussion of the onscreen father-son relationship in Prince's first film, *Purple Rain*, in Sherman M. White, Aaron J. Kimble, and Jerod Lockhart's contribution, that in some ways speaks to many contemporary relationships between African American fathers and their sons. Indeed White, Kimble, and Lockhart's candid approach to this topic is moving, as each of the three men takes the opportunity to tease out elements in the film that resonate with their own lived experiences. Readers learn as much about the writers of this chapter, as they do about the subject being explored. Chapter 3 closes the theme with Shannon M. Cochran's chapter, "Educating to Empower: Gender Performativity Pedagogy Using the Artistry of Prince and Sheila E." Especially instructive is the manner in which Cochran demonstrates how using the artistry of Prince and Sheila E. in the classroom can be an especially effective teaching tool. The section ends with an interview with Prince's youth basketball coach.

"Beauty, Race, and Spirituality," Part II, begins with chapter 5, Cassandra D. Chaney's examination of Prince's "challenging of European standards of beauty" through the women depicted in his video "The Most Beautiful Girl in the World." A close read of this chapter alongside viewing the video will give readers insight into widely discussed beliefs and debates within the

African American community about the kinds of features and attributes that constitute beauty, including but not limited to colorism, hair texture and body type. In chapter 6 Tony Kiene moves to a case study of Prince to examine "urban rage, protest, subversion, and contempt" in his music and artistry. Few artists touched on as many pressing social ills in their music in as clever, innovative, and timely manner as did Prince. The messages in Prince's music are as timely today as they were in previous decades. In chapter 7 Laurel Westrup and Paul N. Reinsch delve into the various aspects of Prince's Batman project, from the motion picture soundtrack to five singles (with remixes and B-sides) and finally a loosely related comic book. Samuel Fitzpatrick's essay concludes the volume with an exploration of one of Prince's protégées, Denise Matthews, aka Vanity of Vanity 6. Easily, the most controversial girl band of their era, Vanity 6's style was not only appropriated by Madonna but served as the inspiration for other female groups.

In no other text has any author explored the topics herein in the manner in which they are tackled by the contributors to this volume. What these authors demonstrate is that the questions central to understanding Prince's work do not lend themselves to exploration within the narrow confines of traditional biography. It is not surprising, then, that while several biographies of Prince now exist, they have been less than impressive about probing and/ or resolving the many intricate and nuanced facets about this cultural icon.

Part I

Black Masculinity and
Gender Performativity

Chapter 1

CHRISTOPHER TRACY'S PARADE

Re-Scripting Black Masculinity in Prince's *Under the Cherry Moon*

ZADA JOHNSON

In the year following the blockbuster success of *Purple Rain*, Prince began working on his second film project entitled *Under the Cherry Moon*, a tribute to classic black-and-white 1930s romantic comedies such as *Swing Time* and *Top Hat*.[1] Filmed on the French Riviera, *Under the Cherry Moon* tells the story of Christopher Tracy, a brash nightclub pianist and gigolo who seduces rich women with the assistance of his best friend and sidekick Tricky (played by Time band member Jerome Benton). In the film Christopher plans to ensnare a young heiress, Mary Sharon, who is destined to inherit fifty million dollars on her twenty-first birthday. However, the two fall madly in love and are faced with confronting Mary's staunchly disapproving father. While *Under the Cherry Moon* tanked at the box office and only enjoyed cult classic popularity among Prince's diehard fans, the film offers a fascinating look into Prince's interpretations (and reinterpretations) of Black masculinity during that time.

The most significant representations of Black masculinity in *Under the Cherry Moon* can be found in Prince's portrayal of Christopher Tracy. While he played the Kid character from *Purple Rain* as somewhat racially ambiguous and enigmatic, Prince's portrayal of Christopher is a more pronounced confluence of African American vernacular culture, Black dandyism, and Black male sexual agency. Subsequently, Prince's performance of Christopher reimagines the representations of Black masculinity

that were emerging in 1980s popular American cinema. Where representations of Black masculinity in movies like *The Color Purple, Beverly
Hills Cop*, and *Krush Groove* were anchored in stereotypes of domestic
abuse, hypermasculinity, aggression, and urban blight, Prince's portrayal
of Christopher Tracy created an alternate space for Black masculinity to
be rescripted and redefined.

This essay examines the way that Prince's performance of the Christopher character challenges common film stereotypes of Black men and
reimagines representations of Black masculinity. Drawing from the literature on Black masculinity and representation, this essay investigates the
way that Prince creates alternate masculinities through *Under the Cherry
Moon*'s dramatic performance as well as the film's musical performances.[2]
Building specifically from Ronald Jackson II's model of the scripting and
rescripting of Black masculine identities in American popular culture, I
argue that Prince's performance of Christopher Tracy rescripts Black masculinity through representations of African American vernacular idioms
and visual representation.[3]

The first part of the essay, "'Once Upon a Time in France . . .': *Under
the Cherry Moon*'s Rescripting of Black Masculinity" examines the way
that Prince uses African American vernacular dialogue and other cultural idioms to signal Christopher as a Black male character. This section
also examines the way that the film's international setting and the Black
dandy–style wardrobe of Christopher and Tricky rescripted the common
stereotypical representations of 1980s Black male characters. The second
part of the essay, "'Meet Me in Another World, Space and Joy': Rescripting Black Masculinity in the Performances and Soundtrack of *Under the
Cherry Moon*" explores the musical performances of the film including
Christopher's opening piano scene, Christopher and Tricky's performance of "Girls and Boys" and Prince and the Revolution's performance
of "Mountains" at the end of the film. Together with the accompanying
songs from *Parade*, this section examines the way that the performances
of the film and music from the soundtrack further reinforce the rescripting of Black masculinity.

The conclusion examines the alternate Black masculinities that *Under the
Cherry Moon* presents in the broader context of the continued struggle to put
nonconformist, multidimensional representations of Black male characters
on the big screen. This section also explores Prince's discussion of *Under the
Cherry Moon* with Detroit DJ Electrifying Mojo as well as past and present
criticisms of the film that reflect the very racial stereotypes that the film
aimed to dispel.

"ONCE UPON A TIME IN FRANCE . . .": *UNDER THE CHERRY MOON*'S RESCRIPTING OF BLACK MASCULINITY

Prince's scripting of Black masculinity in *Under the Cherry Moon* is most apparent in his use of African American vernacular references as well as the visual representation of the film. Through African American vernacular dialogue and Black cultural references, Prince racially scripts the Christopher character as an African American male, a distinction more defined in this film than the Kid character in *Purple Rain*. In addition to African American vernacular dialogue, Prince also uses the visual representation of the French Riviera as well as the visual aesthetics of the Christopher and Tricky characters to rescript the common African American male stereotypes that existed in film during that time. Prince's rescripting practices reflect Ronald Jackson II's model of Black bodies as discursive texts that can be rewritten to subvert the racialized stereotypes that have been inscribed upon them by white dominant culture.[4]

In the opening scenes of *Under the Cherry Moon*, the audience is immediately introduced to the film's main character, Christopher Tracy, playing the piano in a French piano bar. "Once upon a time in France there lived a bad boy named Christopher" a narrator's voice begins, and then follows up with a description of Christopher's desire for women and money. As the scene continues, Christopher woos an attractive female patron in the club with his piano playing, encouraged by his sidekick, Tricky. By the end of Christopher's performance, the woman (who is later identified as Mrs. Wellington, a wealthy divorcee) has left a wad of bills behind at her seat to arrange a meeting with him. After their meeting later that evening, Christopher makes his way back to his apartment with Tricky the next morning, greeting various passersby on his way home. It is within the characterization of these scenes that we learn of Christopher and Tricky's hustling lifestyle as gigolos on the French Riviera. They are young Black men from the United States, who somehow ended up in France and make their living working at an upscale piano bar while cavorting with wealthy women.

Along with establishing the status and motivation of Christopher, these scenes also work to script the Black male cultural identity of the character. Following Jackson's model of the Black male body as a site for discursive messages to be scripted, Prince uses both verbal and nonverbal cues to script Christopher Tracy as an African American male.[5] At the beginning of the film, when Christopher is returning home from a romantic interlude with Mrs. Wellington, he is greeted by a group of neighborhood boys running with a basketball who immediately ask him for money when they see him. In what appears to be a routine exchange between Christopher and the boys, he hands money to each one but asks, "When y'all gone get jobs?" "I got a job, why don't y'all get a job?" he continues as he takes the ball and dribbles while he walks. He then quips, "It's a dishonest job, but still it's a job," while he passes the ball back to the boys. After his exchange with the boys, he continues to walk with swagger (a walking style commonly attributed to African American men as walking with a "bop" or "pimp walking") down the street as he swipes an apple out of the bag of a market shopper, and flirts with a Black French woman purchasing flowers. As he arrives at his apartment building, he greets the French server of the adjoining cafe with "What's up?" and struts into the front door.

Collectively, the gestures and dialogue of these scenes illustrate Jackson's discussion of the process of scripting or assigning various social and cultural meanings to the Black male body.[6] In the case of Christopher Tracy, Prince uses African American vernacular patterns ("when y'all gone get jobs?" "what's up?") to signal the character's racial identity as a Black male. The African American identity of Christopher Tracy is also scripted in the nonverbal cues of Christopher's walk as well as his handling of the basketball as he talks with the young boys from his neighborhood. In this case the nonverbal cues of walking swagger and skill with a basketball (commonly performed by and associated with African American men) are applied to Christopher as additional signifiers of African American male identity.

Prince's use of African American vernacular traditions to shape the Christopher character continues throughout the film, particularly in the scenes that depict his courtship of Mary Sharon. Similar to the black-and-white romantic comedies of the 1930s, Christopher and Mary initially clash when they meet. At the core of their opposition is their contrasting socioeconomic backgrounds: Mary a young heiress from one of the richest families on the Cote d'Azur, and Christopher a hustler from Miami. This difference is often represented in the contrast between Mary's use of standard English and Christopher's code switching between standard English and African American vernacular forms. For example, when Mary has Christopher and Tricky thrown out for crashing her birthday party, Christopher describes her as having no "home training" ("Man, forget it, that girl ain't got no home training"), an African American vernacular phrase often used to refer to people with no manners. When Mary has her father's security guards forcefully remove Christopher and Tricky from her party ("Remove this peasant from my property, I'm having trouble breathing"), Christopher replies, "Well maybe if you took off your chastity belt you could breathe a little mo' better."

In one of the most memorable scenes from the film, Christopher challenges Mary to define the meaning of a phrase he writes on a napkin

("Wrecka Stow") while they are in an upscale restaurant. After much consternation, Mary realizes that the phrase is an African American vernacular idiom for "record store" ("If you wanted to buy a Sam Cooke album, where would you go . . . the wrecka stow"). During their first rendezvous, when Christopher asks Mary why her wealthy father "shits on so many people," she responds by calling him a peasant as she did when they first met. In response, Christopher uses racial references and African American vernacular forms as he boasts about being a better lover than her rich fiancé ("[kissing me] is a little different than it is with your rich boyfriend, ain't it Mama"). He then speculates on the ways Mary would respond to him sexually ("you're probably real quiet at first . . . then you get loud . . . and then you get Black—'oh shit, Christopher shit, oh baby, oh Lord'").

The African American vernacular forms and cultural references that frame the Christopher character illustrate Jackson's discussion of the way that Black men themselves can use the process of inscription to script and rescript expressions of Black male identity and masculinity.[7] As Jackson and Hopson point out, media and popular culture performances have historically inscribed various racial meanings to bodily texts, particularly the Black male body.[8] For the most part, these inscriptions have reinforced the common stereotypical representations of Black men as "dangerous, anti-intellectual, reckless, incompetent, uneducated criminal delinquents, deadbeat dads, incarcerated felons and/or entertainers and athletes."[9] However, the process of inscription can also be used by subjects themselves to redefine the meanings that have been ascribed to them. In the case of Christopher, it appears that African American vernacular and cultural references are intentionally inscribed upon the character to signal an African American racial identity. Perhaps in response to the racial ambiguity of the autobiographical Kid character in *Purple Rain* as well as Prince's own performed racial ambiguity in his early career, the repeated vernacular and cultural referents scripted onto Christopher establish him as a Black male character.

These vernacular and cultural referents are also used to dismantle representations of social hierarchy and elitism in the film. This is illustrated in his greeting of "What's up?" to the formally dressed maitre d' in the beginning of the film as well as the numerous vernacular quips launched at Mary's descriptions of him as a "peasant." In these cases, Prince's use of African American vernacular forms not only scripts the Christopher character as an African American male but is also deployed to subvert representations of social hierarchy and elitist privilege.

Along with African American vernacular and cultural references, the visual representation of *Under the Cherry Moon* is another place where rescripting of Black masculinity takes place. Filmed on the French Riviera (Cote d'Azur), *Under the Cherry Moon* is filled with numerous shots of the scenic French Mediterranean coastline as well as locations within the city of Nice that accompany the film's overall narrative. More than just a backdrop of the film, the Cote d'Azur location of *Under the Cherry Moon* also provides an alternate narrative through which the characters of Christopher and Tricky are rescripted as Black male protagonists.

At the time that *Under the Cherry Moon* was filmed in 1985, the Hollywood movies that featured Black male characters were likely confined to either rural or urban American settings and also confined to stereotypical portrayals of Black men. In movies like *The Color Purple*, Black male characters were not only confined to the rural settings of the American South, but also largely confined to representations as violent abusers of women. Conversely, in the early hip hop movies that were becoming popular in the 1980s (*Beat Street, Breakin', Wild Style*), Black males were often confined to roles as street-savvy protagonists struggling as artists/dancers to overcome urban blight. In comedies like *Trading Places, Beverly Hills Cop, Stir Crazy,* and *Brewster's Millions*, the Black male characters portrayed by Eddie Murphy and Richard Pryor showcased their comedic skills, but otherwise sexually neutralized them when it came to relationships with female characters, particularly white women.

In contrast to these portrayals in these movies, *Under the Cherry Moon's* placement of Christopher and Tricky on the French Riviera extends them beyond the usual characterization of Black male characters at that time, providing an opportunity for stereotypical representations of Black masculinity to be rescripted. As street-smart hustlers from Miami, the Christopher and Tricky characters contain similar backgrounds as many of the Black male characters in other movies of the time; however, the international setting of *Under the Cherry Moon* gives Christopher and Tricky a dimension of agency and worldliness that their counterparts in other movies don't seem to possess. In this regard, Christopher and Tricky's world travel and movement through Cote d'Azur society are reminiscent of the agency demonstrated by African American artists who expatriated to Paris during the early to midtwentieth century in search of racial quality and artistic freedom.

While race or racism is never overtly mentioned in *Under the Cherry Moon*, the movement of both the Christopher and Tricky characters through the multiethnic Cote d'Azur society and their frequent involvement with white women imply a type of freedom that the Black male characters of other 1980s films don't possess. In this case, the absence of overt references to race and racism in the film imply an effort to transcend the racialized stereotypes of typical Black male characterization. That is not to say, however, that the film is without racial undertones. The ultimate demise of Christopher upon the orders of Mary's wealthy father vaguely recalls the violence enacted on Black men for associating with white women in American society. However, Mary's rejection of her father after the death of Christopher and decision to take her money to start a real estate business in Miami with Tricky suggests a denouncement of her father's elitism/racism.

In addition to the film's French Riviera setting, the overall visual presentation of Christopher and Tricky is also a primary site for rescripting Black masculinity. Throughout the film, both Christopher and Tricky are often finely attired in sequined satin and lace suit ensembles accessorized with luxury watches, cuff links, and gold jewelry. The highly stylized dandyish wardrobe of Christopher and Tricky stands in stark contrast to the representations of Black male hypermasculinity in other movies of the early to mid-1980s. Where other Black male characters are commonly wardrobed in standard menswear, overalls, military uniforms (*The Color Purple*, *A Soldier's Story*) or hip hop–inspired street styles (*Krush Groove*, *Breakin'*, *Beat Street*), the sequin and lace ensembles of Christopher and Tricky push beyond conformist notions of Black male masculinity as well as stereotypes of hypermasculinity, opening up new spaces for Black masculinity to be rescripted and therefore redefined.

The rescripting of Black masculinity through representations of dress and visual appearance was not a new endeavor for Prince in the 1980s. Since the beginning of his career in the late seventies, Prince was frequently known to push the boundaries of gender and masculinity conformity, often performing in g-string underwear, knee-high boots and facial makeup. His visual presentation of studded trench coats, Edwardian collars, and Cuban heels in *Purple Rain* is a further testament to challenging mainstream notions of Black masculinity through corporeal rescripting. Along these same lines, the visual representation of *Under the Cherry Moon* challenges the boundaries of gender and masculinity conformity, particularly the stereotypes of Black hypermasculinity that were often portrayed in Black male characters in 1980s film.

This is illustrated in the closeup shot of the Christopher's reclining body that occurs shortly after the opening montage of the film. The morning following his rendezvous with Mrs. Wellington, Christopher is lounging in a grotto along the French Mediterranean coast. The scene opens with a closeup of Christopher's outstretched body as he is writing in his journal. As the camera moves slowly from Christopher's legs to face, the shot reveals his sequined high-heeled boots, matching sequined pants and white ruffled poet's shirt with jeweled cufflinks. From here, the scene cuts to Mrs.

Wellington in bed, waking up to Christopher's smiley-faced note to call him later. Back at the grotto, Christopher finishes writing his journal note and leaves it behind, another closeup shows that the note says, "Goodness will guide me when love is inside me, until then life's a parade! C. Tracy."

From his immediate representation in this long shot, Christopher's wardrobe and his activity both rescript him as a Black male character. His sequined high-heeled boots and matching pants along with his ruffled poet's shirt are a stark contrast to the way Black male characters were wardrobed in 1980s movies (aside from *Purple Rain*). While this ensemble is not usually perceived as a hetero-masculine wardrobe, Prince challenges these understandings by pairing the wardrobe with the otherwise heterosexual pursuits of the character (being a gigolo for women/cavorting with Mrs. Wellington). In addition to his wardrobe, Christopher's activities of leaving a love note behind for the woman he is involved with as well as journaling his thoughts on love and life also rescript the stereotypical hypermasculine and aggressive portrayals of Black male characters. In *Hollywood Black*, film historian Donald Bogle refers to these stereotypes as a culmination of "Hollywood's ongoing fear of strong, sexual, romantic African American men."[10] However, through his wardrobe and actions within this scene Christopher is presented as romantic, artistic, creative, and introspective—a combination of characteristics that were not commonly attributed to Black male characters of that time.

The visual representations of *Under the Cherry Moon* also seem to be directly pointed at challenging the elitist class, particularly as they are represented through the character Isaac Sharon, Mary's wealthy father. Similar to the way that Christopher's usage of African American vernacular often subverted Mary's elitist privilege, his overall visual representation as a character, including his style of dress, appear to challenge the elitist domination and marginalization implied in Isaac Sharon's character. This is illustrated in the scene where Christopher and Tricky are getting dressed to meet Mary at an upscale restaurant and discussing Isaac Sharon's affair with one of Christopher's clients, Mrs. Wellington. As he gets dressed in a tuxedo, he looks in the mirror and tells Tricky ". . . what's good enough for Isaac Sharon is even better for me."

Interestingly, this is one of the few moments in the film where Christopher is dressed in mainstream formal menswear. Here, it seems his visual representation of getting dressed in formal wear as he declares that he is entitled to whatever is "good enough" for Isaac Sharon symbolically challenges Isaac Sharon's elitist domination and marginalization. Earlier in the film, Christopher describes Isaac as "being worth a billion, and he kicked a billion asses to get it too," implying the domination and marginalization of Isaac's elite status. Declaring that he is entitled to whatever is "good enough" for Isaac

Sharon while staring at his reflection dressed in a tuxedo also reinforces his claim that he is just as worthy as Isaac Sharon despite his social status.

During his rendezvous with Mary, Christopher is dressed in perhaps one of the most elaborate ensembles of the film, a sheer lace crop-topped suit embellished with pearls, fringes and sequins. It is in this ensemble that Christopher has his first romantic interactions with Mary and also in this ensemble that he has his first direct confrontation with Isaac Sharon. After their romantic interlude and subsequent argument, Christopher goes to a pay phone to call Isaac Sharon and taunt him about being with his daughter. He also taunts Isaac about Mrs. Wellington, who is laying next to Isaac in bed while he is on the phone ("Get your ass out of that bed, you know them is my draws"). Christopher goes on to tell Isaac, "You rich folks are always taking from people like me. And, that says what? That says now I'm going to take something from you," referring to his plan to wed Mary. Christopher's verbal confrontation with Isaac is reinforced by the contrasting visual representation of his lace and pearl ensemble. In this case, his dandy-like appearance emphasizes his nonconformist challenge to take something from the elitist class and even the score between "people like him" and "people like Isaac Sharon."

In her discussion of Black dandyism as a social phenomenon, Shantrelle Lewis argues that "the Black dandy is deliberate in his use of the Black body to express not only his individualism, but also his relationship to his own community and to mainstream culture, challenging negative perceptions of what he is capable of doing and being."[11] She further notes that the colorful style and material finery of Black dandies are an intentional effort of "appropriating the outward and highly specific signs of class, culture, wealth, education and status" to make his own statements about masculinity and self-worth.[12] Lewis's definition of the Black dandy is exemplified in the visual aesthetics of Christopher, not only when he is dressed in colorful style but also when he is dressed in mainstream formal wear. In both cases, Christopher's visual appearance rails against the confinement of gender conformity as well as the negative perceptions and stereotypes of Black masculinity by presenting its own alternate narratives about the character's entitlement and self-worth. Along the same lines as the traditional Black dandies Lewis discusses, the dandy-like representation of Christopher and Tricky intentionally appropriates both traditional and nonconformist signs of class, wealth, and status to create alternative perspectives of Black male identity and masculinity.

Together, Prince's use of African American vernacular dialogue and visual representations in *Under the Cherry Moon*, primarily with the Christopher character, provides valuable insight into the ways that he rescripts representations of Black male identity and masculinity. Through African American vernacular and cultural referents, Prince establishes Christopher as a Black male character in ways that are more defined than his previous role of The Kid in *Purple Rain* and more defined than the somewhat racially ambiguous persona of his seventies/early eighties musical career. By establishing the character as an African American male, *Under the Cherry Moon* opens both a representational and ideological space to rescript Black male identity and masculinity. African American vernacular forms are also a key site in which the Christopher character challenges the elitist class hierarchies represented in the Mary and Issac Sharon characters.

The film further builds upon the representation of Christopher and Tricky as African American males by placing them in the setting of the Cote d'Azur. In this case, the setting of the film rescripts the stereotypical representations of Black male characters in the movies of that time by incorporating elements of cosmopolitan worldliness and agency. In contrast to the Black male characters of films like *The Color Purple*, *Krush Groove*, and *Beat Street*, the characterization of Christopher and Tricky pushes beyond the common stereotypes of Black men trapped in urban/rural American settings of cyclical abuse, hypermasculine aggression, and urban blight. Finally, the Black dandy–inspired visual representation of both Christopher and Tricky's wardrobe in the film makes its own rescripted statements about Black male identity and masculinity. In this case the sequined satin and lace ensembles of both characters challenge confining stereotypes of Black male hypermasculinity while also subverting the representations of elitist hierarchy and domination within the film.

"MEET ME IN ANOTHER WORLD, SPACE AND JOY": RESCRIPTING BLACK MASCULINITY IN THE PERFORMANCES AND SOUNDTRACK OF *UNDER THE CHERRY MOON*

In addition to the vernacular dialogue and visual representation of the film, the accompanying performances and soundtrack of *Under the Cherry Moon* also offer insight into the ways in which Prince utilized this project to rescript representations of Black male identity and masculinity. Unlike *Purple Rain*, the performances in *Under the Cherry Moon* are fairly sparse, but they still illustrate a reimagining of Black masculinity that is different from typical Black male character stereotypes. Through these performances and the accompanying songs of the soundtrack, we are able to see representations of a cosmopolitan Black male agency and expressive sexuality that was otherwise not afforded to Black male characters of the time. These representations are an interesting contrast in the common stereotypes that Ronald Jackson outlines in his discussion of racial scripts that have been historically associated with the male body (exotic/strange, violent, incompetent/uneducated, exploitable, and innately incapacitated).[13] Instead, the performances and soundtrack of *Under the Cherry Moon* reconfigure these scripts in some cases and directly challenge them in others, presenting new narratives in which the complexities of Black masculinity can be better understood.

From the first musical performance of *Under the Cherry Moon*, the audience is immediately introduced to a representation of cosmopolitan Black male agency that continues throughout the film. In the opening performance, Christopher is wrapping up the final chords of "Under the Cherry Moon" from the film's soundtrack as Mrs. Wellington walks into the bar. Later in the film, we learn that Christopher plays at the piano bar in the Venus de Milo, a fictional French luxury hotel catering to wealthy patrons on the Cote d'Azur. After his toast to the crowd ("Enchanté, the more you drink, the better I sound") he plays an instrumental version of "An Honest Man," a track that he wrote during the time of developing the film that did not make the *Parade* album but is later featured with lyrics on the *Crystal Ball* album. During his performance, he openly flirts with Mrs. Wellington, trading seductive glances with her while he plays. By the end of the performance he has won Mrs. Wellington's affection, and a monetary offer from her for his gigolo services that she leaves behind at her table.

Christopher's opening piano performance at the Venus de Milo establishes his character as a cosmopolitan and worldly figure against the international setting of the French Riviera. In the same way that the wardrobing of the character in expensive sequins, fringes, and ruffles creates a contrasting image to the historical stereotype of Black men as unrefined brutes, the representation of Christopher as an accomplished piano player in a luxury hotel piano bar on the French Mediterranean coast implies a sense of agency, skill, and movement that was not usually ascribed to Black male characters. The cosmopolitan Black male representation of Christopher Tracy's character is further implied by his working knowledge of French (as illustrated by his toast, his understanding of the French waitress who delivers Tricky's messages and later in the film he and Tricky read a French newspaper together) as well as the command he displays during his piano performance while simultaneously flirting with Mrs. Wellington.

The exchanges that take place during Christopher's performance of "An Honest Man" seemingly recalls Jackson's discussion of the way that Black male bodies are often inscribed with exotified and hypersexualized scripts that subsequently render them inferior to white bodies. However, the agency through which Christopher presents his sexualized behavior during this performance suggests that he is reconfiguring the typical inscriptions of Black male exotification and hypersexualization. Throughout the course of his nonverbal interactions with Mrs. Wellington, it is Christopher who is in control, leading their exchanges with his skilled piano playing. In the place of a superficial exotification and/or hypersexualization of the character, these exchanges demonstrate a reconfigured representation of Black male sexual agency. While his placement on the Cote d'Azur and eccentric dress do in fact exotify him to a certain extent, this seems to be countered with displays of control and command over the circumstances of his situation.

It is also interesting to note the single stanza lyrics of "An Honest Man" ("I want 2 be an honest man / I'll be your slave just understand / . . . With U I can be an honest man") in the context of the Christopher character. Though they are not featured in his piano performance, they do appear in a love letter that Christopher writes to Mary once he realizes he wants to pursue a committed relationship with her. Combined with the nonverbal seduction that takes place between Christopher and Mrs. Wellington, the lyrical premise of the song further adds dimensions of passion and romanticism. The impassioned lyrics associated with the song Christopher is playing during this scene is a contrast to stereotypical portrayals of Black male characters as incompetent, emotionally dysfunctional brutes who are incapable of romantic passion and affection. This is not to say the representation of Christopher as romantic figure is without its limitations. His status as a gigolo complicates an understanding of whether or not his intentions of romance are sincere. However, this is countered with the overall plot arc of Christopher eventually falling in love and seeking the type of committed romantic relationship that the lyrics of "An Honest Man" implies.

Along the same lines as the cosmopolitan Black male agency that is embodied in the Christopher character are two very brief performances by Mary and Tricky that take place at her twenty-first birthday party. In the scene where she greets her party guests wrapped in a sheet to eventually reveal her "birthday suit," Mary takes over for the drummer of the live band for a rendition of Afrika Bambaataa's hip hop classic "Planet Rock." The inclusion of a performance of "Planet Rock" at Mary's upscale birthday party signals the cosmopolitan reach of Black music to international and upper-class audiences. This reach also implies the cosmopolitan agency of the Black male artists including Afrika Bambaataa (and Prince, as well as Black jazz musicians from the previous generation) who performed in global markets, making their music known worldwide.

Similar expressions of cosmopolitan agency are implied when Tricky organizes a conga line (an African-derived dance form) at Mary's party, leading the procession of wealthy guests around the grounds of the Sharon estate and eventually pulling Mary in to join the line of revelers. The presence of the conga line at Mary's upscale birthday party, and Tricky's leadership in organizing it, are also signs of the cosmopolitan presence of Black musical and dance forms among upper-class audiences. Tricky's leadership in organizing the conga line illustrates his skill and subsequent agency as a Black male character who can move comfortably through diverse social spaces. Together with similar representations of cosmopolitan agency expressed through the Christopher character, these performances reinforce the alternative narrative of Black masculinity that is presented throughout the film.

In another very brief performance, Christopher plays piano for Mrs. Wellington back at her apartment after they leave together from Mary's birthday party. In this scene, Christopher accompanies the answering machine recording of Isaac Sharon as he interrogates Mrs. Wellington about her whereabouts. In between chords, he comically answers "with me" to Isaac's questions about where Mrs. Wellington has been and "me too" to Isaac's remark about hating her answering machine. When Isaac threatens to kill any man who would rival his affections for Mrs. Wellington, Christopher plays a set of ominous sounding chords on the piano and then feigns an expression of fear. After Issac's message has ended, Christopher plays the last chords of his impromptu performance and then matter-of-factly asks Mrs. Wellington, "He's a little possessive, don't you think?" In this case, Christopher's performance and sardonic banter with Isaac's voice message subverts Isaac's romantic possessiveness over Mrs. Wellington as well as his elitist privilege overall. Christopher's skilled piano playing and quick wit also establish him as a formidable rival to Isaac, signaling that he is not intellectually incapable or inferior.

Perhaps the most memorable performance of the film, Christopher's impromptu performance of "Girls and Boys" at the upscale Le Pavillon restaurant, also exemplifies representations of cosmopolitan Black male agency and Black male sexual agency. Shortly after the "Wrecka Stow" scene, tables are cleared away in the restaurant for ballroom dancing but Christopher and Tricky storm the stage with an oversized boombox. This is all a part of Christopher's plan to "bring Mary Sharon down to our world" and loosen her up from her stuffy elitist persona. Once the music begins, Christopher jumps up on the restaurant's grand piano, does a split and then lays across it seductively as he sings the opening lyrics of the song ("He only knew her for a little while, but he had grown accustomed to her smile"). During the second line of the song ("She had the cutest ass he'd ever seen / He did too they were meant to be") Tricky bends over and smacks his own rear end playfully as he dances on a nearby table.

The performance continues in a lively dance party between the restaurant patrons, Christopher, Tricky, and Mary until Isaac Sharon shows up to retrieve his daughter. Once he arrives, he has his bodyguard destroy Christopher and Tricky's boom box and then calmly orders Mary to come home with him. The scene ends with Mary deciding to leave with her father amid boos from the crowd and Christopher shouting "party poop" at Isaac's control over his daughter. In the same way that the aforementioned performances of the film signal a cosmopolitan Black male agency, Christopher and Tricky's takeover of the upscale restaurant's ballroom dancing audience with their "Girls and Boys" performance further illustrates their skilled ability to move through diverse social spaces. Their ability to replace the restaurant's ballroom dancing time with the boombox-accompanied "Girls and Boys" performance is also a symbolic subversion of the status quo. As Black male characters with cosmopolitan agency, they are not only able to move through diverse social spaces but also able to inscribe their own influences onto these spaces, subverting elitist hierarchies.

The "Girls and Boys" performance also introduces expressions of Black male sexual agency that were not commonly ascribed to Black male characters at that time. As *New York Times* columnist Wesley Morrison points out in *The Last Taboo: Why Pop Culture Just Can't Deal with Black Male Sexuality*, the sexuality of Black male characters was often stifled altogether, that is if they weren't portrayed as sexual aggressors.[14] In "Girls and Boys," performances of both Christopher and Tricky push beyond the stifled sexuality/ sexual aggressor representations by placing the characters in control of their erotic expression. The lyrics of the song tell the story of romantic longing and erotic desire, themes that were not commonly associated with Black male sexuality in 1980s popular film. Christopher's sensuous acting out of these lyrics (laying across the piano while he sings) places him in a position of having control over his own sexual expression. In the verse "she had the cutest ass he ever seen / he did too, they were meant to be," the "he did too" portion of the lyrics celebrates both male beauty and male eroticism. This is underscored by Tricky's sensuous dancing, openly acknowledging his own male beauty and erotic expression.

In the final scenes of *Under the Cherry Moon*, Prince and the Revolution perform "Mountains" from the *Parade* soundtrack over the end credits of the film. As the culminating performance of *Under the Cherry Moon*, "Mountains" pulls the major characters of the film (Prince/Christopher, Tricky,

Mary, Katie) together for a curtain call of sorts while the Revolution plays and dances in the background. The performance of "Mountains" begins with the band descending from the clouds as if to imply that the Christopher character lives on in the afterlife after being shot down by the police at the request of Isaac Sharon. The scenes that follow feature cut-in shots of Mary responding to the lyrics of the song, along with scenes of Tricky and Katy standing together as a couple. There is also a shot of Mary appearing in the reflection of the heart-shaped mirror pin on Prince's jacket, again suggesting the transcendence of Christopher and Mary's love beyond his death. The transcending power of love is further reflected in the note from Christopher's journal that appears in the performance next to a picture of Christopher and Tricky that says "with love there is no death."

In addition to themes of transcendent love in "Mountains," there are also moments of social commentary in the performance. During the lyrics of the second verse ("Once upon a time in a haystack of despair / Happiness is sometimes hard to find / Africa divided, hijack in the air / It's enough to make you wanna loose your mind"), the Revolution performs in front of a huge back drop of letters that read "Africa Divided." In the next scene, two hooded gunmen hold rifles to members of the band, acting out the lyrics about airplanes being hijacked. Referencing the various conflicts that took place in continental Africa during the eighties as well as the numerous airplane hijackings that were occurring around the world, these scenes and their corresponding lyrics address pressing social issues within the context that it is the love of humanity that will ultimately resolve these issues ("But I say it's only mountains and the sea / love will conquer if you just believe").

Themes of transcending love and social commentary in the "Mountains" performance add another layer of dimension to the characterization of Black male characters in *Under the Cherry Moon*. Not only is the Christopher character romantic but he is also concerned with the idea of a love that transcends death as well as the love of all humanity as resolution to the world's pressing social issues. These themes directly challenge the common portrayals of Black men as emotionless brutes as well as the portrayals of Black men as incompetent and uneducated. As an introspective thinker about the possibilities of love, Christopher pushes beyond the standard characterization of Black male characters who were seldom associated with love and romance. In addition, references to current social issues in the performance dispel the stereotype of Black male characters as incompetent and uneducated, portraying them instead as introspective thinkers about the larger world around them.

Along with the performances in *Under the Cherry Moon*, songs from the accompanying soundtrack album *Parade* further reflect the rescripting of Black masculinity that takes place in the film. Similar to the film, African American vernacular forms are used throughout the soundtrack alongside the album's African American musical influences of R&B, blues, funk and jazz. In the album's blues-influenced "Kiss," Prince addresses his would-be love interest as "Mama" while he describes the qualities he likes in a romantic partner ("You can't be too flirty, Mama / I know how to undress me"). Later in the song, he quips, "Act your age, Mama, not your shoe size / Maybe we could do the twirl," referencing an African American idiom ("Act your age, not your shoe size") about behaving maturely. In "AnotherLoverHoleInYoHead," Prince references the African American idiom "like you need a hole in yo head" ("You need another lover like you need a hole in yo head") to challenge his love interest's attempts to leave him. If we accept that the narrative voice in these songs are primarily Christopher's, then the African American vernacular references on the soundtrack further signal his identity as a Black male character. In addition to this, the presence of these idioms combined with the influence of African American musical genres on the album also signal the African American cultural influences of the overall project.

The themes of love that are associated with the Christopher character are expressed in the eponymous "Christopher Tracy's Parade," featuring a lyrical variation of Christopher's note from the grotto scene ("Goodness will guide us if love is inside us"). Representations of romantic love and desire continue in the "Under the Cherry Moon" title track where Prince further explores themes of love and death ("Lovers like us, dear, are born to die / If they don't find us, what we will we do? / I guess we'll make love under the cherry moon / I'll die in your arms under the cherry moon"). Similar to the film, these themes of love establish Christopher as a character who is connected to ideas of love and commitment. As the film eventually reveals, love and commitment become a major motivation for the Christopher character, leading him to abandon his gigolo lifestyle and ultimately sacrifice his life in his pursuit of love.

Also related to themes of love and death, "Sometimes It Snows in April" explores the love and loss of the Christopher character, sung by Prince but expressed in what appears to be the narrative voice of Christopher's best friend, Tricky. In the song, Tricky laments the loss of his friend as he recalls Christopher's brash outlook on life ("He used to say so strong, oh unafraid to die / Unafraid of the death that left me hypnotized / You know staring at his picture I realize / No one could cry the way my Tracy cried"). In this case, the lyrics of "Sometimes It Snows in April" imply yet another dimension of

Black male character types not often portrayed in popular film at that time: the Black male as loving friend to another Black man. This trope appears in several scenes of the film where Tricky expresses his friendship love to Christopher (oftentimes as homoerotic banter). Aside from the friendship between Cochise and Preach in *Cooley High*, the expression of Black male friendship love in *Under the Cherry Moon* and subsequently "Sometimes It Snows in April" is particularly interesting because it is so rarely featured as a dimension of seventies/eighties Black male characterization in film.

In addition to love and commitment there are also tropes of the cosmopolitan Black man in the *Parade* soundtrack. Along with the French phrases infused in the chorus of "Girls and Boys" ("Meet me in another world, space and joy / Vous etes tres belle, Mama, girls and boys"), the album version of the song also includes a female-voiced monologue that repeats some of the song's lyrics in French. The opening of "Do U Lie?" begins with a recording from a French language lesson ("Les enfants qui mentent n'iront pas au paradis" [Children who lie don't go to heaven]). The song also features the instrumental accompaniment of French accordions in the style of French café music. The inclusion of French language as well as French instrumentation on these songs references the cosmopolitan agency of Christopher and Tricky as they move through the diverse cultural society of the Cote d'Azur in the film. In this case, the international dimensions of the music from the soundtrack mirror the worldly knowledge of the film's main characters and their access to international spaces.

Several songs on the soundtrack also reflect the Black male sexual agency that is expressed in the film. As mentioned in the discussion of "Girls and Boys" in the previous section of this essay, the lyrics of these songs underscore the tropes of Black male beauty and Black male erotic expression that proliferate in the film. In "New Position," Prince informs his love interest that they are in need of new sexual adventures to spice up their romantic life ("Got to try a new position, something that'll make it alright / . . . new position / . . . let's go fishing in the river, the river of life"). Later in the song, he assures his love interest that he can make her happy "like a good man should" and make their new sexual adventures "real good" as the background vocals spell out the words "happy" and "pussy." Along the same lines of the film, the themes of sexuality and erotic desire in "New Position" connote a Black male sexual agency that expresses itself freely and on its own terms. In contrast to the often stifled and/or criminalized expression of Black male eroticism in popular culture, the themes of sexuality and desire in both the film and the soundtrack challenge and reimagine the common stereotypes of Black men as sexual deviants.

As key supporting components to the film's narrative, the performances and soundtrack of *Under the Cherry Moon* are an extended expression of the Black masculinity tropes that frame the overall plot. Throughout the performances of *Under the Cherry Moon*, representations of Black masculinity depart from the common stereotypes of the era and are instead rescripted to reinforce themes of social agency, sexual agency, and Black men as equally intelligent/talented as members of elite white society. In the performances that feature Christopher, he is often portrayed as confident, highly skilled, quick-witted, socially minded, erotically charged, and capable of romantic love. As a result, these attributes are a stark contrast from the inscriptions of exotic, violent, uneducated, exploitable, and innately incapacitated that have often characterized Black masculinity both on and offscreen. The "Planet Rock" and conga-line performances of Mary and Tricky further underscore the film's theme of cosmopolitan Black male agency, referencing the worldwide presence of Black male artists such as Afrika Bambaataa (and Prince) while also signaling the social agency that the Christopher and Tricky characters use to move through international spaces.

Critical rescripting of Black masculinity is also present in the Parade soundtrack.[15] In this case, the usage of African American vernacular forms in conjunction with the diverse African American musical influences of the album further establishes Christopher as a Black male character who expresses himself through African American cultural idioms. Likewise, the usage of French language and French-inspired musical instrumentation on the soundtrack references the worldly knowledge of Christopher and Tricky as they interact with the diverse cultural groups of the Cote d'Azur. Lastly, recurring themes of erotic desire, transcendent love, and the friendship love between Tricky and Christopher reinforce the multidimensional expressions of love and desire that Black male characters can simultaneously represent.

CONCLUSION: "SOMETHING TO THINK ABOUT WHEN IT'S OVER"

In a rare 1986 phone interview with Detroit DJ Electrifying Mojo, Prince excitedly discussed the upcoming release of *Under the Cherry Moon* and what he wanted audiences to come away with after viewing it. "There's a message behind it all and I'm hoping people think about it when they leave," he shared with Electrifying Mojo, "That's the main thing, it's a lot of fun, but there's something to think about when it's over." Unfortunately, the response to *Under the Cherry Moon* was not what Prince had hoped; box office numbers paled in comparison to *Purple Rain* and critics were unmerciful in their negative reviews of the film's acting and overall plot. Yet, upon closer inspection of the film's attempts to reconfigure the stereotypical understandings of Black masculinity, there actually is something to think about when it comes to *Under the Cherry Moon*'s ability to put nonconformist and multidimensional Black male characters on the big screen.

In its efforts to present a Black male character steeped in African American vernacular traditions, but still portrayed as confident, worldly, intelligent, and erotic, *Under the Cherry Moon* is actually quite compelling. For those who may only be familiar with Prince's more mainstream performative contexts, this may be a rare moment when Prince's 1980s persona is so closely and clearly associated with African American cultural traditions. Nevertheless, his performance of Christopher as a Black male character is noteworthy in its undertaking to challenge the demeaning and confining stereotypes associated with Black masculinity at that time. Likewise, the overall creative vision of the film to place Black male characters in international surroundings where they are able to subvert social hierarchies of class, race, and privilege is also noteworthy. In this regard, the representations of nonconformist, multidimensional Black male characters in *Under the Cherry Moon* present a unique ideological space for understanding the ways that themes of Black masculinity have been historically constituted and reconstituted in popular culture contexts.

It is not lost on my analysis of the social agency of *Under the Cherry Moon*'s Black male characters that much of this agency is achieved through their interactions with white women. While it would have been nice to see some of the same multidimensional characterization afforded to Black female characters in *Under the Cherry Moon* (there are three minor Black female characters in the film), the response to Black male/white female interactions in the film provides an important site for understanding why what Jackson terms as "liberatory representations" of Black masculinity are so critical in the first place. In his 1986 review, *New York Times* film critic Walter Goodman wrote: "In asking the audience to believe that the womanly Miss Scott-Thomas [Mary] and the lovely Francesca Annis [Mrs. Wellington], as yet another conquest, would have anything to do with a self-caressing twerp of dubious provenance like Chris, 'Under the Cherry Moon' asks rather too much. More convincing is his affection for Jerome Benton [Tricky]. . . ."[16] Similarly, in a 2016 retrospective review, Australian filmmaker Bryn Tilly writes, "And, let's not forget one of the most hideous kisses on screen history when Christopher plants his chimp lips on Mary in the phone booth. . . ."[17]

These racially charged criticisms of Prince's interactions with white female characters illuminate the very racist hierarchies that *Under the Cherry Moon*'s rescripted portrayals of Black masculinity aimed to dismantle. Moreover, the fact that these types of racist perceptions were still very much alive in 2016 reveal the ongoing need to subvert and dismantle these hierarchies. The "message behind it all" that Prince was referring to in his 1986 was probably the film's central theme of love's power to transcend the barriers of class, privilege, and even death. However, in its underlying message of changing the way we think of Black masculinities from debilitated stereotypes to multidimensional human beings, Prince's *Under the Cherry Moon* leaves us with much more to think about as we continue to challenge the hierarchies of representation from both the past and present.

Notes

1. Prince, dir., *Under the Cherry Moon* (Los Angeles: Paramount Pictures, 1986).

2. Ronald Jackson II and Marc Hopson, introduction to *Masculinity in the Black Imagination: Politics of Communicating Race and Manhood*, ed. Ronald Jackson II and M. Hopson (New York: Peter Lang, 2011); Ronald Jackson II, *Scripting the Black Masculine Body: Identity, Discourse, and Racial Politics in Popular Media* (Albany: SUNY Press, 2006); Jared Sexton, *Black Masculinity and the Cinema of Policing* (Cham: Palgrave Macmillan, 2017); Ed Guerrero, *Framing Blackness: The African American Image in Film* (Philadelphia: Temple University Press, 1993); bell hooks, *We Real Cool: Black Men and Masculinity* (New York: Routledge Press, 2004); Manthia Diawara, ed., *Black American Cinema* (New York: Routledge Press, 1993).

3. Jackson and Hopson.

4. Jackson.

5. Jackson.

6. Jackson.

7. Jackson.

8. Jackson and Hopson.

9. Jackson and Hopson, 2.

10. Donald Bogle, *Hollywood Black: The Stars, The Films, The Filmmakers* (New York: Running Press, 2019), 169.

11. Shantrelle Lewis, *Dandy Lion: The Black Dandy and Street Style* (Reading: Aperture Press, 2017), 12–13.

12. Lewis.

13. Jackson.

14. Wesley Morris, "The Last Taboo: Why Pop Culture Just Can't Deal with Black Male Sexuality," *New York Times Magazine*, October 30, 2016. https://www.nytimes.com/interactive/2016/10/30/magazine/black-male-sexuality-last-taboo.html.

15. Prince, *Parade* (Los Angeles: Warner Bros. Records, 1986).

16. Walter, Goodman, "Screen: Prince in 'Cherry Moon,'" *New York Times*, July 3, 1986. https://www.nytimes.com/1986/07/03/movies/screen-prince-in-cherry-moon.html.

17. Bryn Tilly, Under the Cherry Moon," *Cult Projections*, July 8, 2016, http://www.cultprojections.com/deeptrash/under-the-cherry-moon.

Chapter 2

THE AFRICAN AMERICAN FATHER-SON RELATIONSHIP IN *PURPLE RAIN*

A Multigenerational Perspective

SHERMAN M. WHITE, AARON J. KIMBLE, AND JEROD LOCKHART

In the 1984 movie *Purple Rain*, pop icon Prince Rogers Nelson, by his own account, offers viewers a semiautobiographical look at his rise to stardom. Featured prominently throughout the movie is Prince's strained relationship with his father. Although Prince's onscreen relationship with his Dad did not mirror the real-life relationship between father and son, interactions between Prince and Clarence Williams III provide a glimpse into the sometimes complex and dysfunctional dynamic that exists between African American fathers and sons. Some of the challenges African American fathers and sons face are as unfortunate as they are real. Research shows that in an African American household, an absent father is often physically and psychologically removed, which can create an unhealthy and dysfunctional environment for the entire family.[1] The void of an absent father can lead to a lack of social and emotional development in the children; conversely, a father's presence can produce beneficial effects.[2] Patricia A. Thomas, Edythe M. Krampe, and Rae R. Newton state that the influence of the African American father on a son's development is significant.[3]

Like many children, Prince's parents divorced when he was relatively young; essentially, he grew up in a single-parent household with a present father. As depicted in the movie and corroborated outside of the film, his parents' relationship and his relationship with his father was not always healthy and productive, yet he still flourished as a child and young man. The negative effects of parents' divorce and separation can be seen through a child's problem behavior as early as eleven years prior to the family's reorganization.[4] The reality for many children of divorce and separation is that their personal growth and development is stunted and delayed.[5] Some children of divorce and separation carry a variety of problems stemming from the family reorganization well into adulthood.[6] Prince's active adolescence showed a diverse interest in sports and the arts. He was a member of his high school basketball team, and he wrote poetry. Some of his poems became songs. His precociousness and elevated consciousness were mature beyond his years, as illustrated through his communication by way of music and artistry. Though he communicated to the world through his songs and actions, he and his onscreen Dad struggled with their father-son communication. Specifically, the same level of freedom of expression and open lines of communication were not evident between father and son.

As depicted in the movie and corroborated by Prince in subsequent interviews, John Rogers Nelson exerted control in their household. Those who seek to control, even when done inadvertently, can create a barrier to the success of the ones under that control.[7] Ultimately, the movie shows that creativity can be born out of chaos. Denis Dutton and Clifford J. Rogers suggests that genius is like a train coming down the tracks that cannot be stopped.[8] If personal growth and fulfillment can be born out of chaos, success and all its trappings are possible. We suspect that the making of the movie had a much deeper cause and higher meaning: The immensely private Prince, someone who granted few interviews and rarely discussed his family, made a nearly two-hour movie that granted access to not only his artistry but also his personal life. For what reason? We suggest that the movie's purpose was to send a message of hope to a marginalized population of people who may have felt voiceless and powerless and inevitably doomed. This is the genius of Prince. His music was his platform, the movie was his medium; but every aspect of his life, from his sexuality, gender, and race, was transmitted through his artistry. His lyrics were his communications to the world. His words, actions, lifestyle, and ultimately his accomplishments were not merely for the purpose of entertainment or selfish self-expression; it was to inform, enlighten, and uplift. All of it is a message for those who need to receive it.

THEORETICAL FRAMEWORK

The amount of scholarly research related to Prince significantly increased after his passing.[9] Since his passing in April 2016, academia has seen a growing body of scholarly literature featuring his accomplishments as a musician to articles on his race, sexuality, and gender.[10] To our knowledge, there exists no work that examines or discusses in any detail the relationship that Prince had with his father as depicted in the movie, and how that relationship may have influenced his creativity and musical genius.

The movie is strategic and deliberate in its message, and with his fame rising rapidly, Prince knew his message would reach those who might benefit most. Just as he and his band The Revolution belted out the closing number "Baby I'm a Star" in the final scene, the declaration was not prophetic or speaking of what could be; Prince was stating a universally accepted fact.[11] The movie's ending celebrates both the fictional character's success and Prince's real-life status as a megastar. The current research supports the theory that other parallels in the movie exist as it relates to fiction and reality—specifically, the father-son relationship depicted in the film.

Exploratory

Matthew Oware's "Decent Daddy, Imperfect Daddy: Black Male Rap Artists' Views on Fatherhood and the Family" examines the influence of the absentee father, engaged father, and active father in their children's lives.[12] Parenting can be difficult and not necessarily something that is considered second nature for everyone. There is evidence of this in the movie. Oware states that even well-intended African American fathers may fall short more often than they would like when it comes to providing for the social, emotional, and financial needs of their children. There are two possible reasons for this: (a) society's shift from vocational trades training in secondary education to service-oriented jobs and (b) African Americans' need to take more personal responsibility for the neglect they show their families.[13] These two polar opposite positions reflect their thinking of the roles society and one's own self-efficacy play in their social and professional lived experiences.

Nancy J. Holland added a critical article to the body of literature in her examination of how the deconstruction of hierarchical oppositions of good versus evil and male versus female is a direct byproduct of the influence of Prince. Seemingly, everything about Prince is a study in contrasts. The question of what the role of the artist and his work is is answered through the words and actions of the artist.[14] One can easily say that the African American male should right his wrongs; it is a rather reasonable statement to make.[15] As the movie illustrates, relational dynamics can be complex and interwoven with one's experiences. After all, for someone to change oneself, they have to understand specifically what needs to be changed and how to change it so that they may better themselves and the world in which they live.[16]

Autoethnography

Prince, the man and artist, evolved throughout his life and his transformation is evident in his music.[17] Art imitates life, and Prince's music is an accurate reflection of his beliefs, value system, and the personal development he experienced. At the age of forty-three, Prince converted to Jehovah's Witness. After his conversion, he not only toned down some of the suggestive lyrics in his new songs, he edited some of the lyrics from his previously recorded songs.[18] Cassandra D. Chaney's "Prince Rogers Nelson: From 'Dirty Mind' to Devout Jehovah's Witness" examines how Prince's personal growth and development is shown in his lyrics and onstage performances. Personal growth and development are an ongoing process, and it can take place in different environments. Prince showed that growth in the midst of a chaotic environment is possible. Music allows you to simultaneously project and release oneself onto others.[19] As stated earlier, the actions and intent exhibited in the movie should be considered intentional because there are direct parallels from the movie to Prince's personal life.

Deidre T. Guion Peoples examines how the Brewer Optimal Distinctiveness Theory (ODT) and SIT influenced Prince's musicianship.[20] ODT is the simultaneous need to be part of a group while still retaining one's individuality inside of the group. It was known that Prince did not grant many interviews, but his position on this matter changed when he became a Jehovah Witness later in life, suggesting that his connection to his faith was stronger than his individual needs and desires. Prince's decision to provide the world with an up-close look at his childhood, with all the challenges and misfortune coupled with great discoveries that so many others experience, was a tremendous victory for the world.[21] In fact, the ease with which Prince comfortably and confidently moved across multiple social identities was equally important to his vast legion of fans and admirers, as it made the disenfranchised feel as though there was a place for them, a safe place where others understood and accepted them.

Kimberly C. Ransom stated that autoethnography allows the author to explore his/her experiences while allowing the author to explore the experiences of the subject.[22] Likewise, Heewon Chang highlighted that autoethnography is not about focusing on self alone, but about searching for the understanding of others culture/society.[23] Tony E. Adams, Stacy Holman Jones, and Carolyn Ellis identified that autoethnography aims to capture people in the process of figuring out what to do, how to live, and the meaning of their struggles.[24] As such, the author immerses him- or herself into the experiences and life of the subject and ties together commonalities and shared experiences.

Ransom introduces a conceptual falsetto framework (CFF) that resists the societal need to singly classify the Black Childhood Experience (BCE) in one singular vein.[25] This is an important addition to the current literature simply because of the duality that existed in Prince's life, specifically his sexuality. CFF calls for one to imagine a BCE that is unique in its experiences for the individual.[26] Ransom reflected on her experiences as an adolescent turned scholar and the influence Prince had on her social and emotional development. It is here that we look to extend the current body of literature that exists regarding Prince.

What follows is a collaborative autoethnographic exploration, where the writers immerse themselves in the lived experiences of Prince and discuss their BCE and the influence their father-son relationship had on their growth and development in the context of discussing the influence that the father-son relationship as portrayed in the movie may have had on Prince's growth and development. Each of us experienced adolescence in three different decades, seventies, eighties, and nineties, and thus experienced distinctly different relationships with their African American fathers.

Aaron J. Kimble—1990s

Growing up in Opelousas, Louisiana, it took Prince's music a little longer to reach my small, rural town. I was nine years old when I was introduced to Prince. It was both interesting and confusing for a host of reasons, not the least of which because, growing up in a very religious household, I was forbidden to enjoy his music. It was not until a few years later, at the age of thirteen, that I was able to freely listen to his music, view his movies, and enjoy his brilliance uninterrupted. It was as an adult that I realized our BCE had some commonalities. I grew up with an emotionally absent father and even today, at the age of forty, this aspect of my childhood affects me almost daily. I related to this story line, almost as if my story was predestined to mirror the Kid's story in *Purple Rain*. Sharing this father-son experience in our BCE, Prince could understand how the on-again, off-again relationship I had with my father influenced my development. The movie portrayed an emotionally unavailable and abusive father that may have stymied Prince's talent somewhat but stopped short of derailing it. Just as my growth was not stunted due to the unhealthy relationship between my father and me, Prince's growth was not stunted due to the unhealthy dysfunction that he was forced to endure.

On some level, I think all children want their parents' approval; I was no exception, neither was Prince. In the scene where he discovers the music his father wrote, it is as if he discovered something about himself that he never knew existed, as though he understood why he was compelled to write. Children of emotionally involved fathers find themselves asking questions such as, who am I? How did I get here and where am I going? and I was no exception to this. How does one answer these questions if he does not have the fortunate discovery and revelation Prince experienced in the movie? Without knowing oneself, one cannot fully develop one's total person. Prince's talent was so immense it could not be contained, but he was also able to better understand his total person. Coupled with understanding the legacy of talent that existed in his family, that helped facilitate his growth and development.[27]

Jerod Lockhart—1980s

At ten years old, I literally stumbled across Prince and his music. While shopping in a Sears department store, I saw an album cover of Prince's that seemed to appear from out of nowhere. The album was either Prince's self-titled album "Prince" in 1979 or his 1980 album "Dirty Mind" to be exact. I thought I was looking at an attractive woman. Getting a closer look, I became confused and somewhat in disbelief when I realized the person I thought I was looking at was not the person that was actually photographed on the cover at all.

Androgyny was always a significant element of Prince's life: from his heels, hair, makeup and his obliviousness to those around him discussing his sexuality. Confused, I asked myself how someone such as Prince can be attractive to me if I am only attracted to women. If one thinks about what was happening in the eighties, one will realize how a person's sexuality was often used to define them, a dynamic to which Prince did not fall prey. At a time when HIV and AIDS dominated the headlines, Prince paraded his indifference to society's slow evolution of understanding front and center and created enough tailwind that there was room for those who choose to join him. It was then that I did not question my sexuality or anyone else's. I got to this point through Prince, but how did Prince get to this point?

Directly or indirectly, our paternal relationships help develop the persons we become.[28] My father was, for all intents and purposes, not in my life at any significant level at all. There was contact between him and myself, but it was limited and few and far between. The emptiness, the void, created more questions than answers. As a young man, I vowed that my children would not experience this void. Growing up in Chicago's South Shore neighborhood in the 1980s was not for the meek or faint of heart. Gangs were prevalent. There were many times when I longed for my father. There were many things I had to figure out on my own.

I would go on to have a hedonistic, spiritual, and heroic relationship with Prince. The movie helped answer some questions that I did not realize I had. For instance, just as in the movie the character Prince played was not responsible for his parents' marriage failing, for his father's and mother's physically combustible relationship, I realized that I was not responsible for my parents' dysfunctional relationship. I realized I was not the reason my father was absent, and that I was still growing and capable of growing well into adulthood, just as Prince did. Everyone has the ability to grow and develop well beyond their childhood years. Today, I am a fifty-year-old father of two, married to my college sweetheart for twenty-five years. I can easily say that providing for my family is the greatest honor of my life.

Sherman White—1970s

The father-son relationship in the movie extends the characterization of the dysfunctional Black family. That dysfunction is not something that I am familiar with, as it relates to my BCE. I grew up in a loving and nurturing home with my parents and siblings. When the movie debuted, I had just graduated from a high school in Chicago's south suburbs. I had my whole life ahead of me. Thirty-six years later, at the age of fifty-four, I remember nearly every detail from that evening.

Originally, my friends and I went to the 7:00 p.m. show, but due to the overwhelming demand to see the movie, the next three shows were all sold out. As the evening progressed, the hundreds of people present swelled to thousands. The crowd was peaceful enough but when the theater manager made the announcement that there would be "no more shows tonight," the mood and temperament suddenly changed. The crowd became anxious and agitated. Soon, the crowd rushed the theater, and the weight of the crowd crushed the ticket agent's window. Wisely, the manager added a special midnight show to prevent further unrest. I remember thinking, "with all these people here, this movie must be good." I was not disappointed.

The colors, the music, the story, had me completely engulfed from the outset. Then, at approximately eleven minutes into the movie, Clarence Williams III walked onto the screen and the world was introduced to John L. Nelson,

Prince's father. I saw immediate similarities between the person portrayed on screen and my father: strong, commanding, the ability to possess a room. That is where the similarities ended, however.

The scenes where the father was on screen were all eerily common. He was depicted as a dark, solemn person that could be aloof, detached, and punishing. The reasons for these character traits vary, but what is unquestioned is the influence it can have on one's son. A son is taught by the father, but who is teaching the father who himself is from a household with an absent father or male role model? This is the BCE and reality for far too many African American sons. They have no one to model their behavior after.[29] So, how do you hold someone accountable for things that are emotionally beyond their control?

The movie illustrates the importance of the father-son relationship. The only family member Prince has a conversation with in the nearly two-hour movie is with his father. It is also interesting that he did not include his siblings as characters in the movie, further emphasizing the importance of the father-son relationship. The movie's singular focus of the importance of the father-son relationship is aligned with the current research.

PRINCE'S PERSONAL GROWTH AND DEVELOPMENT

Sherman White

In spite of his circumstances, Prince excelled. Seeing the father-son relationship unfold on the screen gave me a greater appreciation for Prince, the man, more so than Prince the entertainer. My true understanding of what made him so remarkable did not take place until I saw the movie. It afforded me two things: (a) how meaningful the father-son relationship is to a household and (b) an understanding that success can still derive from chaos. Prince's rise supports M. J. Thier's position that control impedes development, but it does not extinguish development. It can potentially slow it down and delay it, but the growth will take place.

Writing is a very personal thing. Those who do it often sacrifice any level of anonymity and privacy they may have. Writing can be cathartic and at the same time overwhelming. A writer has to be bold to bare all and inform, enlighten, and entertain others. The movie showed Prince holed up in his basement writing. His desire to release what was inside of him, what was passed on to him through his lineage, had to be released.[30] I suggest that this is where his personal growth and development was spearheaded. When one lives in a household where control is exerted upon everyone and it is stifling and persistent, a person's creativity and growth can suffer.[31] However, Prince succeeded when the BCE of so many others suggests he should not have, because geniuses rises above the rules—and the impact of the movie, the influence of his life, and the iconic status he achieved suggests the genius title is appropriately given to Prince.[32]

I do not know very much about my father's BCE. What I do know has me wondering how he achieved so much when so few things tangibly had been given to him. As shown in the movie, the talents Prince had, writing, playing instruments, and singing were talents he shared with his father. As an adult, I witnessed my father being given a microphone and speaking eloquently and entertainingly without any prepared remarks seemingly forever when prompted, which is a talent that I am told I also have. How amazing it must have been for Prince when he discovered his father's musical compositions. It was as if the missing piece of his personal puzzle was added. His father was more than just a man from a failed marriage. He was more than just a man who the movie cast as demanding and punishing. Prince realized he had something in common with his father, something healthy, something good. I know that is how I felt as I sat there in awe of my father as he was asked to entertain an entire banquet room without any advance notice. Even in the uniqueness of every child's BCE, this piece should be a part of everyone's experience.

The movie is the strongest reference we have of Prince's childhood as told on his own terms and in his own words. None of the recent articles have produced anything definitive regarding their father-son relationship. The interviews in which members of his family participated while he was alive and since his passing cannot be considered impartial sources of information. Even with the increase in scholarly research on his life and music, Prince's own words on the matters of his family, his relationship with his father, and its influence on his development do not exist. A movie made more than forty years ago may very well be the most accurate source of information on the growth, development, and greatness of Prince, because it is in his own words and actions.

AFRICAN AMERICAN FATHERHOOD

Aaron J. Kimble

The African American father conundrum often consists of diametrically opposed positions within the African American community. Statistics reveal that African American fathers have higher rates of nonmarital childbearing and divorce than any other ethnic group.[33] As technology continues to integrate into our lives, many African American fathers find themselves left behind and left out as our society has transitioned from low and semiskilled jobs to careers that involve higher levels of education and training.[34]

Conventional wisdom suggests that African American fathers could strengthen their families and communities by simply being present and presenting themselves as role models and leaders; however, the movie showed that simply being present does not right all that plagues the African American household. My experience as a child is unfortunately all too familiar and common in the African American community. Because my biological father was deliberately absent, my stepfather, whom I refer to as my father, often absorbed the brunt of my emotional trauma and abandonment issues. One must first understand how this phenomenon came about and why it still exists.[35] Centuries of concentrated laws, practices, written and unwritten protocols designed to suppress the African American male were successful. These efforts and laws, with some still in place as recent as the late twentieth century, negatively influenced the socioemotional health of the African American father and his self-efficacy as it relates to his position in his household and community. Regardless of how true it may ring to one's ear, it is unfair to dismissively say "do better" to someone when doing "better" is not possible because the information and resources one would need to do better are not shared and applied evenly. Sometimes a person is doing their absolute best with the resources available to them.

Jerod Lockhart

My parents divorced when I was two years old, and I had very limited interaction with my father throughout my formative years. I have vague memories of him visiting, which reflecting back now, I understand how confusing that must have been to my younger self. Like any child that has witnessed some form of trauma, there were times that I felt powerless. Just as in the movie, my parents fought and there were some particularly violent episodes that I witnessed. After one extremely violent incident, my father was no longer allowed in our home.

My memories of my father from when I was a very young child then fast-forward to my adult years, when I had a wife and family of my own. As a young adult, there was a large gap of virtually no interaction with him at all. In fact, throughout my entire life I would see my father less than a handful of times a year. My BCE includes a shared experience along with other African American sons that our fathers resorted to abusive behavior toward their families as a way to overcompensate for their lack of fulfilling what society considers their responsibility as head of a household.[36] In the movie Prince's father falls into the same category, as the movie shows him being abusive to his wife.

I assume that my father felt some form of guilt, as is often the case in absentee fathers.[37] As a young man, I was not concerned with how successful he was or would become. I simply wanted to be with my dad and enjoy the moments we had together. In the movie, Prince's father is rarely seen making eye contact whenever he spoke with his son. The inability to look someone in the eye can suggest deception, as though a person is attempting to be someone he is not, albeit if only for a moment as long as a visit with his son.

Sherman White

The family has an important role in society and that is why all laws of the countries in the contemporary world have protected it through various moral and legal norms.[38] Abandoned, victimized, unprotected, and hurt are emotions a son feels when he is the child of an absent father. Of these four emotions, abandonment may be the most damaging to one's socioemotional health. When the victim is a child, these negative consequences are stronger both physically and psychologically on his development.[39] These are all-powerful and influencing emotions—influencing in the fact that a child's first role models are his parents. The decline of the African American family and the father as the head of household brought about antisocial behavior and further alienation from mainstream society.[40]

As nature would have it, a son's role model is his father. When the father is absent and/or detached, the son loses his compass, his identity; but because of his innate desire to survive, he is still able to move forward. Through centuries of systemic alienation from the nation African American males call home, significant strides have been made in education and income. Both of these areas are determinants of growth. There are more African American males that the Internal Revenue Service classifies as high net worth now than there were fifty years ago. There are also more African American males earning postsecondary degrees now than there were fifty years ago.[41] Between 1990 and 2008, the number of African Americans with a college degree has increased by 57 percent, with 88,000 African American males obtaining a professional degree (retrieved from www.jbhe.com). Growth has taken place; however, there were some long, harrowing, and painful steps in between then and now.

DISCUSSION AND CONCLUSION

Our goal was to examine the father-son relationship Prince had with his father and how that relationship may have influenced his personal growth and development. Examining it through a collaborative ethnographic lens gives the reader insight into our BCE, as well as providing understanding into the personal growth, triumph, and development of Prince. Just as it is important to prevent the negative internal and external influences that are around us, it is equally important to understand that they do exist.[42] When one understands that these negative influences exist, they can confront these challenges, rise above them, and achieve the personal growth and development they are capable of having. It is in the uniqueness of one's BCE that growth and development blossoms or festers.

By using a multigenerational approach, the authors wanted to gauge diverse perspectives that spanned three decades in order to elucidate if there were any generational differences in the lived experiences of each author's perspective and overall worldview. Each author experienced a different reaction to the movie based on his relationship with his father. We learn in the movie that one's growth is not a singular event, involving only one person; directly or indirectly, others have to be involved. There has to be some external source that allows a person to fuel their internal engine. Prince understood himself and his gift for writing better when he understood it came from his father because he understood himself better. In the movie, they were reconnected through their writings.

Prince wanted his movie to communicate to his fans in the same manner his music did. Movies can inform, enlighten, or educate. This movie does all three, and we see that Prince lived his life in an unforgiving manner so that others could understand themselves better, how they became who they are, even where they are, and that everyone has their own level of genius in them.

Revisiting the past was both nostalgic and painful for us; however, the process was necessary to channel our personal experiences relative to the father-son relationship as depicted in the movie. While undertaking the research, we were able to experience a "self-discovery" on how our father-son relationships influenced our personal growth and development. Having gained a level of self-awareness, we have come to the conclusion that as adults, we have a choice of letting the past dictate our future or being empowered to become the masters of our fate, the captains of our soul.

For the past five generations, there have been critically acclaimed and celebrated films that illustrate the impact of a father-son relationship. Future research could focus on how the African American father-son relationship is depicted in film and examine the thoughts and feelings of audience members regarding the father-son relationship and its influence on the son's growth and development. Also, additional research could examine the emotional void created by the emotionally absent African American father and how it influences the father-son relationship.

The limitations of an autoethnographic study is that it requires a sometimes painful honesty by the author and a willingness to self-disclose. The "do no harm" requirement in research applies to the author in an autoethnographic study just as much as it does for the participants in other research studies. Qualitative research that is rooted in generalizations can lead to false conclusions. Having said that, each author met the expectation set forth of open and honest disclosure as it relates to the topics discussed in this chapter. Hopefully, this chapter will spur additional research, perhaps of a scientific nature, that examines the impact that father-son interactions have on the personal, professional lives of both the son and the dad.

There is uniqueness in one's BCE, and there are also strong threads of commonalities from one to the other. This chapter sought to examine those commonalities and to understand the influence that comes from internal and external forces as we continue to grow and manage our own father-son relationships well beyond our childhood years.

Notes

The authors would like to express our sincere appreciation to Kimberly C. Ransom, Assistant professor at the University of Illinois Urbana-Champaign. Dr. Ransom's experience as a subject-matter expert on ethnographic research related to Prince proved to be invaluable as the authors collaborated on this chapter.

1. Patricia A. Thomas, Edythe M. Krampe, and Rae R. Newton, "Father, Presence, Family Structure, and Feelings of Closeness to the Father among Adult African American Children. *Journal of Black Studies* 38, no. 4 (2008): 529–46.

2. Thomas, Krampe, and Newton, "Father, Presence, Family Structure."

3. Thomas, Krampe, and Newton, "Father, Presence, Family Structure."

4. Linda Pagani, Bernard Boulerice, Richard E. Tremblay, and Frank Vitaro, "Behavioural Development in Children of Divorce and Remarriage," *Journal of Child Psychology and Psychiatry* 38, no. 7 (1997): 769–81

5. Pagani, Boulerice, Tremblay, and Vitaro, "Behavioural Development in Children."

6. Paul R. Amato and Jacob Cheadle, "The Long Reach of Divorce: Divorce and Child Wellbeing across Three Generations," *Journal of Marriage and Family* 67, no. 1 (2005): 191.

7. M. J. Thier, "Create Success out of Chaos," *Journal for Quality and Participation* 18, no. 5 (1995): 6–9.

8. Denis Dutton, "What Is Genius?," *Philosophy and Literature* 25, no. 1 (2001): 181–96; Clifford J. Rogers, "Clausewitz, Genius and the Rules," *Journal of Military History* 66, no. 4 (2002): 1167–76.

9. Adrian A. Bautista, "A Flâneur in the Erotic City: Prince and the Urban Imaginary," *Journal of African American Studies* 21, no. 3 (2017): 353–72.

10. Bautista, "A Flâneur in the Erotic City."

11. Marie A. Plasse, "'Joy in Repetition?': Prince's *Graffiti Bridge* and *Sign O' the Times* as Sequels to *Purple Rain*," *Journal of Popular Culture* 30, no. 3 (1996): 57–61.

12. Matthew Oware, "Decent Daddy, Imperfect Daddy: Black Male Rap Artists' Views on Fatherhood and the Family," *Journal of African American Studies* 15 (2011): 327–51.

13. Oware, "Decent Daddy."

14. Nancy J. Holland, "Prince: Postmodern Icon," *Journal of African American Studies* 21 (2017): 320–36.

15. James Gordon Williams, "Black Muse 4U: Liminality, Self-Determination, and Racial Uplift in the Music of Prince," *Journal of African American Studies* 15 (2011): 296–319.

16. Williams, "Black Muse 4U."

17. Cassandra D. Chaney, "Prince Rogers Nelson: From 'Dirty Mind' to Devout Jehovah's Witness," *Journal of African American Studies* 21, no. 3 (2017): 425–42.

18. Chaney, "Prince Rogers Nelson."

19. Chaney, "Prince Rogers Nelson."

20. Deidre T. Guion Peoples, "Nothing Compares to You: Prince and the Theory of Optimal Distinctiveness," *Journal of African American Studies* 21, no. 3 (2017): 443–60.

21. Peoples, "Nothing Compares to You."

22. Kimberly C. Ransom, "A Conceptual Falsetto: Reimagining Black Childhood via One Girl's Exploration of Prince," *Journal of African American Studies* 21, no. 3 (2017): 461–99.

23. Heewon Chang, *Autoethnography as Method* (Walnut Creek: Left Coast Press, 2018).

24. Tony E. Adams, Stacy Holman Jones, and Carolyn Ellis, *Autoethnography: Understanding Qualitative Research* (New York: Oxford University Press, 2015).

25. Ransom, "A Conceptual Falsetto."

26. Ransom, "A Conceptual Falsetto."

27. Dutton, "What Is Genius?"

28. Cherine Habib, "The Transition to Fatherhood: A Literature Review Exploring Paternal Involvement with Identity Theory," *Journal of Family* 18, no. 2 (2012): 4–21.

29. Julia S. Jordan-Zachery, "Making Fathers: Black Men's Response to Fatherhood Initiatives," *Journal of African American Studies* 13 (2009): 199–218.

30. Rogers, "Clausewitz, Genius and the Rules."

31. Thier, "Create Success out of Chaos."

32. Rogers, "Clausewitz, Genius and the Rules."

33. Armon R. Perry, Dana K. Harmon, and James Leeper, "Resident Black Fathers' Involvement: A Comparative Analysis of Married and Unwed, Cohabiting Fathers," *Journal of Family Issues* 33, no. 6 (2011): 695–714.

34. Kristen Harknett and Sara S. McIanahan, "Racial and Ethnic Differences in Marriage after the Birth of a Child," *American Sociological Review* 69, no. 6 (2004): 790–811.

35. Perry, Harmon, and Leeper, "Resident Black Fathers' Involvement."

36. Jay C. Wade, "African American Fathers and Sons: Social, Historical, and Psychological Considerations," *Families in Society* 75, no. 9 (1994): 561–70.

37. Oware, "Decent Daddy."

38. Marius E. Radu, "The Crime of Family Abandonment in the New Criminal Code," *Euromentor Journal* 5, no. 3 (2014): 84–92.

39. Radu, "The Crime of Family Abandonment."

40. Radu, "The Crime of Family Abandonment."

41. Reginald A. Noël, "Race, Economics and Social Status," US Bureau of Labor Statistics, Spotlight on Statistics, May 2018, https://www.bls.gov/spotlight/2018/race -economics-and-social-status/home.htm.

42. Celia Doyle, "Surviving and Coping with Emotional Abuse in Childhood," *Clinical Child Psychology and Psychiatry* 6, no. 3 (2001): 387–402.

Chapter 3

EDUCATING TO EMPOWER

Gender Performativity Pedagogy Using the Artistry of Prince and Sheila E.

SHANNON M. COCHRAN

"What I'm going to do is preach freedom."
~PRINCE

As an educator who seeks to use self-reflection and practical theory in my classroom, I incorporate that which I see as both "high" and "low" art, as novelist and activist Alice Walker points out in her groundbreaking essay "In Search of Our Mothers' Gardens." For Walker, Black women have historically been relegated to the margins of society and, thus, their creativity has been negated and not recognized in American society. However, Black women, and I argue Black people in general, have resourcefully expressed themselves in imaginative ways such as quilting, gardening, and singing, expressions that should be considered art in the same way as a Michelangelo painting or Shakespeare poem.[1] Further, Black feminist and womanist theories suggest that "theory" is not developed solely via academic scholarship but also through texts such as a novel, a quilt, a garden, or a song, and through the bodies of human beings. This chapter examines the star personas of musical artists Prince and Sheila E. to illustrate the advantage of using both cultural producers as pedagogy in the classroom. In demonstrating how Black feminism and textual analysis are used to theorize body politics, Prince's and Sheila E.'s gender performativity is incorporated into my gender and cultural studies courses, revealing just how instrumental they are as texts of teaching.

The use of textual analysis in the classroom has been an effective tool to examine culture. According to Douglas Kellner, "Textual analysis should use a multiplicity of perspectives. . . . This requires a multicultural approach that sees the importance of analyzing the dimensions of class, race and ethnicity, and gender and sexual preference within the texts of media culture, while studying as well their impact on how audiences read and interpret media culture."[2] Culture is imperative to understanding who we are as a society. Stuart Hall, in *Representation: Cultural Representations and Signifying Practices*, argues: "It is participants in a culture who give meaning to people, objects and events. Things 'in themselves' rarely if ever have any one, single, fixed and unchanging meaning . . . we give things meaning by how we *represent* them."[3] Thus, representation in culture "is an essential part of the process by which meaning is produced and exchanged between members of a culture."[4] Historically, the representation of Black bodies in US visual and narrative cultures has been pejorative, for the most part, serving as ideology that benefits white supremacy and adds to Black people's oppression. Scholars have argued that depictions of Black bodies in US visual and narrative cultures have been "controlling" and damaging rather than complex representations of who they really are.[5] Thus, "Black sexual politics" as disseminated in visual and narrative cultures shapes how Black people are perceived and treated.[6] Patricia Hill Collins argues: "But, because African Americans have historically been harmed by these contradictory sexual politics, the stakes are much higher to develop a critical consciousness. The refusal to discuss in *public* the profound influence of Western constructions of a deviant Black sexuality on African American men and women leaves a vacuum in contemporary African American politics."[7] Such imagery is damaging because it has historically affected the economic, political, and social mobility of Black bodies in both the United States and the world.

Because the representation of Black bodies in visual and narrative cultures affects anything from self-regard to US social policy, it is imperative that consciousness-raising strategies be implemented to combat how white supremacy, domination, and racism are used in this arena.[8] Conversely, representation can also allow us to examine how Black bodies have resisted and negotiated their status in US society and even on a global scale. Kobena Mercer argues that the "Colonial fantasy attempt to 'fix' the position of the black subject into space that mirrors the object of white desires; but black readers may appropriate pleasures by reading against the grain, overturning signs of otherness into signifiers of identity."[9] Reading against the grain has also meant disrupting established extensions and tools of white supremacy and dominant culture. Thus, gender rules and expectations have been established not only to subjugate women, but to sustain a racist agenda that argues that Black bodies are inherently deviant. Black feminist, womanist, and feminist theories have examined the ways in which gender is constructed and disseminated. In "'Night to His Day': The Social Construction of Gender," Judith Lorber argues:

> gender is constantly created and recreated out of human interaction, out of social life, and is the texture and order of that life . . . gender cannot be equated with biological and physiological differences between human females and males . . . the gendered practices of everyday life reproduce a society's view of how women and men should act.[10]

She goes on to say, "Gendered social arrangements are justified by religion and cultural productions and supported by law, but the most powerful means of sustaining the moral hegemony of the dominant gender ideology is that the process is made invisible . . ."[11] Examining and deconstructing established white patriarchal gender roles is a way to combat the use of representation as a tool of oppression. The objective here is to identify the ways in which Prince and Sheila E. have negotiated their bodily performances to allow for autonomous and innovative cultural expression. Moreover, doing so allows students to acknowledge how representation is part of the "process by which meaning is produced and exchanged between members of a culture."[12] Textual analysis is an approach to learning that can allow students accessibility to popular texts and theoretical paradigms. Additionally, I believe it important to remind students that there is no definitive way of reading a text and that each person arrives at a text with, and is influenced by, their own personal, cultural, racial, sexual, and other histories.

"SHE DON'T NEED A MAN'S TOUCH": SHELIA E.'S COMMAND OF MUSIC INSTRUMENTATION

A 2018 viral video on the internet and posted on the social media platform Facebook showcases a small Black girl playing drums as her classmates and teachers surround her enthusiastically cheering her on. The small child is sitting in a chair and playing the drums so intensely that she often leaps up to reach some of the top cymbals. Her fancy white-and-black dress moves with her small body as she pounds effortlessly on the drums. Perhaps one of the most compelling moments of the video is when one of the adults pulls the child's hair away from her shoulders, onto her back so that it will not interfere with her playing, as the girl is now standing with her shawl slipping down her shoulders. The child seems oblivious to her surroundings as she continues to master the drums. Based on the number of views, the video continues to be very popular at the time of this project. What seemingly captivates many viewers is not only that the drummer is a small child, but also that the musician is a girl. Moreover, visually, the little girl embodies everything that US society deems feminine regarding her clothing, hair, and so on; however, her actions contradict this femininity in that she is doing something that little girls have not been expected to do according to traditional beauty standards and gender rules in the United States.

In the comments section of the viral video, many of the viewers remarked on how she resembles a specific popular artist. They comment that she could be the "next Sheila E." By invoking the name of the iconic cultural figure Sheila E. in this presentation, viewers make the parallel between the artist and the child and articulate that the child's playing is so good that it must have been influenced by the artist. One viewer commented, "If Sheila E. and Prince had a daughter," another tags Sheila E's Facebook fan page in the conversation and attempts to bring her attention to the video: "Sheila E., I thought you would enjoy this."[13] That Sheila E. would be thought of by many after viewing this powerful presentation of the girlchild prodigy speaks volumes to her artistry and impact as a woman musician.

When I first heard Sheila E., there was something about her music, her voice, and particularly the 1984 song, "The Glamorous Life," that moved me. As a child, I enthusiastically sang and danced to the record. It was one of my favorites and one of the first records that I remember owning. "The Glamorous Life" was on heavy rotation at radio stations at the time and, even though incredibly talented Sheila "Sheila E." Escovedo had been in the music industry for some time, this song catapulted her into pop culture stardom. It had a catchy beat, she was singing lead, and it was the age of the music video. Seeing her was mesmerizing to me as a young girl. There was something about "The Glamorous Life" that I found captivating as a girlchild. The fact that a woman was playing drums and percussion and the way she played them really stood out to me. Moreover, that she played the drums in high-heeled shoes and continuously flirted with the camera during the video was fascinating. Even though she was performing for the video at the cue of a director, the young me was unaware of that at the time. She did not just play the drums, she *commanded* them. This was not something commonly seen in visual culture—a master female percussionist. On one hand, you see a very feminized woman on screen and on the other hand, you see a woman performing a role that has been traditionally reserved for male musicians. Sheila E. has commented on her struggles entering the

world of music by identifying the many times she was dissuaded from playing percussion because she was not male. She contends, "In my family I'd
never experienced any of the prejudices of being in an 'man's world' playing
a 'man's instrument.' It was only when people started commenting that I
realized there could even be a gender attached to any musical instrument.
. . . I didn't understand the logic."[14]

Rarely have women been viewed and treated as serious musicians outside
of being pianists, especially in contemporary R&B times. At the time Sheila
E. flooded the airwaves with the "Glamorous Life," there were women players like Klymaxx and Patrice Rushen. Klymaxx was a band that comprised
of six members and Patrice Rushen was not shown playing any instruments
in most of her videos in the early 1980s. In the video for her 1982 hit song
"Forget Me Nots," Rushen is dancing and singing rather than shown playing
any instruments, an unfortunate underrepresentation of her musical prowess.
By contrast, white all-girl bands were hypervisible and found favor during
this time; namely, those like the Go-Go's and the Bangles (who scored a hit
in 1986 with "Manic Monday," a song written by Prince). However, musical instrumentation was not, on the whole, portrayed in popular culture as
something at which women were adept. Moreover, soloist gendered percussionist instrumentation was rare.

Sheila E. did not actually begin her career with Prince; however, it was
his entourage, platform, and sound that propelled her during the mid-1980s.
Although Sheila E. first played the drums onstage at the tender age of five,
and even played with the late, great George Duke and his band professionally,
"The Glamorous Life" is still considered her breakthrough and biggest hit.
Even though Sheila E. and Prince were intimately connected, the song and
her overall musicianship are what forever ties Sheila E. to the Prince music
family forever. Although the lyrics, written by Prince, about a girl who wants
to lead a glamorous life but realizes that it would not be worth it without
love, might appear to cave to societal gender expectations and standards, the
instrumentation of Sheila E. is what transcends gender boundaries. Moreover, the protagonist's cynicism regarding love, including her notion that
"love will only conquer my head," is certainly not a characteristic that women
are expected to possess in a Cinderella and fairytale–induced US society.
Prince put a spin on the song that upsets the traditional romance narratives
one normally would hear. With her instrumentation, Sheila E. made the song
a classic, among my generation anyway. Even had Apollonia, the intended
singer of the song, sung it, it is doubtful that the song would have enjoyed
the popularity that it did simply because Apollonia was not a musician for
that matter. I argue that Sheila E.'s outstanding instrumentation is what took

the song to the commendable level that it achieved, reaching #1 on the US dance charts and earning her two Grammy Award nominations and three MTV Award nominations. Moreover, the visual of her instrumentation is powerful and might have appealed to those cheering for female artistry and expertise at the time.

Sheila E.'s musical expertise is exemplified in her ongoing performances of the song, and her gender performativity is reflected in her command of instrumentation and her legacy as a master of drums and percussion. Even though the video for "The Glamorous Life" was an impressive visual performance, Sheila E.'s live and *modern* onstage performances are even more notable. Most of her contemporary performances showcase her advanced gender performativity. For example, in a performance at a Prince concert in Oakland, California, in February 2011, Sheila E. performed "The Glamorous Life" that included a dynamic drum solo. The vision of her in a long white evening gown playing drums and percussion, playing the instruments, is captivating yet informative. Hair pulled back, but hanging, Sheila E. is no longer the young woman in the 1984 music video, cued by a director. She is a mature woman whose beauty, boldness, and stylish confidence rival those of younger artists today. Here she is a one-woman show bringing alive the song I loved as a girlchild with lightning-quick movements and heavy, but delicate hands pounding the drums as her hair whips back and forth. There is no winking of the eye or flirting into the camera as she did in the 1984 video. She is preoccupied with making the music that she does so well and mastering the sounds that permeate the coliseum. Sheila E.'s bodily performance is not what it was when she started her career and at the height of popular music video. She has gained traction as a legendary master musician in world culture. What is becoming more obvious, and rightfully so, is her practice in elevating her skill rather than emphasizing her physical appearance in music video culture. This performance is reflective of this.

At this moment, and like Prince who will soon follow her on stage that night, Sheila E. is doing something that is unconventional. She is breaking societal rules and not adhering to established gender expectations. She is acting "unladylike," so to speak. The dress in which she is draped screams feminine gender rules, but her body language and actions belie perceived traditional and expected feminine behavior. Her percussion playing is masterful. Her gender performativity is obvious but discreet. She bends and moves in a way that a "lady" is not supposed to in the dress she is wearing. Her legs bend and open more than society would deem appropriate for a "lady" in such an elegant gown. Moreover, she knocks the drum down in a very forceful and "unladylike" gesture before leaving the stage. The huge

iconic Prince symbol, which Prince continually and publicly admitted was
a combination male and woman, on the floor of the stage, returns her from
whence she came. And just like that the show is over. This performance is a
fine example of Sheila E.'s gender performativity that I make available to my
students. By using her body to theorize gender in the classroom, I attempt
to envision innovative ways to think about visual and popular culture while
introducing Sheila E. to generations of students that may or may not be
familiar with her brilliance. Prince's affirmation of a woman musician, Sheila
E., is more than admirable. It was *bold*. Along with others such as Wendy
Melvoin and Lisa Coleman, Prince assisted Sheila E. in becoming visible in
a male-dominated arena.

"DOESN'T MY BODY LOOK GOOD?": GAZING PRINCE'S RECONSTRUCTION OF MASCULINITY

The legendary Prince's willingness to write songs for others and affirm women
musicians is commendable, but they are only a fraction of the imprint he left
on the world of music and culture. For me, it was seeing the dark hair on the
brown skin on the self-titled album in 1979. I cannot recall where I saw this
album. However, even though I was too young to remember, it probably was
in my late uncle Gary's hip music collection. I remember thinking how beautiful Prince looked with his long hair, mustache, thick eyebrows, and chest
hair against a sky-blue background. The look was a little unusual to me at
the time, but just a little. My father shared similar features with Prince at the
time. The light skin, long hair, and mustache were what I was used to seeing
every day during this time in my life, but my father did not look like Prince.
In my girlchild and socially conditioned eyes, Prince was very "pretty." Also,
my father was not the author of record on which he sang, "I want to be your
lover . . . I want to be your mother and your sister too." Prince's lyrics in his
hit song "I Want to Be Your Lover" were bold at this time and like nothing
I had ever heard before in the music I was exposed to. Prince's adoption of
identities that were other than masculine was certainly innovative in the
realm of rhythm and blues and pop music authored by Black males. While
scholars who study masculinity have pointed out that the personas of some
musicians during this time were within the realm of "feminized masculinity,"
they were mainly white and many of them were British.[15] David Bowie and
the Sex Pistols have been mentioned in this discourse, but for the most part
Prince is left out of such critical examinations. As a child, I knew that he was
special to me because he shared certain features with my father and his music

was familiar to my environment. Eventually, my father chopped off his long hair and adopted another hairstyle. Meanwhile, Prince grew in popularity becoming a trendsetter in fashion, one who stretched gender boundaries and, in the process, reoriented people's thinking about masculinity and gender.

Prince's gender performativity has redefined what manliness is supposed to resemble. I maintain that, even in death, he continues to serve as an example of how gender, for the most part, is socially constructed. I began using Prince in the classroom as a graduate teaching associate in my Women's and Gender Studies' courses during the early 2000s. I longed for an example of gender performativity that transcended the lessons that were typically offered and discussed in Women's and Gender Studies circles in academia. I wanted to draw upon my experiences in a way that Black feminist and womanist theories suggest and illustrate to students that they, too, can reach within themselves and incorporate their lived experiences for learning. My childhood wonderment and excitement of the fierce instrumentation of Sheila E. and the bodily performance and aesthetics of Prince suddenly made sense to me in a way that it had not before and translated to a powerful nonconformity to gender standards. Also, as Black feminist and womanist theories suggest, I set out to use the body to teach gender theory. Certain figures like pop star Madonna have figured prominently in the discipline, a favorite teaching tool of many, but she did not speak to me, not in the least. Prince would help me teach gender performativity in a way that would encourage students to rethink firmly entrenched US ideals of masculinity and maleness. Therefore, he, along with Sheila E., have been staples in my courses. Using their artistry and bodies as texts, I illustrate not only that gender is socially constructed but also how powerfully the two artists have performed gender in ways that resist and transcend societal expectations and rules. In doing so, Prince is one of the most innovative self-expressionists of the modern era. In "What Is This 'Black' in Black Popular Culture," Stuart Hall contends that ". . . black popular culture is a contradictory space. It is a sight of strategic contestation."[16] Black American music has a history of being a form of resistance. Examining music as a form of representation is empowerment. Thus, I borrow from Lawrence Levine's suggestion that one should generally refrain from "searching too narrowly for signs of political consciousness and revolutionary activity" and that "protest has been too easily depicted in exclusively political and institutional terms" regarding Black Americans' resistance through music.[17] Music can be not only a site of negotiation but one of protest as well. I maintain that Prince and Sheila E. protest white patriarchal boundaries of gender in their personas and artistry and that, consequently, their gender performativity is revolutionary and a form of protest.[18]

Prince as an example of gender performativity is ideal because no matter who Prince was linked to in his personal life, it did not matter. I suggest to students that Prince's gender *performance* has nothing to do with his intimate life. The gender performativity that I examine here does not go that far. It does not have to. It should not. My objective is to protect Prince's private life while examining his bodily narratives and performance that he made accessible and available to the world. Making a more powerful example, Prince's body is also theorized through his star persona and his personal style and fashion. Of course, I go back to the 1979 album cover and my first memory of Prince, but I trace how he has chosen to craft himself with hair, clothing, and accessories. Overall, Prince's aesthetics inform and help shape his gender performativity.

Early in his career, Prince started out with a curly Afro, then quickly moved to a straight and relaxed lengthy look. By the time the world saw him as the star character in the music drama film *Purple Rain* in 1984, his look veered somewhat from the 1979 album cover.[19] It was still straightened and lengthy, but it was loosely curled and cropped on the sides and stylishly hung in front sweeping his attractive face. In the film and his star performances, Prince intentionally did things that drew attention to his body. He would run his hand through his hair and touch his body often. In the opening musical scene in the film, Prince runs his hand through his hair and, consequently, draws the audience's attention to it. Even though this scene is early on, it sets the tone for his bodily politics and performance in the film. I must admit, loving television the way that I did as a small child in the 1970s and 1980s, the image of Prince, an African American male, on his motorcycle in *Purple Rain* challenged Henry Winkler's cool-biker character, Arthur "The Fonz" Fonzarelli from the television sitcom *Happy Days* (1974–84). The television series' version of a streetwise "heartthrob" who attempted to upset, yet somehow blend in, a romanticized 1950s white America, was a dominant image in visual culture. Henry Winkler played a character whose intent was to embody strength, courage, and manliness. He was portrayed as a "cool" and smooth character. When *Happy Days* ended in 1984, Prince changed, for me, what expectations of masculinity on a motorcycle should resemble on screen. The "coolness" that Prince brought to the screen as he rode his bike was, in my view, incomparable. The Fonz's studio leather jacket costume paled in comparison to The Kid's sharp black outfit that accented his shoulder-length, loosely curled hair. Although Prince was performing a perceived masculine act in riding a large motorcycle, the contrast of his long flowing locks and high-heeled shoes could be viewed as crossing gender boundaries. In the early to mid-1980s, the Jheri curl was popular in the United States among many Black males including artists such as Michael Jackson and Ready for the World, to name a few. Therefore, Prince—and even other figures within the Minneapolis music culture who chose to straighten their hair and add length—transcended these gender boundaries during this time. From the beginning, Prince's hair was revolutionary due to his willingness to style it according to his own desires and his ability to create his own hair politics that transcended US gendered beauty conventions. Thus, its aesthetic appeal should be viewed in connection to its revolutionary quality. During the *Purple Rain* period, Prince's layering and sweeping of his hair across his face and particularly his eyes, added to an ambiguous sexiness that he portrayed throughout his life as a cultural figure. While such a hair style was not common for Black males in US visual culture, celebrity women such as the late singer Aaliyah have popularized and worn it. Hence, Aaliyah consequently made the style her signature look during the peak of her career in the mid-1990s. Prince's former bandmate, Wendy Melvoin, wore a similar eye-hiding hairstyle in *Purple Rain* and after. However, Prince's possession of the style protests gender rules and expectations because he was a Black male. Men have worn similar styles; however, coupled with his overall bodily performance, Prince's hair takes on specific meaning and disrupts gender spaces in US visual culture.

Later in the 1980s and 1990s, Prince evolved and continued to construct his personal style by wearing his hair in a way that was unique and defied gender boundaries. Even though he did drift back and forth to wearing his hair long during his career, for a large part of the 1990s and 2000s, Prince kept cropped and stylish cuts; hair styles that, at the time, were not characteristically worn by Black males. To demonstrate the power of Prince's aesthetics, I provide my students with other examples of hairstyles and cultures for comparison. West Coast rap artists have been known for reflecting fashion, including, hairstyles worn by African American males in areas such as Los Angeles, Long Beach, and Compton, California. Artists such as Snoop Dogg and DJ Quik have worn their hair in styles from the Jheri Curl to the straight and lengthy look. Another personal favorite image for this in-class example appears on the cover of his 1998 *Rhythmal-ism* album, where producer and recording artist DJ Quik's hair is straight and lengthy. This was not atypical of him, however. DJ Quik's hair is not like Prince's hair. Thus, I have students do a critical analysis of why Prince's fashion and DJ Quik's fashion might differ and why Prince's gender performativity is breaking boundaries and DJ Quik's is adhering to them based on regional preferences and ideals. While both men are beautiful in their presentation, DJ Quik is not viewed as departing from the West Coast rap societal gender norms for having his hair straightened. He also does not have his hair cut in one of the precision cuts that Prince wore later in his career and incorporated into his

public persona. Prince's precision and point cuts are what made him excep-
tional in his presentation of hair as a male. It is not uncommon for celebrity
women to be complimented on hairstyling. For example, many people have
admired actress Halle Berry for having short hairstyles in the beginning of
her film career. However, Prince does not get the credit that he deserves for
being a pioneer in hairstyling and fashion. The fact that he decided to wear
his hair in ways and styles that have been deemed feminine by US gender
standards, is considered revolutionary because it protests established gender
boundaries and rules. His success at it, as is evident by his overall enormous
fan reception, affirms the revolutionary quality of his decisions and testi-
fies to his power as an iconic cultural figure. A pictorial example of his hair
fashion and precision cut is draped on the walls of Paisley Park, his private
estate and recording studio in Chanhassen, Minnesota. While visitors are
exposed to his entire career in images, the artwork from his 2009 triple
album, *LOtUSFLOW3R*, glares at visitors from the "Inspiration and Influence
Hallway" wall of the mansion. Adorning his trademark purple, Prince gazes
into the camera as beautiful and gold neckwear lies on his chest. Images of
the musicians who influenced him are to his left in the artwork and those
who he influenced are to his right. Prince's face is characteristically perfectly
pretty with subtle makeup as the curls in his precision cut hair style are soft
but pronounced. One large curl gently swoops the right side of his forward.
What is even more evident and reflected in the artwork and on the walls of
Paisley Park is the reality that Prince could pull off any style he chose to wear.

Returning to his natural state and wearing an Afro before his death suggested to some that he had come full circle. While Prince wore an Afro at the
beginning of his career, it should be noted that it was during the 1970s and
when the Black Power Movement was ending. However, I argue that Prince's
adorning of the hairstyle at the end of his career can be regarded as Black
Power aesthetics because he was involved in racial and social justice issues
through his philanthropy and artistry, as is evident in his commitment to
the Freddie Gray case. Gray was an African American male who lost his life
at the hands of members of the Baltimore Police Department in April 2015.
His death sparked protest and insurgency across the nation, and Prince was
so moved that he penned a song because of the incident and in dedication to
Gray. Prince's fashioning of his hairstyles throughout his career and eventually
settling on the afro that he began with could reflect a turnaround and "coming home" in the eyes of some of his fans and spectators. In one of his final
television talk show appearances on *The Arsenio Hall Show* in March 2014,
Prince slowly and modestly walked onto the set wearing deep purple and
styling his afro.[20] It is important to note that Hall has told his audience that

Prince encouraged him to return to television through his talk show because of its relevance and impact on culture. Even though his music crossed into the mainstream during the middle of his career and was received by the world, Prince remained dedicated to issues regarding race. Thus, his natural afro can be viewed as politicized in the moment in time that he wore it.

"PURPLE REIGN, PRETTY LACE, AND PERFECT RUFFLES"

In *Purple Rain*, Prince's black outfit that he wears while on the motorcycle contrasts the purple and white lace clothing and makeup in the opening scene of the film. The film, which many would argue propelled Prince into mainstream culture, could be regarded as an example of how Prince's fashion transcended gender and crossed boundaries in a way that established him as the architect of his own of masculinity. As a child, I knew that the image on the self-titled album was different, if not special. I saw a male with a mustache posing for the camera, but now I see that Prince was not posturing in a way that would be considered macho by traditional US gender standards. Even though his lower arms are not visible in the image, his upper arms appear so that his hands might even be crossed or at least positioned close together. Prince does not seem concerned about being macho, in a traditional sense, in this image. In "True Confessions: A Discourse on Images of Black Male Sexuality with Isaac Julien," Mercer and Julien argue that "'Macho' is the product of these historical contradictions, as it subjectively incorporates attributes associated with dominant definitions of manhood—such as being tough, in control, independent—in order to recuperate some degree of power or active influence over objective conditions of subordination created by racism." They conclude that "'Macho' may therefore be regarded as a form of misdirected or 'negative' resistance, as it is shaped by the challenge to the hegemony of the socially dominant white male, yet assumes a form which is in turn oppressive to black women, children and indeed, to black men themselves, as it can entail self-destructive acts and attitudes."[21] That Prince resisted a "macho" narrative and consequently the dominant narrative of what *he* should be, in his persona, is one of the things that endeared him to me: the fact that he was his own person and governed his persona. He did not care to fit in or assimilate to what was happening in United States and world culture. He did not allow typical forms of machoism to dictate how he should carry himself. Thus, he wore makeup, (some) clothing, and high-heeled shoes that are characteristically perceived to be feminine attire in accordance to US gender rules and expectations.

In the opening scene of *Purple Rain*, a silhouette of Prince quickly turns into the visual of his performance of "Let's Go Crazy" that showcases his curly hair and white outfit. Throughout the film he wears white lace and ruffles. For the most part, lace and ruffles have traditionally been portrayed and read as feminine in US culture. Thus, Prince's adorning of lace upsets gender conventions and expectations. During this time in his career, lace and ruffles were common features in his apparel, adding to his aesthetics and the characteristics of his star persona. One telling piece of ruffled clothing in his wardrobe exists as an artifact that I assessed when I visited Paisley Park in 2019. Prince's clothing from the *Around the World in a Day* album cover that he also did with The Revolution reflects the lace and ruffled look that he possessed during this era of his career. In addition to the societal gender-blurred styles worn by all members of the group in 1985, Prince wore a beautiful sky-blue and white two-piece outfit with white ruffles in the "Raspberry Beret" video. Gazing upon this outfit in person was something surreal to me. It had been one of my favorites and most memorable of his. As a child, *Around the World in a Day* was one of my favorite albums and I was visually mesmerized by Prince's style at the time. It was a creative and stunning extension of his Purple Rain attire. An important aspect of the legend strikes me when I gazed upon the beautiful costume in person; how petite and delicate Prince really was. The small and beautiful outfit reflected to me his gender performativity. Petite Prince wore ruffles and constructed his own manliness on his own terms. He used the ruffles and his body to not only construct a star persona, but to also force viewers and listeners of his craft to negotiate the ways that we see gender in the United States.

The white lace with purple and blue that he wore in the opening scene of *Purple Rain* and in the "Raspberry Beret" video was replaced by even more intricate and complex pieces as his career ascended and the times changed. What remained the same, of course, were the high-heeled shoes to which he was so attached and wore well. When Prince appeared on George Lopez's show, *Lopez Tonight*, in April 2011, he wore a red outfit with slim high-heeled shoes.[22] The shoes were matching his bright red outfit; soft red slacks with a red blouse covered by a hip red blazer. His sharp clothing reflected his unique aesthetic; however, his shoes were eye-catching and fashion-trending for a male in the public eye during this time.

My recognition of Prince's aesthetics and challenge to established gender rules and expectations allows him to become a "text" of analysis and a teaching tool in my classroom. Using imagery of Prince informs my pedagogy on gender construction and socialization. There are many images of Prince from which I choose to engage my students in gender performativity theory, but often the choice is theirs to make. The objective is to have them identify the multiple ways that Prince defies societal expectations of masculinity and femininity while creating alternative definitions of gender performance. His gender performativity allows one to see how narratives of femininity and masculinity are scripted in society and on the body. These narratives are expected to be performed by certain sectors of society. If one does not adhere, they are considered outside of the "appropriate" gender. In American society, rarely do males succeed in fashioning themselves the way that Prince did without encountering backlash. My intent is not to undermine the reality and severity of discrimination and violence targeted to the LGBTQIA+ community; my aim is to point out that Prince succeeded in doing something that few heterosexual and cisgender Black males can do in America; wear makeup, sport high-heeled shoes, and lace, and still be revered and accepted on his own terms. This speaks to his larger-than-life persona and transcendent societal impact. This impact can influence students and humans. Prince was a large celebrity figure, which makes him an important text to examine and assess how he can and did influence others.

Prince defied gender standards in numerous ways. One other way would be through the act of "gazing" that has been a component of Women's and Gender Studies. Feminist film critic Laura Mulvey argued that there existed a "male gaze" through which objects are viewed. Mulvey contended that this gaze possesses the power of males (typically assumed white and heterosexual), which sees the object (assumed women) as passive. Using cinema as her primary text, she argues, ". . . the fascination of film is reinforced by preexisting patterns of fascination already at work within the individual subject and the social formations that have moulded him . . . An active/passive heterosexual division of labour has similarly controlled narrative structure . . . Man is reluctant to gaze at his exhibitionist like."[23] Black feminist and womanist theories have challenged this theory and intervened with such arguments that suggest that it tends to be Eurocentric and that certain communities can and do possess an oppositional gaze. In *Black Looks: Race and Representation*, bell hooks introduces the notion of this specific gaze by contending that for Black women, there is "power in looking."[24] Looking relations in visual culture continue to be examined and negotiated. Here, I have expanded hooks's targeted possessors of the gaze, Black women, to include the Black community in general. I argue that Prince's gender performativity includes a repositioning of the gaze. An example of this is found in his characterization in *Purple Rain*. He constantly runs his hands through his hair and even shakes his buttocks for his fictional concert crowd in an act that drew the viewing audience to his body. Prince positioned himself as subject of the gaze in a way that presented himself, his hair and body, as desiring and beautiful to his audience. This is not believed typical and expected of masculine behavior in US visual culture. Prince often exposed his small frame for the world to see; showing his bare midriff and even more of his nude body (as reflected in the blatant but subtle sexually oriented image on the cover of the 1988 *Lovesexy* album). By posturing himself in visual culture in a way that is not deemed masculine by US gender standards, Prince pushed his petite body into spaces where it would historically be marginalized and ostracized. By forcing viewers to gaze upon his body, Prince restructured masculinity through his star persona. In Prince's world, the gaze is neither gendered nor passive. He is the focus of the camera entirely too much for it to be anything other than aesthetically appealing. Overall, Prince allows for subjectivity in visual culture by upsetting theories on gazing and looking practices.

Drawing from my personal experience, I use one of my admired songs by Prince as an example to demonstrate to students how his gender performativity further upsets the traditional theories on gazing. When Prince released the song and video for "Insatiable," I did not realize how useful they would become in demonstrating the component of Prince's gender performativity that dealt with "gazing" and the power of looking.[25] From his 1991 *Diamonds and Pearls* album, "Insatiable" tells the story of two people making a, presumably sex, video. The woman is the director of the video and Prince is the one being filmed as he croons, "Turn the lights off . . . no one knows how to handle my body . . . the way you truly do." The music video has him taking his clothes off and touching his body, gyrating his hips to the rhythm of the music, swirling on the floor and performing for the camera as he sings, ". . . I can't help it Martha. I can't help what you do to me. You are insatiable . . ." True to Prince's sexy lyrics at the time, the song and video take the audience on a journey about lovemaking; however, unlike some songs that are about romance, Prince places himself in a manner that most male songwriters and singers are unwilling to: being vulnerable to women. I love the legendary Motown all-male group Temptations and I admire hearing the late Eddie Kendricks, my favorite Temptation, sing about being in love; however, Prince's positioning is different from Kendricks singing, "You're my everything." According to traditional US gender standards, Prince is placing his body in a way that would be deemed non-masculine and sexually vulnerable to women. Historical US gender rules and expectations would deem it disempowering for a male to do so in visual culture.

Further, the lines, ". . . insatiable is my name when it comes to you . . . Do you really want all of my clothes off . . . you say you want my hips in the air?" gives power to the director of the camera but it also provides Prince agency in his own video. Prince's sexual vulnerability, but with power, enhances his gender performativity and reflects how gender is a social construct. Yet again, Prince writes himself as beautiful and the subject of the gaze in a way that is rarely done by US gender rules and standards. As much as I argue that Eddie Kendricks possessed sensitivity in his star persona, I cannot imagine him singing and telling a woman to place his "hips in the air." I feel that it would attract backlash from fans and music executives even during the prime of his success in the 1960s. Thus, Prince's performativity broke boundaries in ways that are deemed empowering to him. Moreover, Prince embodied beauty in a way that one cannot truly describe or ascribe gender or any other labels to. Centering himself as the subject of the gaze was not isolated to "Insatiable," which is only an example. He presents himself and the woman directing the camera as players and subjects in the video; going against the grain and maintaining subjectivity. Through his star persona and performances, Prince presented himself in ways that were indescribable and mesmerizing for those viewing and consuming his image, softer and gentler than how men are encouraged to present themselves. Even as Prince changed and grew deeper in religion, his aesthetics were still presented as always stunning and pleasing to the eye. His fashion was unique and never failed. He was a visionary who set trends and redefined how gender should operate in visual culture. Using his petite body, Prince reimagined how self-expression could be used to define one's self in a world that dictates what is aesthetically acceptable.

> Despite everything, no one can dictate who you are to other people.
> ~PRINCE

It appears that I am always in class and teaching when important news comes. I received the devastating news that one of the most important persons who was instrumental in shaping my intense love of music, my dear Uncle Gary, had passed away and transitioned when I was teaching on November 9, 2010. So much news, it seems, comes while teaching. And so it was on April 21, 2016. Students had been giving presentations in one of my African American Studies classes that day. One student eagerly presented on musician Janelle Monáe's artistry and chose to include Prince's positive affirmation of her and how important this was to her worth as an artist and cultural figure. Even though her project was on Monáe, the student felt it was imperative to mention Prince. It *was* crucial that she mention and discuss him. I could tell that my student felt it vital information, a way of validating Monáe and securing her own affirmation and study of Monáe's artistry. She was right, at least for this audience. As a class, we congratulated Monáe because being affirmed by Prince was a very big deal. All my students applauded Monáe, a person who was not physically present in class. That is how big a deal it was to be affirmed by the iconic Prince.

Approximately an hour after class ended, I was standing outside of the classroom chatting with students when the same student rushed back toward us and asked if we had "heard the news." She was distraught and lacked composure. Thus, I knew that something was terribly wrong. I tried to calm her as I asked her what was wrong. It seemed as if the world stopped when she answered. The news outlets were saying that Prince died. What? How could this be? I knew that I had to be strong for the students who were around me at the time. They were looking at me for answers. I did not know what to say or do. I instructed one to take out his mobile device to see what was going on. It was confirmed that we had indeed lost the softspoken and beautiful legend that day. My mind drifted to the pretty face on the 1979 album cover. It drifted to my childhood. No. Not Prince. It still stings like I knew him personally. I still mourn the loss of Prince, I still mourn the loss of my dear Uncle Gary: two people who heavily affected the way that I see the world; two men who showed me that my own lived experiences are important in whatever I do. Uncle Gary was one of the biggest supporters of my life and career. He cheered me and we both cheered Prince's once-in-a-lifetime incredible artistry.

The character Billy, played by Billy Sparks in *Purple Rain*, tells The Kid, "Nobody digs your music but yourself!" Even though he was trying to reach Prince's character in the film, this statement is reflective of how Prince treated his own artistry. He *did* dig his music and composed it for his own taste; however, people loved it. I love Michael Jackson. Indeed, the girlchild in me still hurts over the loss of both Michael and Prince; however, I feel a special hurt because deep down I sensed that Michael might have cared too much about what others thought of him. In my eyes, Prince did not. Prince did not seem to care about what other people thought. That pretty face with the long hair and mustache on the album cover conveyed that to me, even as a small child, that day in 1979. His career was built on being himself; being different from what was expected. Unlike so many other celebrities, he smiled, wrote, moved, sang, dressed, lived, the way that Prince *wanted* to. That is the ultimate lesson to learn. A life lesson. That is what is important to teach; to tell. This is the true success and joy in teaching Prince. To teach that self-love and positive self-regard are essential to navigating this world.

I cannot always be with students to help them process the death of such an impressive and important iconic cultural figure as Prince, but I can encourage their learning by providing them with tools to critically think about the world in which we live. Whoever the person, whatever the experience, *live it*. My uncle "gave" me Prince by exposing me to his artistry and I, in turn, give Prince (and Sheila E.) to students by allowing them the chance to practice theory through his empowering persona, aesthetics, and artistry. The gender performativity of Prince can be used to teach gender theory and body politics. Teaching Prince as "text" is instrumental in demonstrating to students not only how gender is constructed and fluid, but how confident self-regard is extremely important and an act of resistance.

With the white-operated corporate control of hip hop and the genre's dominance in global visual culture, it is imperative that students know that it is all right to go against the grain in relation to the harmful racial bodily narratives that have persevered in culture. It is all right to be oneself in a world that continuously dictates what and who should be standard. Like Prince, students must be encouraged to transcend rigid boundaries in every aspect of their lives and find total happiness within. Dare to live as one would desire. Students should be given the analytical tools that encourage them to challenge and conquer oppressive institutions of power. Prince was a master musician but more than that he was an architect of self-expression. This is praiseworthy and important when analyzing him and teaching him to new generations. I teach to inspire and educate to empower, and I must continue to share the genius and exceptionality of Prince with generations to come. In an interview on *BET Tonight* in 1998, Prince said, "What I am going to do is preach freedom."[26] He was specifically discussing his business struggles and consequent contractual freedom from Warner Bros; however, this freedom should be discussed when thinking about his theory on self-regard. At another moment during the interview, he affirmatively said, "I love me!" Preach, Prince, Preach!

Notes

1. Alice Walker, *In Search of Our Mothers' Gardens* (New York: Harcourt Brace Jovanovich, 1983).

2. Douglas Kellner, "Cultural Studies, Multiculturalism, and Media Culture," in *Gender, Race, and Class in Media*, edited by Gail Hines and Jean M. Humez, 3rd ed. (Los Angeles: Sage, 2011), 15.

3. Stuart Hall, *Representation: Cultural Representations and Signifying Practices* (Los Angeles: Sage, 2009), 3.

4. Hall, *Representation*, 5.

5. Patricia Hill Collins, *Black Feminist Thought: Knowledge, Consciousness, and the Politics of Empowerment* (New York: Routledge, 1991).

6. Patricia Hill Collins, *Black Sexual Politics: African Americans, Gender, and the New Racism* (New York: Routledge, 2005).

7. Collins, *Black Sexual Politics*, 44–45.

8. K. Sue Jewell, *From Mammy to Miss America and Beyond: Cultural Images and the Shaping of US Social Policy* (New York: Routledge, 1993).

9. Kobena Mercer, *Welcome to the Jungle: New Positions in Black Cultural Studies* (New York: Routledge, 1994), 135–36.

10. Judith Lorber, "'Night to His Day': The Social Construction of Gender," in *Race, Class, and Gender in the United States: An Integrated Study*, edited by Paula S. Rothenberg (New York: Worth Publishers, 2004), 54–58.

11. Lorber, "'Night to His Day,'" 54–58.

12. Hall, *Representation*, 5.

13. West Elementary, Facebook untitled video, Retrieved May 17, 2018, https://www.facebook.com/wes.hcboe.net/videos/1226047950864900.

14. Sheila E., *The Beat of My Own Drum: A Memoir* (New York: Atria Books, 2014), 98.

15. Thomas Keith, *Masculinities in Contemporary American Culture: An Intersectional Approach to the Complexities and Challenges of Male Identity* (New York: Routledge, 2017), 252.

16. Stuart Hall, "What Is This 'Black' in Black Popular Culture?," in *Black Popular Culture*, edited by Gina Dent, (Seattle: Bay Press, 1992), 26.

17. Lawrence Levine, "Antebellum Period (African American Music as Resistance)," in *African American Music: An Introduction*, edited by Mellonee V. Burnim and Portia K. Maultsby, (New York: Routledge, 2006), 587.

18. Levine, "Antebellum Period," 587.

19. Albert Magnoli, dir., *Purple Rain* (1984; Burbank: Warner Bros., 2002), DVD.

20. Arsenio Hall, dir., *The Arsenio Hall Show*, March 5, 2014, CBS Television Distribution.

21. Mercer, *Welcome to the Jungle*, 143.

22. George Lopez, dir., *Lopez Tonight*, aired April 14, 2011, Panamort Television.

23. Laura Mulvey, "Visual Pleasure and Narrative Cinema," in *The Feminism and Visual Cultural Reader*, edited by Amelia Jones (New York: Routledge, 2003), 44–48.

24. bell hooks, *Black Looks: Race and Representation* (Boston: South End Press, 1994), 115.

25. Prince and the New Power Generation, "Insatiable," recorded December 1989, track 3 on *Diamonds and Pearls*, Warner Bros., compact disc.

26. Tavis Smiley, dir., *BET Tonight*, BET, 1998.

Chapter 4

CONVERSATION WITH AL NUNESS (PRINCE'S BASKETBALL COACH)

JUDSON L. JEFFRIES

Although Al Nuness grew up in Illinois, he is best known for the imprint he made on the University of Minnesota. After having starred at Proviso East High School in Maywood, Illinois, in the early to mid-1960s, Nuness attended Iowa Central, a junior college, where he played basketball and became the school's first JC All-American. As his time in Iowa was coming to an end, a prominent alumnus of the University of Minnesota convinced him to enroll at his alma mater. For many, going from a junior college to a Big Ten university would have been quite the challenge; not so for Al Nuness. While playing for the Golden Gophers, the 6'3" guard was twice named an All-Big Ten player and voted team captain in 1968–69. By the end of his two-year playing career, Nuness averaged 15.4 points per game, scoring 740 points in just two years, while averaging nearly five rebounds a game, playing for the great Bill Fitch, who years later went on to coach the Boston Celtics to an NBA championship.

Nuness was also named the team's MVP in his senior season. In the fall of 2016 Nuness was inducted into the University of Minnesota Hall of Fame. Prior to that, Nuness had been inducted into the Halls of Fame at his Maywood, Illinois, high school, Proviso East, and at Iowa Central.

At some point after his playing days ended, Nuness caught the coaching bug, becoming the first African American full-time assistant coach in any sport, at the University of Minnesota. Later he coached and taught at Central High School in Minneapolis, and in 1976 Nuness was named Minnesota Coach of the Year.

Nuness has had the kind of career that many people dream of. He has enjoyed as much success in corporate America as he did in athletics. He has held executive positions with Pillsbury, Jostens, and the Minnesota Timberwolves, to name a few. Over the past several years, Nuness's name has been associated with Hopkins High School, a local high school in a Minneapolis suburb where he serves as mentor, guidance counselor, and teacher.

Judson L. Jeffries: Brother Nuness, it took me a long time to track you down, but here we are finally. Thank you for taking time out of your hectic schedule to talk to me.

Al Nuness: You're very welcome. When I received the 2017 issue of the *Journal of African American Studies* in the mail where you featured Prince, I figured it was only a matter of time before we spoke.

JLJ: I would venture to say, Brother Nuness, that the overwhelming majority of people who are familiar with your name do not realize that you were once Prince's basketball coach.

AN: No, they don't, but that has changed some because of the few interviews I did after Prince passed.

JLJ: Please share with my readers one or two of your earliest memories of Prince, Brother Nuness.

AN: Okay, I'll have to think about that for a moment. Well, here we go; back when I was coaching at Central High School in South Minneapolis, I'll never forget. Prince, his brother Duane, and friend Paul were students at the junior high school down the street. I would be in my office and the next thing I know I would hear a dog barking. He'd be barking up a storm. I walk out of my office to see what's going on and come to find out Prince, Paul, and Duane have brought this dog in the building. Not only did they bring a dog in the building, which was not allowed, but they'd be in the gym shooting hoops. I'd have to chase them out.

JLJ: So, why did they have to sneak in Central High School's gym, didn't their junior high school have a gym?

AN: That's a good question. I don't know if Bryant had a gymnasium or not.

JLJ: Bryant?

AN: Yes, that was the junior high school Prince attended.

JLJ: Oh, I see. Now, who is this Paul guy you referred to earlier?

AN: Paul Mitchell and Prince were very good friends, thick as thieves. I think at one time, Prince may have even lived with the Mitchells, if memory serves me correctly. That's how close they were.

JLJ: Now, Brother Nuness, back in 2004 Dave Chappelle does this hilarious skit of Prince and his crew squaring off against comedian Charlie Murphy and his boys on the basketball court. Murphy is narrating the whole thing. Murphy says when Prince broached the subject of playing some ball, he and his boys burst out laughing, thinking Prince was kidding around. I guess he thought Prince couldn't play, because as you know, Prince was very short, especially for a guy. From what I understand, he was only 5'3" or 5'4". Murphy, known for telling great stories, said that he and his boys changed into some athletic gear and met Prince and his crew on the court, only to see that Prince and his people still had on the clothes they had performed in. Anyway, he said Prince could straight up ball. How true is that?

AN: Okay, I can't comment on the story Murphy told about what folks were wearing and whatnot, but what I can say is, Prince could ball!

JLJ: Prince could ball, Brother Nuness?

AN: Oh, absolutely, Prince could definitely ball; no question about that!

JLJ: Ok, give me some context please.

AN: Let's put it like this. In the seventh, eighth, and ninth grades, no one was better than Prince. Prince was a dominant player during those years, and I'm not exaggerating when I say that.

JLJ: Whaaaaat?

AN: I'm serious, no one was better. He wasn't a great shooter but was quick as greased lightning and a great passer. He could also D up a person.

JLJ: He could D up a player, Brother Nuness?

AN: Oh, yeah, he could D up the opposing guard, absolutely.

JLJ: What are we talking about, Brother Nuness, when we say D up an opposing player? You mean like Muggsy Bogues?

AN: That's a great comparison, that's exactly what I mean!

JLJ: I'll be darned.

AN: Oh yeah, listen! The team Prince was on in the eighth grade (AAU Park Avenue Youth Club) won the championship that year.

JLJ: I take it that Prince was a point guard.

AN: Yes, Prince played the point. He understood very well how to play the point guard position.

JLJ: Oh really?

AN: Listen to me. When Prince and the other guys I had got to the ninth grade, they were better than all of my tenth graders.

JLJ: The ninth graders were better than the tenth graders?

AN: Oh yeah, oh yeah! In fact, when they became juniors, they were my starters at South Minneapolis High School.

JLJ: Okay, so Prince started for you while in the eleventh grade?

AN: Actually no, he didn't. In fact, Prince didn't try out in his junior year. Prince started two years at the tenth-grade level.

JLJ: I don't get it; how did that work?

AN: Because he started playing at the tenth-grade level while in the ninth grade.

JLJ: But as a ninth grader he would have still been in junior high school at the time.

AN: [laughter] I know it.

JLJ: So, if he is in the ninth grade, how did that work?

AN: Easy. I brought the ninth graders over to Central where I was coaching and moved them up.

JLJ: So, Prince started for two years and then didn't try out when he got to the eleventh grade?

AN: Nope, didn't try out.

JLJ: You have any idea why? Did he prefer to concentrate on his music or what?

AN: That's a very good question, I never asked him why. What I do know is that the other kids grew taller and matured. Prince just didn't grow much. And by that time, the other kids had passed Prince in ability and skill.

JLJ: Did he think he might be cut if he tried out?

AN: I don't think he thought he would be cut, because he wouldn't have gotten cut, but he was no longer going to be a starter. I think he understood that. But no, he wouldn't have been cut, he'd have made the team.

JLJ: What do you remember about Prince, the kid?

AN: Prince was very quiet, he was somewhat of an introvert, but he was a jokester. You wouldn't expect him to be a jokester, but he was.

JLJ: What was your initial reaction when you heard the news that Prince had died, Brother Nuness?

AN: I was hurt, no doubt about that. A lot of people are unaware of the good things that Prince did in communities throughout Minneapolis. Prince never really changed. His friends always remained his friends. Plus, Prince never left Minneapolis. He didn't move to LA or New York, he stayed right there in Minneapolis. That says a lot about him.

JLJ: Thank you for taking the time to talk to me, Brother Nuness, I really appreciate it.

AN: You're welcome, I appreciate what you are doing.

Part II

Beauty, Race, and Spirituality

CONCEPTUALIZATION OF BEAUTY IN PRINCE'S "THE MOST BEAUTIFUL GIRL IN THE WORLD" VIDEO

CASSANDRA D. CHANEY

INTRODUCTION

> When he [Prince] wrote that song [The Most Beautiful Girl in the World], he had all women in mind.
> —MAYTE GARCIA, THE EX-WIFE OF PRINCE

Beauty is personal and subjective. The Chinese teacher, editor, politician, and philosopher Confucius (551–479 BCE) says: "Everything has beauty, but not everyone sees it." The British actor, model, dancer, and humanitarian Audrey Hepburn (May 4, 1929–January 20, 1993) feels this way about beauty: "The beauty of a woman is not in a facial mode but the true beauty in a woman is reflected in her soul. It is the caring that she lovingly gives, the passion that she shows. The beauty of a woman grows with the passing years." The Spanish painter, sculptor, poet, and playwright Pablo Picasso (1881–1973) admits the following regarding beauty: "Beauty? To me it is a word without sense because I do not know where its meaning comes from nor where it leads to." The American poet, author, and editor Martin Buxbaum (1912–1991) feels this way regarding beauty: "Some people, no matter how old they get, never lose their beauty—they merely move it from their faces into their hearts." Finally, Markus Zusak (b. 1975), the Australian author of the book *I Am the Messenger*, makes this comment regarding beauty: "Sometimes people are beautiful. Not in looks. Not in what they say. Just in what they are." Given these complementary and sometimes conflicting definitions of beauty, it is important to recognize that perceptions of beauty are frequently based on assessments of phenotypical characteristics, inward virtues, as well as what a culture widely promotes.

This chapter focuses on how Prince Rogers Nelson perceived beauty. Upon examining the words, visual imagery, and women in his video "The Most Beautiful Girl in the World," I assert that Prince challenges European beauty norms by highlighting cross-cultural standards of beauty, which validate the race, age, and marital and parental status of women throughout the world. In the section that follows, I will highlight key scholarship related to beauty, perceptions of beauty, and culture.

RELEVANT SCHOLARSHIP ON BEAUTY

An extensive body of extant scholarship has examined beauty. For example, scholars have explored the psychology of beauty, the construction of mainstream beauty standards, as well as how beauty myths are harmful to women.[1] Other studies have examined how individuals with body types that fall outside of the mainstream perceive popular beauty advertisements and are demanding greater inclusion in society.[2] Recently published doctoral dissertations have examined the relationship between beauty, cosmetic use, and brand loyalty, the salience of the beauty salon for African Americans, as well as the increase in cosmetic surgery among Asians.[3]

However, what is beauty? *The Shorter Oxford Dictionary* defines *beauty* as "That quality or combination of qualities which affords keen pleasure to the senses, especially that of sight or which charms the intellectual or moral capacities."[4] Admittedly, this definition is vague because it fails to define pleasure or the charm of "intellectual or moral capacities," however, this definition recognizes the multidimensionality of beauty ("quality or combination of qualities") as well as beauty's ability to activate thoughts (intellect) or behaviors (moral capacities). Moreover, I believe it important to acknowledge fundamental realities regarding this construct, especially as it relates to Prince's conceptualization of beauty. Valentine provides a valuable framework for the relationship between the object of the beauty and the one who observes beauty: "The nature of the object found beauti-ful can never be ignored; it is the relation of the object and the observer that is the important thing."[5] A return to Valentine's perspectives will occur later, but I believe it important to mention here that "the relation of the object and the observer" are connected.

THE SALIENCE OF BEAUTY

Beauty, or commonly held perceptions regarding what is beautiful, deter-mine the frequency and quality of social interaction as well as the emo-tions that are associated with this construct.[6] In one of the first scholarly works to examine the relationship between facial recognition and beauty, Cross, Cross, and Daly[7] reveal that women recognize female faces more frequently than male faces; however, males recognize the male and female faces with equal facility. Moreover, whites recognized the white faces more frequently than the Black faces, while the Black subjects equally recognize the Black and white faces. It is especially noteworthy that perceived facial beauty facilitated recognition.[8]

The following year, Dion, Berscheid, and Walster's[9] work notes under-graduate male and female students are significantly likely to believe attrac-tive individuals possess more socially desirable personality traits than physically unattractive stimulus persons and are expected to lead better lives (for example, be more competent husbands and wives and more suc-cessful occupationally) than unattractive stimulus persons. Individuals also associate physical beauty with status. Webster and Driskell[10] reveal that physical attractiveness (beauty) affects both cognitions about indi-viduals and their interaction patterns.

Evolutionary, as well as cultural, pressures may contribute to individual perceptions of facial attractiveness, and facial symmetry is important. The work of Rhodes, Proffitt, Grady, and Sumich[11] finds a positive relationship between facial symmetry and appeal as a life partner, which suggests facial symmetry, might affect human mate choice. Other studies note the attractive-ness of a symmetrical face of facial attractiveness are remarkably consistent, regardless of race, nationality or age, and attractiveness of certain body fea-tures links to optimal health.[12] Thus, a symmetrical face and a symmetrical lip ratio (1:0:1:0) are most attractive in females.[13] Essentially, theoretical and empirical findings suggest that in addition to health, human beauty standards are universal, and attractiveness links to visual characters of the face and body as well as vocal and olfactory signals.[14]

CULTURE, THE MEDIA, AND BEAUTY

Perceptions of beauty are not static and are influenced by two forms: communications media (print vs. television) and visual media (advertising vs. entertainment).[15] Scholars note cultural differences in beauty and how these ideas play a key role in evaluating one's own appearance as well as the appearance of others.[16] As a media genre, advertising offers a unique opportunity to study the construction of beauty ideals across cultures. Firth, Shaw, and Cheng's[17] analysis of content of advertisements from women's fashion and beauty magazines in Singapore, Taiwan, and the United States reveal beauty in the US focuses on "the body," whereas in Singapore and Taiwan the defining factor of beauty relates more to a pretty face. Researchers have also identified significant differences between US and Korean evaluations of attractiveness in others due to several predictor variables, such as media exposure, sociocultural pressures to be thin, sociocultural pressures to be attractive, perceived influence of outside sources in the development of ideal beauty, and gender.[18] This argument was supported by Jung and Lee[19] in that there are often large negative discrepancies between actual and ideal body images perceived by individuals who place a low cognitive importance on appearance (such as USA) and those who place a high cognitive importance on it (such as Korea).

Environment greatly determines which female forms are preferable and deemed attractive. To make this point clear, Tovée, Swami, Furnham, and Mangalparsad[20] found striking differences in attractiveness preferences for female bodies between United Kingdom (UK) Caucasian and South African Zulu observers. In the UK, a high body mass is correlated with low health and low fertility, and the converse is true in rural South Africa. Furthermore, these scholars report significant changes in the attractiveness preferences of Zulus who move to the UK, which suggests these preferences are malleable and can change with exposure to different environments and conditions. Additionally, Britons of African origin, birthed and reared in the UK have exactly the same preferences as the UK Caucasian observers. These results suggest that humans have mechanisms for acquiring norms of attractiveness that are highly plastic, which allow them to track different ecological conditions through learning.[21]

EUROPEAN STANDARDS OF BEAUTY

While campaigns such as Dove's Real Beauty challenge traditional beauty norms,[22] television and print representations generally associate a thin body with beauty. For example, music videos, frequently viewed by young people, generally prize a thin physique; however, exposure to these images are associated with unhealthy eating habits and low self-esteem.[23] To support this, Harrison[24] reveals that exposure to fat-character television, thin-ideal magazines, and sports magazines predicts eating-disorder symptomatology for older women and exposure to fat-character television predicts body dissatisfaction for younger males. A subsequent study supports negative effects of the thin ideal among young adults. Specifically, college women exposed to thin-ideal magazine images had increased body dissatisfaction, negative mood states, and eating disorder symptoms as well as decreased self-esteem.[25]

In addition to a thin body, the media promotes certain skin tones, hair lengths, and facial features as ideal. In their examination of media-based appearance standards for Asian and Latina women in *Seventeen* magazine (aimed for female audiences), Boepple and Thompson (2016) find significant differences in the skin tone and hair length of women featured in those magazines. They reveal medium to lighter-skin tones, long straight hair, and small facial features (such as nose, lips) to be optimal beauty standards for Black, Latina, and Asian women. Even popular television programs, such as *Being Mary Jane* and *How to Get Away with Murder*, depict African American women with straight hair and average body types. Furthermore, women with natural hair and overweight body types are associated with immorality and unhappiness, while African American female characters with medium skin colors are beautified, but those with darker skin colors are portrayed in a negative light.[26]

RACE AND BEAUTY

Scholars note race determines how women perceive beauty. Poran[27] examined the responses of 157 college women (forty-eight Latinas, fifty-two Black women, fifty-one white women, and 6 "others") to determine the ideas that these women had about beauty as well as how they perceive cultural standards of beauty. Results indicate significant differences in Latinas', Black women's, and white women's relationships with their bodies, and their relationships to dominant cultural standards of beauty. Other studies note racial differences in the internalization of beauty standards based on media messages. Dye's[28] work finds Caucasians report higher internalization, higher body dissatisfaction, and higher preoccupation with weight, dieting, and eating restraint than African Americans.

While some may assume that members of stigmatized groups, such as African American and Asian women, may be more likely to experience negative self-evaluations after exposure to mainstream beauty standards, this may not necessarily be the case. As part of a longitudinal study that examines early and late adolescent girls' interpretations of mainstream teen magazines, this research focuses on how the African American audience's interpretive frame enables them to analyze and distance themselves from selected aspects of a consumption object with which they regularly engage. This study involves in-depth interviews with sixteen African American girls, ages thirteen to eighteen, who are regular readers of one of the top three teen titles: *Seventeen, YM,* or *Teen.* This work reveals older African American girls did *not* defer to the magazines' authority in defining their conception of femininity, which instead was strongly influenced by culture and frequently defined in direct opposition to the mediated ideal.[29]

One study examines whether fifty-four Asian, fifty-two Black, and sixty-four white women's exposure to mainstream standards of beauty would influence them to compare themselves to these idealized images. The results indicate Black women did not find mainstream standards relevant to themselves and reported positive self-evaluations of themselves and their bodies. Asian women, on the other hand, responded differently than Black women and were more likely to endorse mainstream beauty standards in a similar fashion to white women. Furthermore, Asian women also experienced greater dissatisfaction with their bodies than did Black women (Chin Evans & McConnell 2003). Recent studies suggest Asian American women feel they must present a bicultural identity by being exotic and American.[30] Women often feel dissatisfied with their appearance after comparing themselves to other women who epitomize the thin-ideal standard of beauty. A study conducted by Evans[31] finds women report self-dissatisfaction and less optimism about their possible future life outcomes after exposure to a thin-ideal female target that ostensibly had a successful life than when the target ostensibly had an unsuccessful life.

AGE AND BEAUTY

Aging causes unique body changes and many individuals feel sociocultural pressure to resist those changes. Since dissatisfaction with one's body can be significantly detrimental to well-being, Jankowski, Diedrichs, Williamson, Christopher, and Harcourt's[32] work finds that while older adults have aging concerns, the ability to navigate their physical environment and maintain stable, loving relationships were more important than physical attractiveness. The findings of this study support Krekula's[33] qualitative interviews with women seventy-five-plus years of age in which these women possess the ability to relate to youthful and age-related beauty norms, and establish an idealized version of middle-aged womanhood.[34]

In addition, while sixty-year-old women from different sociocultural areas recognize beauty based on social standards, these women appreciate aesthetic appeal and associate beauty in old age with caring for self and relationships.[35] Although ideas on beauty vary with personal preferences and cultural standards, there is substantial agreement as to what constitutes human beauty. However, Maymone, Neamah, Secemsky, Kundu, Saade, and Vashi[36] find contemporary standards of beauty are less narrow than they were in 1990. In particular when compared to 1990, a wide variety of skin colors and inclusion of older age groups represent among those deemed to be the most beautiful.

METHODOLOGY

This study utilizes a content analysis process to determine beauty in Prince's "The Most Beautiful Girl in the World" video. Conducting a content analysis involves deciding on a body of material to analyze, which in this work will involve song lyrics as well as systematically determining the themes and frequency of themes present in a particular song. Essentially, this method allows the researcher to "discover features in content of large amounts of material that might otherwise go unnoticed."[37] In addition to the words, this study also analyzes visual content in Prince's "The Most Beautiful Girl in the World" video. This methodology (visual content analysis) usually involves "isolating framed images (in publications) or sequences of representation (scenes or shots in television or film)" and classifying the text according to specified dimensions, or variables.[38] In this study, visual content analysis involves examining the race, body type, hairstyle, marital status, life accomplishments, and age of the women in the video. In essence, a content analysis makes it possible for the author to reveal themes in the "data" that the majority of people would not notice, allowing me to describe what is seen as well as to determine the meaning of what is seen in the context of a broader sociological phenomenon.

Procedure

The procedure involves viewing this video ten times a day from August 12–18, 2017, which was the week before the start of the semester. In total, I viewed the video seventy times (ten times per day over seven days) because it was consistent with a content analysis methodology. On the first day, I viewed the video ten times but did not take notes. My purpose in doing this was to "construct a world in which the text makes sense" and notice features of the video that I had not previously. To ensure scholarly rigor, I made the decision to view the video an additional sixty times.[39] Next, I wrote descriptive notes of the physical appearance of the individuals in the video as well as the physical environment. Then, I conducted a line-by-line and word-by-word analysis of the words Prince uses to describe beauty. During this process, I noted the number of times that certain words and/or phrases were used (for example, "Could you be") as well as the divergent conceptualizations of beauty that Prince provided. An example of these divergent conceptualizations is Prince's description of beauty as both an internal and external construct.

"THE MOST BEAUTIFUL GIRL IN THE WORLD"

"The Most Beautiful Girl in the World" is the lead single from Prince's 1994 EP *The Beautiful Experience* and 1995 album *The Gold Experience*. It was his first release since changing his name to an unpronounceable symbol. With the consent of Prince's usual record distributor Warner Bros. Records, this song was released by NPG Records and Edel Music, and independently distributed by Bellmark Records (under the control and guidance of Music of Life) as a one-off single, topping five different charts. The single was released in February 1994 in the United Kingdom and remains Prince's only #1 single in the UK Singles Chart, and was shortly followed by an EP of remixes titled *The Beautiful Experience* that also charted at #18 in the United Kingdom. The version released on *The Gold Experience* is a different mix of the song. A year after Prince met his first wife, Mayte Garcia, he released the song "The Most Beautiful Girl in the World." When an interviewer asked Garcia, "Are you the most beautiful girl in the world?" she replied, "When he wrote that song, he had all women in mind." The chorus of the song "The Most Beautiful Girl in the World" is as follows:[40]

> Could you be the most beautiful girl in the world?
> Could you be?

It's plain to see you're the reason that God made a girl
Oh, yes you are

PRESENTATION OF THE FINDINGS

Lyrical Content Analysis. For Prince, female beauty is: (a) attainable; (b) spiritual; (c) external; (d) internal; (e) powerful. Attainable relates to words and/or phrases regarding the possibility for women to be beautiful. An example of this theme is the phrase: "Could you be the most beautiful girl in the world?" [mentioned four times]. *Spiritual* relates to words and/or phrases that indicate womanly beauty is because of a Higher Power (God). An example of this theme is the phrase: "It's plain to see you're the reason that God made a girl" [mentioned four times]. External relates to words and/or phrases regarding feminine aspects of beauty. An example of this theme is the phrase: "Who'd allow, who'd allow a face to be soft as a flower? Oh" [mentioned one time]. *Internal* relates to words and/or phrases that associate beauty with qualities that are not visible to others. An example of this theme is the phrase: "Cuz baby this kind of beauty is the kind that comes from inside" [mentioned one time]. *Powerful* relates to words and/or phrases regarding the strength of female beauty as well as the ability of female beauty to render males weak. Examples of this theme are the following phrases: (a) "How can I get through days when I can't get through hours?" (b) "I could bow (bow down) and feel proud in the light of this power." (c) "I can try but when I do I see you and I'm devoured,

Table 5.1 – *Themes, Conceptualization of Beauty and Prince Lyric Associated with Beauty*			
Theme	**Conceptualizations of Beauty**	**Prince Lyric Associated with Beauty**	**Frequency**
Attainable	Words and/or phrases regarding the possibility for females to be beautiful.	*"Could you be the most beautiful girl in the world?"*	4
Spiritual	Words and/or phrases that indicate female beauty is because of a Higher Power (God).	*"It's plain to see you're the reason that God made a girl."*	4
External	Words and/or phrases regarding feminine aspects of beauty.	*"Who'd allow, who'd allow a face to be soft as a flower? Oh."*	1

| Internal | Words and/or phrases that associate beauty with qualities that are not visible to others. | "Cuz baby this kind of beauty is the kind that comes from inside." | 1 |
| Powerful | Words and/or phrases regarding the strength of female beauty as well as the ability of female beauty to render males weak. | • "How can I get through days when I can't get through hours?"
• "I could bow (bow down) and feel proud in the light of this power."
• "I can try but when I do I see you and I'm devoured, oh yes." | 3 |

oh yes" [mentioned three times]. [See Table 5.1 for Theme, Conceptualizations of Beauty and Prince Lyric Associated with Beauty and Frequency of Lyrics.]

Visual Imagery Analysis. This video presents several representations of beauty, based on race, body type, hairstyle, marital status, life accomplishments, and age. Specifically, this video shows one Asian female (who escorts the women into The Beautiful Experience to take their places in the seat to receive Prince's gaze), two white women, one Asian woman, and three Black women. In regards, to body type the Asian woman, the white women, and one Black woman were average-sized (normal frame); however, one African American female (singer) had a plus-size build. The Asian female wore her past-shoulder-length, natural hair; the Black female (gymnast) wore her hair in a past-shoulder-length, relaxed hairstyle; one white female sported a short red wig (which covered her short, brunette hair); and one white female wore locks. The women in this video were single and one white female was a bride (wearing a wedding dress and veil). In regard to life accomplishments, the women in this video were a bride, a spouse, a mother, a singer, a gymnast, and a politician. Women in this video were young, middle-aged, and one Black female represented the old demographic. [See Table 5.2 for Prince's Conceptualizations and Demonstrations of Beauty.]

Table 5.2 – *Prince's Conceptualizations and Demonstrations of Beauty*	
Conceptualization of Beauty	**Demonstration of Beauty**
Race	• White • Asian • Black • Ambiguous
Body Type	• Average (Normal) Build • Large Build (Black woman)

Hairstyle	• Asian woman with long, natural hair • White woman wearing a wig • White woman with locks • Black woman with long, natural hair • Black woman with shoulder-length natural hair • Black women with short, natural
Marital Status	• Married • Single
Life Accomplishments	• Marriage • Motherhood • Entertainment (Comedians & Actors & Directors) • Gymnastics • Politics
Age	• Very young (child, approximately 5-6 years old) • Young (late teens; early 20's) • Middle-Age (30's or 40's) • Older (60+ years of age)

DISCUSSION

The focus of this chapter is to examine how Prince perceives beauty in his "The Most Beautiful Girl in the World" song and video. Before discussing how Prince conceptualizes beauty, it is important to remember that this construct relates to "that quality or combination of qualities which affords keen pleasure to the senses especially that of sight or which charms the intellectual or moral capacities."[41] An analysis of the content and visual imagery in this video demonstrates several qualities that are associated with beauty.

One may recall the video commencing with a female on a large television screen, who says, "Welcome to the dawn. You've just accessed The Beautiful Experience. This experience will cover Courtship. Sex. Commitment. Fetishes. Loneliness. Vindication. Love and Hate. Please enjoy your experience." Initially, when women enter into what appears to be a large warehouse, it is evident that "The Beautiful Experience" is an actual location. However, as the video progresses, it becomes evident that upon entering this locale, women experience emotions that make it possible for them to appreciate where they currently are, where their lives will take them, and allows them to see themselves through the eyes of Prince, who regards each of them as "the most beautiful girl in the world." By definition, an experience is "the observing, encountering, or undergoing of things generally as they occur in the course of time."[42] The women in this video enjoy success as wives, mothers, comedians, actors, sports figures, and politicians and take pleasure in the success of others; however, it is important to note they experience this enjoyment the moment that they sit in the chair and become the focus of Prince's gaze. The following nine individuals enjoy a place in the chair: (1) bride; (2) Black female singer (large frame); (3) Black female gymnast; (4) Family of three (white husband and father; racially ambiguous wife and mother; child that is racially mixed); (5) white female comedian; (6) white female producer who wears her hair in locks; (7) Elder Black female.

Prince rejects Eurocentric standards of beauty by advocating the multidimensional ("quality or combination of qualities") nature of beauty as well as beauty's ability to activate thoughts (intellect) or behaviors (moral capacities).[43] The multidimensional nature of beauty is evident in the various ages, races, and body shapes of the women represented, as well as the beauty of interracial marriage and family formation.[44] For example, the female that holds the gown of the bride is Caucasian, dons a black and white asymmetrical jacket, and has androgynous facial features. Consider also that while the groom in the video is African American, the race of the bride is ambiguous and can represent an amalgam of African American, European, and Latino heritages. Furthermore, while the husband and father of the family of three appears to be white, the wife and mother, like the bride, represent an ambiguous racial heritage. Even the young (five or six years old) mixed-race child of this couple hints at the increased "browning" of America over the past decades, as well as the beauty of multiculturalism.[45]

By asking, "Could you be the most beautiful girl in the world?" Prince advises that regardless of race, age, phenotypical characteristics, life accomplishments, and marital or parent status, it is indeed possible for all women to be beautiful. This question can be especially meaningful for women who feel dejected because they can never meet Eurocentric beauty standards frequently promoted in commercial advertising, and thus question their own beauty.[46] By helping women understand the attainable nature of beauty, Prince accomplishes two things: (1) he helps women appreciate their own beauty; and (2) he helps women see themselves as he sees them. Prince also sings, "It's plain to see you're the reason that God made a girl." Through these words, this artist links beauty to spirituality (a Higher Power, or God), or as a triumvirate in which belief in the power of God as creator influences how individuals perceive beauty, which in turn, determines the kinds of relationships that they build with others.[47]

Prince also acknowledges the feminine or external aspects of beauty via these words: "Who'd allow, who'd allow a face to be soft as a flower? Oh."

Although facial symmetry is associated with perceived attractiveness, for Prince outward beauty is external and is synonymous with the beauty in nature (such as a flower).[48] Stated another way, just as a flower cannot produce itself, external beauty is similarly a creation of God. Furthermore, when Prince sings, "Cuz baby this kind of beauty is the kind that comes from inside," he juxtaposes internal beauty from external beauty. In particular, the phrase "this kind of beauty" compares the kind of beauty that one can see (external) with qualities that are not visible to others. This internal quality of beauty transcends aesthetic appeal because it focuses on the characteristics that make women intrinsically unique. Essentially, by lovingly gazing inward, women appreciate where they are as well as where they want to be. Conversely, Prince recognizes the power of beauty and its ability to make separation difficult ("How can I get through days when I can't get through hours?"); cause males to willingly succumb to its power ("I could bow [bow down] and feel proud in the light of this power"), and be totally overcome ("I can try but when I do I see you and I'm devoured, oh yes"). By speaking of beauty in these ways, Prince acknowledges that although males are generally physically stronger than women are, the power of these strong men immediately diminishes when in the presence of womanly beauty.[49]

As marriage is a goal for most people, including African Americans, Prince highlights this traditional value when he presents a young bride (wearing a white wedding dress and veil) and an African American male that gazes lovingly at his bride as they marry.[50] In addition, Prince heralds the beauty of childbirth and committed love when he features a female giving birth while her husband kisses her head and holds her hands firmly. In addition, although Asian women feel pressure to merge Americanism and exoticism, it is noteworthy that an Asian woman leads and escorts the bride away from Prince's gaze.[51] Thus, as the escort to "The Beautiful Experience," this Asian female is the conduit by which non-Asian women can truly see and appreciate their own exotic beauty. Moreover, Prince challenges Eurocentric standards of beauty (such as long straight hair and a thin body frame) by celebrating multiple forms of beauty. Consider how Prince features an African American woman with a large frame who sings and smiles adoringly at him, and to whom, he returns her gaze. By featuring a Black woman whose body stands in contrast to the thin-frame Eurocentric idea of beauty, Prince pushes the boundaries of Black beauty by acknowledging the capacity for all body types to be pleasing to one's sight. As it relates to the current representations of Black female identity featured in mass media, although large, this physically attractive Black female does not neatly fit within the Mammy prototype because Prince recognizes she has the capacity to be beautiful.[52] Returning to the attainability of beauty that I previously mentioned, Prince also reminds women that true beauty recognizes the possibility of who they can become. Even though Black female athletes have not reaped the same social and economic standing as their counterparts, Prince presents a Black female who gazes with awe at the image of herself as an award-winning gymnast.[53]

While Black women frequently feel pressure to wear their hair in ways that fit society's standards of beauty, Prince suggests Caucasian women are not exempt from this pressure, and mask their natural beauty.[54] To make this point, Prince shows a Caucasian woman who wears makeup, a white feathered boa, a dress that hugs her figure, and high-heels. Although this female is a successful entertainer (based on the animated laughs that she receives while performing), her authentic beauty is masked. Consider that although her hair is styled in a reddish-toned, bob (shoulder-length) hairstyle, she takes off her wig to reveal her natural hair, which is shorter than the wig and brunette in color. Furthermore, Prince challenges the European beauty standard of long straight hair by highlighting a white woman whose hair is in the traditional African American hairstyle of locks. While some might argue that a white woman wearing her hair in this manner is a misappropriation of Black culture, it could also mean something more. Since hairstyles may be forms of political expression, a Caucasian female wearing her hair in a style traditionally donned by African/African American women (locks) may hint at white women's unquestionable acceptance of Black culture via imitation.[55]

Prince battles society's ageism by featuring a mature African American woman who watches with pride, as a young, white woman, who is provocatively dressed (in a formfitting gown that shows her cleavage) receives an award and expresses her gratitude. This mature Black woman also beams with pride, as a Black woman, who resembles the late R&B/pop/soul/gospel singer Whitney Houston (1963–2012), becomes the forty-third president of the United States. By presenting women on both ends of the career spectrum (entertainer versus politician), Prince subtly yet powerfully advocates that society have equal respect for both forms of beauty.

To resist traditional beauty norms that emphasize youth, sexuality, and the reproductive capacity of women, the mature African American woman is sporting a short, tapered hairstyle and is wearing a suit and tie. By dressing the matriarch of the video in clothing traditionally worn by men, Prince pushes the boundaries regarding what true feminine beauty is. In other words, by wearing makeup with a suit and tie, this mature woman acknowledges her right to wear clothing that reflects what she deems attractive, the all-encompassing nature of beauty (respecting her masculine and feminine qualities), as well as the power of knowing her value in society. It is also important to note this mature African American female wave back to the children, who are different ages and genders, and engage in a hand game with them. By engaging in this shared activity, this mature Black female minimizes the age gap between herself and the youth, and even hints at her ability to be "young at heart," or young in mind, body, and spirit. The positionality of this mature Black woman is salient, as well. As this mature Black woman and the children around her gaze upward, she stands in the center of the children, and serves as a visual focal point and foundation from which true beauty stems. Furthermore, her positionality as mature beauty is evident when the Asian female respectfully escorts her from her seat, rather than pressure her to vacate it.

CONCLUSION

At the beginning of this manuscript, I provide several definitions of beauty. In general, these subjective assessments of this construct recognize the intrinsic nature of beauty (Confucius), questions regarding the meaning of beauty (Picasso), the ability of beauty to change and grow over time (Hepburn and Buxbaum), as well as the ability of beauty to just be (Zusak). However, Prince encourages us to make a conscious effort to recognize beauty in terms of what we can and cannot see. An important part of this effort is to recognize the connection between how women see themselves, how Prince sees them, and how the world sees them. In essence, Prince's conceptualization of beauty publicly recognizes that female beauty has a higher source (God), the capacity of all women to be beautiful, aspects of beauty that attract others, the unseen nature of beauty, as well as the ability of beauty to render individuals powerless. Although Prince is a musical giant and the man who focuses his gaze on various women, even he becomes unapologetically weak when he witnesses the multidimensional complexity of womanly beauty before him. Prince starts this video with the words: "Welcome to the dawn. You've just accessed The Beautiful Experience. This experience will cover Courtship. Sex. Commitment. Fetishes. Loneliness. Vindication. Love and Hate. Please enjoy your experience." Regardless of whether Prince conceptualizes dawn as the start of life or the start of new experiences, he soulfully urges women to appreciate each phase of their lives and to see themselves as beautiful through each of them. Although humans value physical attractiveness, *The Beautiful Experience* reminds women that their entire existence, which is distinct from their physical appearance, is valuable to him and others. Most important, Prince challenges European beauty norms by highlighting cross-cultural standards of beauty, which validate the race, age, and marital and parental statuses of women throughout the world.

When Prince left the earth on April 21, 2016, President Barack Obama said, "Few artists have influenced the sound and trajectory of popular music more distinctly, or touched quite so many people with their talent."[56] Anyone that doubts the validity of Prince's immeasurable talent or the depth of his influence need only read a few comments on his "The Most Beautiful Girl in the World" video, which is on YouTube. Case in point: One commenter whose name is Johnston6999 says, "My favorite Prince song! He is telling us every women has a gift to the next generation! My heart is saddened by his Loss :(" In addition, Boyd Daniels writes, "Proper respect to all women in every color race and body type!! 🙋‍♀️🎦👒✒️🕳️👍🌿✌️💘" Consider the connection Deanna Woods makes regarding the gift that Prince gave the world and how that gift frequently affects her today. She says, "Prince wanted all women to know that they have beauty and this was his gift to us. This song helps me feel better when I am feeling bad about myself." This brilliant singer, songwriter, and performer may no longer be physically with us, but the message in this video is unapologetically clear: All women are beautiful because their experiences are beautiful. When we imitate Prince by opening our minds and hearts to what women are and can become, we make a conscious effort to see beauty in all its forms, and recognize that every woman alive has the capacity to be "The Most Beautiful Girl in the World."

Notes

1. See Ethel D. Puffer, *The Psychology of Beauty: Creation of Aesthetic Experience* (Comet Content Providers, 2015); Charles Wilfred Valentine, *The Experimental Psychology of Beauty* (Routledge, 2015); Cherika Fills and Praphul Joshi, "European Standards of Beauty and the Relation of These Assimilated Beauty Ideals among African American Women" (*National Social Science Proceedings* 58, no. 2, National Technology and Social Science Conference, 2015), 83; Imani Perry, "Buying White Beauty," *Cardozo Journal of Law & Gender* 12 (2005): 579; Sheila Jeffreys, *Beauty and Misogyny: Harmful Cultural Practices in the West* (New York: Routledge, 2014); Naomi Wolf, *The Beauty Myth: How Images of Beauty Are Used against Women* (New York: Random House, 2013); Jane Sprague Zones, "Beauty Myths and Realities and Their Impacts on Women's Health," *Gender through the Prism of Difference* (2000): 87–103.

2. See Josée Johnston and Judith Taylor, "Feminist Consumerism and Fat Activists: A Comparative Study of Grassroots Activism and the Dove Real Beauty Campaign," *Signs: Journal of Women in Culture and Society* 33, no. 4 (2008): 941–66; Anna Kirkland, "Think of the Hippopotamus: Rights Consciousness in the Fat Acceptance Movement," *Law & Society Review* 42, no. 2 (2008): 397–432.

3. See Jaleesa Reed, "The Beauty Gap: Black Women and the Relationship between Beauty Standards and Their Decision to Purchase MAC Cosmetics" (PhD diss., University of Georgia, 2015); Shane Quantisa Weaver, "Resurrecting Black Beauty Culture: A Critical Analysis of the Black Beauty Salon through Contemporary Film" (PhD diss., Bowie State University, 2015); Minyi Liang, "Extreme Beauty" (PhD diss., California State University, Northridge, 2017).

4. Charles Wilfred Valentine, *The Experimental Psychology of Beauty* (New York: Routledge, 2015), 3.

5. Valentine, 3.

6. Anthony C. Little, "Facial Attractiveness," *Wiley Interdisciplinary Reviews: Cognitive Science* 5, no. 6 (2014): 621–34; Anthony C. Little, Benedict C. Jones, and Lisa M. DeBruine, "The Many Faces of Research on Face Perception," *Philosophical Transactions of the Royal Society B* (2011): 1634–37.

7. John F. Cross, Jane Cross, and James Daly, "Sex, Race, Age, and Beauty as Factors in Recognition of Faces," *Attention, Perception, & Psychophysics* 10, no. 6 (1971): 393–96.

8. Cross, Cross, and Daly.

9. Karen Dion, Ellen Berscheid, and Elaine Walster, "What Is Beautiful Is Good," *Journal of Personality and Social Psychology* 24, no. 3 (1972): 285–90.

10. Murray Webster Jr. and James E. Driskell Jr., "Beauty as Status," *American Journal of Sociology* 89, no. 1 (1983): 140–65.

11. Gillian Rhodes, Fiona Proffitt, Jonathon M. Grady, and Alex Sumich, "Facial Symmetry and the Perception of Beauty," *Psychonomic Bulletin & Review* 5, no. 4 (1998): 659–69.

12. Bernhard Fink and Nick Neave, "The Biology of Facial Beauty," *International Journal of Cosmetic Science* 27, no. 6 (2005): 317–25; Gillian Rhodes, "The Evolutionary Psychology of Facial Beauty," *Annual Review of Psychology* 57 (2006): 199–226.

13. Rhodes et al.; Paul I. Heidekrueger, Sabrina Juran, Caroline Szpalski, Lorenz Larcher, Reuben Ng, and P. Nicolas Broer, "The Current Preferred Female Lip Ratio," *Journal of Cranio-Maxillofacial Surgery* 45, no. 5 (2017): 655–60.

14. Karl Grammer, Bernhard Fink, Anders P. Møller, and Randy Thornhill, "Darwinian Aesthetics: Sexual Selection and the Biology of Beauty," *Biological Reviews* 78, no. 3 (2003): 385–407.

15. Basil G. Englis, Michael R. Solomon, and Richard D. Ashmore, "Beauty before the Eyes of Beholders: The Cultural Encoding of Beauty Types in Magazine Advertising and Music Television," *Journal of Advertising* 23, no. 2 (1994): 49–64.

16. Sara Docan-Morgan, "Cultural Differences and Perceived Belonging During Korean Adoptees' Reunions with Birth Families," *Adoption Quarterly* 19, no. 2 (2016): 99–118; Jaehee Jung and Seung-Hee Lee, "Cross-cultural Comparisons of Appearance Self-Schema, Body Image, Self-Esteem, and Dieting Behavior between Korean and US Women," *Family and Consumer Sciences Research Journal* 34, no. 4 (2006): 350–65.

17. Katherine Frith, Ping Shaw, and Hong Cheng, "The Construction of Beauty: A Cross-Cultural Analysis of Women's Magazine Advertising," *Journal of communication* 55, no. 1 (2005): 56–70.

18. Kim L. Bissell and Jee Young Chung, "Americanized Beauty? Predictors of Perceived Attractiveness from US and South Korean Participants Based on Media Exposure,

Ethnicity, and Socio-cultural Attitudes toward Ideal Beauty," *Asian Journal of Communication* 19, no. 2 (2009): 227–47.

19. Jung and Lee.

20. Martin J. Tovée, Viren Swami, Adrian Furnham, and Roshila Mangalparsad, "Changing Perceptions of Attractiveness as Observers Are Exposed to a Different Culture," *Evolution and Human Behavior* 27, no. 6 (2006): 443–56.

21. Tovée et al.

22. Johnston and Taylor.

23. Marika Tiggemann and Amy Slater, "Thin Ideals in Music Television: A Source of Social Comparison and Body Dissatisfaction," *International Journal of Eating Disorders* 35, no. 1 (2004): 48–58.

24. Kristen Harrison, "The Body Electric: Thin-Ideal Media and Eating Disorders in Adolescents," *Journal of Communication* 50, no. 3 (2000): 119–43.

25. Nicole Hawkins, P. Scott Richards, H. Mac Granley, and David M. Stein, "The Impact of Exposure to the Thin-Ideal Media Image on Women," *Eating Disorders* 12, no. 1 (2004): 35–50.

26. Jennifer Holloway, "How to Get Away with Whitewashing: Evaluating the Effects of the Black Is Beautiful Movement on Beauty Standards Through *Being Mary Jane* and *How to Get Away with Murder*" (PhD diss., Georgetown University, 2016).

27. Maya A. Poran, "Denying Diversity: Perceptions of Beauty and Social Comparison Processes among Latina, Black, and White Women," *Sex Roles* 47, no. 1 (2002): 65–81.

28. Heather Dye, "Are There Differences in Gender, Race, and Age Regarding Body Dissatisfaction?" *Journal of Human Behavior in the Social Environment* 26, no. 6 (2016): 499–508.

29. Lisa Duke, "Get Real!: Cultural Relevance and Resistance to the Mediated Feminine Ideal," *Psychology & Marketing* 19, no. 2 (2002): 211–33.

30. Katy Snell and Wan-Hsiu Sunny Tsai, "Beauty for Asian American Women in Advertising: Negotiating Exoticization and Americanization to Construct a Bicultural Identity," *Advertising & Society Quarterly* 18, no. 3 (2017).

31. Peggy Chin Evans, "'If only I Were Thin Like Her, Maybe I Could Be Happy Like Her': The Self-implications of Associating a Thin Female Ideal with Life Success." *Psychology of Women Quarterly* 27, no. 3 (2003): 209–14.

32. Glen S. Jankowski, Phillippa C. Diedrichs, Heidi Williamson, Gary Christopher, and Diana Harcourt, "Looking Age-Appropriate while Growing Old Gracefully: A Qualitative Study of Ageing and Body Image among Older Adults," *Journal of Health Psychology* 21, no. 4 (2016): 550–61.

33. Clary Krekula, "Contextualizing Older Women's Body Images: Time Dimensions, Multiple Reference Groups, and Age Codings of Appearance," *Journal of Women & Aging* 28, no. 1 (2016): 58–67.

34. Teri Del Rosso, "There's a Cream for That: A Textual Analysis of Beauty and Body-Related Advertisements Aimed at Middle-Aged Women," *Journal of Women & Aging* 29, no. 2 (2017): 185–97.

35. Thais Caroline Fin, Marilene Rodrigues Portella, and Silvana Alba Scortegagna, "Old Age and Physical Beauty among Elderly Women: A Conversation between Women," *Revista Brasileira de Geriatria e Gerontologia* 20, no. 1 (2017): 74–84.

36. Mayra B. C. Maymone, Hind H. Neamah, Eric A. Secemsky, Roopal V. Kundu, Dana Saade, and Neelam A. Vashi, "The Most Beautiful People: Evolving Standards of Beauty," *JAMA Dermatology* (2017).

37. According to W. Lawrence Newman, "content analysis is a technique for examining information, or content, in written or symbolic material (e.g., pictures, movies, song lyrics, etc.). Maymone et al., 34.

38. Theo Van Leeuwen and Carey Jewitt, eds., *The Handbook of Visual Analysis* (Thousand Oaks: Sage, 2001).

39. Klaus Krippendorff, *Content Analysis: An Introduction to Its Methodology* (Thousand Oaks: Sage, 2018), 28.

40. "Mayte Garcia on ex-husband Prince hiding their son's death," ABC News, April 8, 2017, YouTube, https://www.youtube.com/watch?v=AlhMwFHJIRE.

41. Valentine.

42. "Experience (1)," dictionary.com, http://www.dictionary.com/browse/experience?s=t.

43. Jandel Crutchfield and Sarah L. Webb, "How Colorist Microaggressions Have Eluded Social Work: A Literature Review," *Journal of Ethnic & Cultural Diversity in Social Work* (2018): 1–21; Yndia S. Lorick-Wilmot, "Performing Identity in Public," in *Stories of Identity among Black, Middle Class, Second Generation Caribbeans* (Cham: Palgrave Macmillan, 2018), 197–238.

44. Moffett, Tahirih Z. "Generational Change in Perspective on Interracial Marriage: A Narrative Approach to the Lifelong Sociocultural Experiences of a Caucasian Individual in a Caucasian-African American Interracial Marriage" (PhD diss., Chicago School of Professional Psychology, 2018); Yan-Liang Yu and Zhenmei Zhang. "Interracial Marriage and Self-Reported Health of Whites and Blacks in the United States," *Population Research and Policy Review* 36, no. 6 (2017): 851–70.

45. Janet M. Currie, "Inequality in Mortality over the Life Course: Why Things Are Not as Bad as You Think," *Contemporary Economic Policy* 36, no. 1 (2018): 7–23; Daniel T. Lichter and Zhenchao Qian, "Children at Risk: Diversity, Inequality, and the Third Demographic Transition," in *Low Fertility Regimes and Demographic and Societal Change*, edited by Dudley L. Poston Jr. (Cham: Springer, 2018), 169–91.

46. Khurram Sharif, Asif Raza, and Amit Das, "Fashion Model Profiles: The Intersection of Self, Ideal and Preferred," *Asia Pacific Journal of Marketing and Logistics* 30, no. 1 (2018): 23–42.

47. Bradley P. Holt, *Thirsty for God: A Brief History of Christian Spirituality* (Philadelphia: Fortress Press, 2017).

48. Alex L. Jones, "The Influence of Shape and Colour Cue Classes on Facial Health Perception," *Evolution and Human Behavior* 39, no. 1 (2018): 19–29.

49. David A. Frederick, Lily M. Shapiro, Tonicia R. Williams, Christiana M. Seoane, Rachel T. McIntosh, and Emily W. Fischer, "Precarious Manhood and Muscularity: Effects of Threatening Men's Masculinity on Reported Strength and Muscle Dissatisfaction," *Body Image* 22 (2017): 156–65.

50. Robert H. Lauer and Jeanette C. Lauer, *Marriage and Family: The Quest for Intimacy* (New York: McGraw-Hill, 2004); Cassandra D. Chaney, "The Character of Womanhood: How African American Women's Perceptions of Womanhood Influence Marriage

and Motherhood," *Ethnicities* 11, no. 4 (2011): 512–35; Richard F. Gillum and Kristen D. Dodd, *Soul Mates: Religion, Sex, Love, and Marriage among African Americans and Latinos* (Oxford: Oxford University Press, 2016): 244–45.

51. Katy Snell and Wan-Hsiu Sunny Tsai, "Beauty for Asian American Women in Advertising: Negotiating Exoticization and Americanization to Construct a Bicultural Identity," *Advertising & Society Quarterly* 18, no. 3 (2017).

52. Donnetrice C. Allison, ed., *Black Women's Portrayals on Reality Television: The New Sapphire* (Lanham, MD: Rowman & Littlefield, 2016); Nina Cartier, "Black Women On-Screen as Future Texts: A New Look at Black Pop Culture Representations," *Cinema Journal* 53, no. 4 (2014): 150–57; Imani M. Cheers, *The Evolution of Black Women in Television: Mammies, Matriarchs and Mistresses* (New York: Routledge, 2017).

53. Steven N. Waller, Dawn M. Norwood, LeQuez Spearman, and Fritz G. Polite, "Black American Female Olympic Athletes Have Not Reaped the Same Social Standing and Economic Benefits That Their Counterparts Have since the 1968 Olympics in Mexico City," *Sport Science Review* 25, no. 1–2 (2016): 53–72.

54. Yndia S. Lorick-Wilmot, *Stories of Identity among Black, Middle Class, Second Generation Caribbeans* (Cham: Palgrave Macmillan, 2018), 197–238.

55. Kobena Mercer, "Black Hair/Style Politics," *Black British Culture and Society: A Text Reader*, edited by Kwesi Owusu (New York: Routledge, 2000): 111–21; Cheryl Thompson, "Black Women, Beauty, and Hair as a Matter of Being." *Women's Studies* 38, no. 8 (2009): 831–56.

56. Jon Pareles, "Prince, an Artist Who Defied Genre, Is Dead at 57." *New York Times*, April 21, 2016, https://www.nytimes.com/2016/04/22/arts/music/prince-dead.html.

Chapter 6

WELCOME TO THE DAWN

The Racial, Sexual, Spiritual, and Political Sociology of Prince / ♀ (1978–96)

TONY KIENE

> Whatever may be the conditions of a people's political and social
> factors . . . it is generally within the culture that we find the seeds of
> opposition, which leads to the structuring and development of the
> liberation movement.[1]
> —AMILCAR CABRAL

This work is about the political and social character of Black popular culture. In particular, it is a study that examines about how sociopolitical Black culture is oppositional to and represents a critique of the dominant society and culture, which historically has asserted its control through social, political, and economic tools that dehumanize and oppress Black people. As a social and political dimension of Black urban life, much of Black popular culture springs up organically, but at the same time out of a necessity, as an agent of resistance to hegemonic forces. It represents a rejection of liberal bourgeois beliefs and behavior and reasserts its identity while creating new forms of knowledge through discourse and action.

The purpose of this essay is to use Prince, arguably the most talented musician of my generation, as a case study. My theoretical argument is that, as a cultural and political critic, Prince articulates—through the racial, sexual, and cultural politics of his music—elements of urban rage, protest, subversion, and contempt while exhibiting alternative forms of behavior and expression. The purpose here is to illustrate this through an analysis of his artistry and the musical phenomenon he spawned, which has come to be known as the "Minneapolis Sound." Prince's "Minneapolis Sound"—not to be confused with the influential alternative rock scene that emerged from the City of Lakes at roughly the same time—melds multiple genres and is characterized in large part by the pioneering use of synthesizers and drum machines, rumbling bass, dynamic guitar, and nimble rhythms.

My study will include Prince's song lyrics, musical styles, and the visual images portrayed in his videos and films. I will also examine some of his interviews, public statements and actions, as well as what both critics and supporters have said about this controversial artist from April 1978 (when he released his debut album on Warner Bros. Records) to November 1996, when he was officially "emancipated" from Warner Bros. after a lengthy and contentious dispute with the label. This newly found "freedom" represents a milestone that Prince himself referred to as "The dawn of the next phase of my life as a musician."[2]

Four principal themes will be addressed. The first will focus on Prince's views regarding violence and racism. In this area I incorporate Frantz Fanon's work, which conceptualizes violence as taking on a myriad of forms beyond simply the physical form. For Fanon, the subjugation of one population by another other is perpetuated by way of violence, which includes cultural, social, and political forms of repression. In *The Wretched of the Earth* he writes that the ruling elite "is the bringer of violence into the home and mind of the native."[3] My intention here is to illustrate how Prince conceived of his own utopian idealism and codes of behavior, resisting what he viewed as culturally imposed moral standards and social constructions. And while Prince wasn't necessarily advocating for Fanon's concept of "collective catharsis"—during which the oppressed attempt to reclaim their self-identity and independence through violence against their oppressor—his music consistently encouraged a vigorous and uncompromising opposition to cultural repression. I will also examine how he critiques the racist/capitalist society and transgresses rigid cultural borders constructed on the basis of race.

The second theme concentrates on the use of sexuality in Prince's music and imagery. This component will encompass both the prevalence of sex in Prince's music as well as his philosophy of sexuality in opposition to the social constructions of sexuality that have traditionally shaped American norms and values. Attention will also be paid to his liberated expression of sexual themes as well as his uninhibited androgynous qualities.

The third theme features Prince's vision of the future and his admonitions about the increasingly chaotic and violent world we live in, from which he underscores the supreme need to resist the threats to our freedom, justice, and our very survival. Finally, the fourth theme will discuss the continuing political and spiritual evolution of Prince into the 1990s and identify how he has come to represent a sort of postmodern spiritual politics through his music and the changing of his name to ♀̣ .

THE POWER AND THE GLORY . . . THE MINNEAPOLIS STORY

Growing up in an overwhelmingly white city during the 1960s and 1970s was not at all easy for Prince and other Black Minnesotans who frequently caught hell from the oppressive political apparatus of the racist/capitalist state. Police brutality, excessive poverty, and numerous other forms of systematic racism prevailed in north Minneapolis as well as parts of the city's south side. Prince, along with many other Black and white youth in Minneapolis, would carve out a social and cultural identity that not only rejected many of the values of white society, but also those of the Black bourgeoisie. As such, the world around Prince would deeply affect his social ideology and its relationship to his musical career and the tutelage of others.

During Prince's early years, there was a vital, yet marginalized Black music scene in Minneapolis. For the Black jazz, blues, and soul bands that did exist, being recognized and making a living at their craft proved difficult. In downtown Minneapolis, most club owners employed openly racist practices and refused to book Black acts.[4] With the rare exception of downtown clubs like The Foxtrap, most Black musicians in the Twin Cities were relegated to playing in dives or strip joints along Hennepin Avenue, the Seven Corners bohemian district near the University of Minnesota's West Bank, and St. Paul's Rondo neighborhood.

First KUXL in the 1960s, and later the poorly powered KMOJ—the only Black radio stations in the city—provided Prince and his peers small doses of the outstanding Black acts from the era, which included James Brown, Ray Charles, Jackie Wilson, Sam Cooke, The Temptations, The Supremes, Aretha Franklin, Parliament/Funkadelic, Earth, Wind & Fire, Stevie Wonder, and Marvin Gaye. Nonetheless, white concert promoters and radio stations dominated in Minneapolis, and as such, Prince and his friends were also inspired by the likes of David Bowie, Joni Mitchell, Grand Funk Railroad, Fleetwood Mac, Led Zeppelin, Elton John, and Chicago. Toss in the profound influence multiracial bands such as Sly and the Family Stone, Santana, The Jimi Hendrix Experience, Tower of Power, Rufus, and War, and Prince's musical palate was piled high and deep (as he might say). It was Prince's ability to master and fuse "Black" funk with "white rock" in addition to genres such as jazz, R&B, punk, new wave, and others that enabled him to revolutionize pop music in the 1980s.

Beginning with the release of his first album *For You* in 1978, in a career that spanned four decades, Prince created and perfected what is known as the Minneapolis Sound. During the 1980s, some argued that this creation not only surpassed Detroit's "Motown Sound" for current supremacy on the Black music scene, but established itself as the most eminent music scene in the world. Although Prince always "knew he was bad," such talk was not always something that sat well with him. He contended that no artist or sound was better than any other, they were all just different.[5]

The Minneapolis Sound was in essence Prince's very own musical genre, from which he sought out, cultivated, and produced numerous other music groups and artists. This list includes, but is not limited to, the likes of The Time, Vanity 6, Sheila E., Jill Jones, Taja Sevelle, The Family, Mazarati, Madhouse, and Tony Lemans. Prince also went on to write and/or produce for dozens of up-and-coming artists as well as established legends like Chaka Khan, Stephanie Mills, George Clinton, Mavis Staples, Joe Cocker, Patti Labelle, and Stevie Nicks. Prince, although universally accepted as a musical genius, has also been referred to in derogatory terms by critics, politicians, and religious groups, some of which have even used the term anti-Christ to describe him. There is little doubt that Prince fueled some of this disdain himself with monikers such as a "Rude Boy" and "His Royal Badness." From the very beginning, it seemed as if Prince had a very strong mistrust and even blatant contempt for different forms of social and cultural authority. He has also displayed an acute dislike and unwillingness to participate in interviews and cooperate with the press.[6]

It did not take long for the outside world to view Prince as perhaps the most enigmatic figure in music, which was very much Prince's own doing. Through his music, lyrics, visuals, and rather infrequent public statements, Prince skillfully constructed a mystique surrounding personal life. In many of his earlier interviews, Prince has admitted to essentially playing the role of "trickster," spreading disinformation about things from his childhood experiences to his racial background.[7] It was always his music that Prince wanted people to concentrate on. The other more personal matters, he believed, were nobody else's business.[8] One popular music author writes:

> Prince hates categorization and has deliberately developed an ambivalent position between black and white, male and female. But the media have just flailed around all the more wildly for a peg on which to hang him. Prince is the "new Hendrix," the "next Michael Jackson,"

the "black Bowie." No surprise then that he has become increasingly reticent in his dealings with the media.[9]

By combining sexuality with spirituality, effeminacy with machismo, and Black with white, Prince "broke all the rules" in an attempt to reject the absolutist rationale of Western political constructions such as race, sex, class, and morality. For example, in the song, "My Name Is Prince," he proclaims "I know from righteous, I know from sin. I got two sides and they're both friends."[10]

THE POLITICS OF CULTURE—HEGEMONIC
AND COUNTER-HEGEMONIC

It was the Italian Marxist, Antonio Gramsci who popularized the term *cultural hegemony*, which can be summarized as

> An order in which a certain way of life and thought is dominant, in which one concept of reality is diffused throughout society in all its institutional and private manifestations, informing with its spirit all taste, morality, customs, religious and political principles, and all social relations, particularly in their intellectual and moral connotation.[11]

Prescribing a hierarchical form of order, the concept of cultural hegemony allows the dominant group (politicians, intellectuals, the wealthy) to ordain and establish itself at the top of the political, economic, and social orders. According to Gramsci, "The apparatus of state coercive power 'legally' enforces discipline on those groups who do not 'consent' either actively or passively."[12] The most important function of the state apparatus (which includes state and judicial governments, the police and other law enforcement, and the military) is that it exists in order to repress and restore order to the society should the masses no longer consent to the hegemonic codes.[13] As will be demonstrated, a central element of Gramsci's thought is that while there is "spontaneous" and unreflective consent by the society to the social order, competing ideas always exist and will necessarily manifest themselves. In essence, cultural hegemony is produced, lost, and fought over.[14]

Regarding the perspective of colonization theory, the Martinican psychiatrist and philosopher Frantz Fanon wrote about the significance of cultural estrangement. When the dominant culture begins to take root, it dramatically affects the culture of the colonized and oppressed population. Fanon argues that this is the primary function of cultural estrangement (or cultural genocide). In order for the colonizer to succeed, it must not only implant its own system of culture, but also supplant and vilify the cultural life of the colonized. Fanon states:

> colonialism is not simply content to impose its rule upon the present and the future of a dominated country. Colonialism is not satisfied merely with hiding a people in its grip and emptying the native's brain of all form and content. By a kind of perverted logic, it turns to the past of the oppressed people, and distorts, disfigures and destroys it.[15]

As with Gramsci, which I will later illustrate, Fanon contends that it is the development of, claim to, and assertion of the oppressed people's culture that will necessitate its liberation.

Historian Ronald T. Takaki employs Gramsci's notion of cultural hegemony, adapting it to fit nineteenth-century American society. Takaki describes how white men of power, whom he refers to as "culturemakers" and "policymakers," influenced and shaped American culture and ideology. He further explains that the historical foundations of the American economic and political structure were largely established by the violent appropriation of Native American lands and the exploitation of African slave labor. In order to justify these actions, culturemakers and policymakers socially constructed indigenous populations as noble savages and slaves as subhuman.[16]

This argument assumed that both of these nonwhite groups were uncivilized, lacking any refined form of history, culture, or social structure. Therefore, they were considered intellectually inferior to whites, while still possessing extraordinary physical capabilities. These populations were also branded as sexually powerful beings that were incapable of any sexual morality.[17] This racialized discourse has been routinely and intensely imbedded in American society since its earliest days. And today, such social constructions remain consequential in the oppression of marginalized populations.[18] Nonetheless, there exists within the oppressed groups, counter-ideologies that continue to resist the dominant models of thought, attitudes, and behavior.

For Gramsci, these competing ideas would manifest themselves in the role of the political party, or what he labeled the "Modern Prince." It is the responsibility of the Modern Prince to develop, affirm, and confirm a "popular collective will" amongst the masses.[19] But as he does so, the people attempt to resist all forms of political, economic, and cultural imposition. Fanon emphasizes the essential role that culture must play in the fight for liberation. He insists that the battle for the people's culture is equivalent to their battle for freedom. Fanon proclaims, "There is no other fight for culture which can develop apart from the popular struggle."[20] West African revolutionary leader Amilcar Cabral also acknowledged the importance of culture as resistance to domination, writing, "... culture is the vigorous manifestation on the ideological or idealist plane of the physical and historical reality of the society that is dominated or to be dominated."[21] A significant aspect of both Fanon's and Cabral's thought, in addition to the importance of culture as a general social and political way of life, is their acknowledgment of popular culture via music, art, poetry, prose, and performance. Fanon writes:

> The Native rebuilds his perceptions because he renews the purpose and dynamism of the craftsmen, of dancing and music and of literature and the oral tradition. His world comes to lose its accursed character. The conditions necessary for the inevitable conflict are brought together.[22]

Essentially this prescribes that cultural forms such as music, writing, and performance redefine and assert themselves as political.[23] Supporting this position, have been a number of recent scholarly and journalistic works that highlight the political and social character of popular music and culture.[24]

Focusing extensively on the political uses of Black popular cultures and Black male deviance, Anthony J. Lemelle notes that much of "Black culture is resistant to mainstream American social organization—our survival as a people has necessitated it."[25] Incorporating Gramsci's concept of cultural hegemony, Lemelle further argues that in attempting to break out from the socially constructed barriers of their hegemonic reality, Blacks became branded as criminal.[26] Moreover, he and others suggest that in violating the legal and moral codes of society, Blacks have been labeled as social deviants, sexual outlaws, the "bad nigger."[27] Prince, because he is persistently critiquing and challenging the legal, moral, and sexual codes of the society in which he lives, he is both relegated to but also deliberately adopts this role of social and sexual reprobate.

The arguments raised by thinkers like Gramsci, Fanon, and Cabral with regard to cultural hegemony and authority raise a series of interesting questions. Is dissent ignored? Is it co-opted? Is it incorporated and assimilated into the larger culture? Todd Gitlin, a scholar and former Students for a Democratic Society member, argues that the dissent of people challenging cultural hegemony is completely co-opted and consumed by the capitalist culture.[28] In contrast, Historian Eugene D. Genovese argues that the hegemonic capitalist culture, in order to necessitate its survival, must absorb and assimilate dissent at the cost of a certain degree of social change to the dominant arrangement.[29] Interestingly, both Gitlin and Genovese are writing in the tradition of Gramsci, illustrating that Gramsci is open to different interpretations. Still, I tend to agree with Genovese and believe that Prince, along with other cultural icons and social movements, have and will continue to oppose and affect the social order.

URBAN VIOLENCE—RESISTING
CULTURAL IMPOSITION AND DOMINATION

Fanon conceptualized a multifaceted theory of violence. Not only does violence manifest itself in the physical form, it assaults the rights and dignity of others in psychological, spiritual, mental, and emotional ways as well.[30] In addition to the poverty, racism, and alienation that Prince encountered as a youth, it was the notion of an abstract moral code of behavior for which he had little use. Prince recalled in a 1981 interview with a British music journalist that he grew up in a circle of friends that were "free minded," expressing their independence in many ways including through their music, language, dress, comedy, and other forms of behavior.[31] This level of consciousness was instrumental in helping Prince envision his own brand of utopian idealism, which he describes in "Uptown," the lead single to his 1980 album *Dirty Mind*.

Uptown is, in fact, a real neighborhood centered at the intersection of West Lake Street and Hennepin Avenue in south Minneapolis, which is known for the rebellious spirit of its inhabitants.[32] For Prince, it was also a state of mind and the kind of surrounding in which he wanted to exist. In the song "Uptown," Prince refers to a place where "Soon as we got there, good times were rolling. White, Black, Puerto Rican, everybody just a freakin.'"[33] He also utilizes a couple of lyrical bridges in the song to underscore, the first of many personal manifestos that would permeate Prince's songwriting well into the future:

> Where I come from
> We don't let society tell us how it's supposed to be
> Our clothes, our hair we don't care
> It's all about bein' there.[34]

Although several music critics would champion Prince's rebellious nature, others considered his racial and sexual utopia an attempt to escape the harsh reality of the world.[35] Nevertheless, Prince's music not only suggested that he was very much in tune to the reality that surrounded him, but adamant about critiquing it.

In the track "Sexuality," from the 1981 album *Controversy*, Prince calls for the "reproduction of a new breed" of leadership, chastising the small-minded leaders and aimless members of society as "tourists."[36] In a social treatise near the end of the song, Prince explains:

> Don't let your children watch television until they know how to read. Or else all they'll know how to do is cuss, fight, and breed. No child is bad from the beginning. They only imitate their atmosphere. They're in the company of tourists, alcohol, and US history. What's to be expected is three minus three.[37]

Prince would go on to express similar themes of societal discontent on his fifth Warner Brothers release, 1982's breakthrough album *1999*.

The album's title track, an apocalyptic party anthem, revisits the Cold War angst of *Controversy*'s "Ronnie Talk to Russia" the year before. Prince's critical assessment of society, along with sex (oftentimes in the same song), dominates the record with songs such as "Let's Pretend We're Married," "DMSR," "Free," and "All the Critics Love You in New York." At the end of "Let's Pretend We're Married," perhaps Prince's filthiest song to date, he shouts another spoken-word manifesto reminiscent of those in "Uptown" and "Sexuality," which declares:

> Whatever you heard about me is true. I change the rules and do what I wanna do. I'm in love with God, he's the only way, 'cause you and I know we gotta die someday. Think I'm crazy? You're probably right, but I'm going have fun every motherfuckin' night. If you like to fight, you're a double drag fool. I'm going to another life, how 'bout you?[38]

Then, in the *1999* song "Lady Cab Driver," Prince relates his confusion, loss, fear, and pain in a cruel and isolated world to the woman whose taxi he has just hailed. During the early part of this ride, he desperately sings to her, "Trouble winds are blowin', I'm growing cold. Get me out of here, I feel I'm gonna die."[39] Later in the song, when his driver gives him another ride "so to speak," this one of a sexual nature, Prince expresses his discontent with society through each pelvic thrust. While the lady cab driver, voiced by Prince protégé Jill Jones, passionately squeals in response, Prince asserts such things as:

> This is for the cab, you have to drive for no money at all . . . This is for politicians who are born to believe in war. . . . This one's for the rich, not all of them just the greedy. The ones that don't know how to give

. . . Not knowing where I am going, this galaxy's better not having a place to go. Now I know.[40]

Years later, Prince would revive similar themes about "tourists," corrupt politicians, and the like, in the song "New Power Generation," where he sings:

> You'd think that if you tell enough lies
> They will see the truth
> I hope they bury your old ideas
> The same time they bury you.[41]

This song is from *Graffiti Bridge*, the 1990 sequel to Prince's first film, *Purple Rain*. Written and directed by Prince, *Graffiti Bridge* challenges the evils of hatred, greed, authoritarianism. In the film, a display board that hovers above Prince's nightclub Glam Slam dispatches messages such as "No one man will be ruler."[42]

Although many of Prince's political expressions in musical and visual mediums are rather straightforward, there are some less archetypal, nuanced examples as well. Prince artfully paints a picture of America in the early 1980s in *Controversy*'s "Annie Christian." He uses religious symbolism to personify the song's mythical main character "as the anti-Christ" who brings about death and destruction to the nation."

"Annie Christian" characterizes the climate of racism, violence, reactionary politics, and social chaos that embodied the early years of the "Reagan revolution." The song makes references to the Atlanta Black child murders, the assassination of John Lennon, capital punishment, and gun control. In his attempt to survive the madness outside, Prince sings over the ominous, avant garde tones of the music, "Annie Christian, anti-Christ. Until you're crucified. I'll live my life in taxi cabs."[43]

In another acute social statement, 1985's "America" from the album *Around the World in a Day*, Prince addresses topics such as capitalism and communism, urban poverty, jingoism, and cynicism. One verse describes the plight of "little sister," who struggles to survive in her one-room project tenement on minimum wage. The final verse speaks to a growing sense of nihilism in the country, particular among young people, the poor, and people of color.[44] Regarding Jimmy Nothing, a character in the song who never went to school, Prince proclaims:

> They made him pledge allegiance
> He said it wasn't cool

Nothing made Jimmy proud
Now Jimmy lives on a mushroom cloud.[45]

Prince also takes on America and its institutions, including the public school system, the corporate oligopoly, and the military-industrial complex. In 1992's *The Sacrifice of Victor*, which among other things, touches on the assassination of Dr. Martin Luther King Jr. and the urban unrest of the 1960s, Prince references an ordeal that many Black children experienced in US cities during the turbulent years following *Brown v. The Topeka Board of Education*. Prince's sister Tyka recalled in an interview that she and her older brother were among the first Black children from North Minneapolis to "participate" in the "busing" phenomenon aimed at integrating the public schools.[46] In addressing this experience in *The Sacrifice of Victor*, Prince suggest that he and his peers were merely pawns in a political game, while evoking their fear of white hostility and the trauma of being called a racial slur. In one verse, Prince sings:

1967, in a bus marked Public Schools
Rode me and a group of unsuspecting political tools
Our parents wondered what is was like to have another color near
So they put their babies together to eliminate the fear.[47]

Although Prince may have experienced other trials and tribulations in the public schools, he still emphasized the importance of education and discipline, which was instilled by his surrogate mother Bernadette Anderson. For Prince, education was critical to free and independent thinking. In other words, it is a matter of how to think as opposed what to think.

Throughout his career, Prince has been extremely disparaging of politicians who in his words "are born to believe in war."[48] Two songs from 1991's *Diamonds and Pearls* make direct references to the Persian Gulf War that began earlier in the year. In "Live 4 Love," Prince portrays himself as a fighter pilot in a moral crisis as he approaches his target, noting: "My mission, so they said was just to drop the bombs / Just like I got no conscience, just like I got no qualms."[49]

Then, in "Money Don't Matter 2 Night," Prince's lyrics attack the motives and principles of the US war machine, demonstrating America's position that oil, profit, and property are more valuable than the lives of its people, much less people throughout the world. In the song's final verse, Prince asks:

Hey now maybe we can find a good reason

To send a child off to war
So what if we're controlling all the oil
Is it worth a child dying for?[50]

While these particular references to war were made in real time during what became America's most visible conflict since Vietnam, Prince had already laid the foundation for such scrutiny in "Partyup" from 1980's *Dirty Mind*. Inspired by antidraft demonstrations of the late 1960s and early 1970s, "Partyup" insists on the right not to be killed by or to kill those who they "don't even know." Prince calls out the "half-baked" politicians who spread "all lies, no truth," ultimately asking "Is it fair to kill the youth?"[51]

While Prince's rebellious attitude regarding matters of race, sex, class, and war were applauded by many fans and critics alike, others chastised the vision of his radical idealism, which decidedly incorporated both taboo sexual themes and sacred imagery and principles. Lyrics such as, "People call me rude / I wish we all were nude / I wish there was no Black or white / I wish there were no rules,"[52] from the title track of his fourth album *Controversy*, prompted criticism from many circles that viewed Prince's romanticism as naïveté and escapist as opposed to revolutionary.[53] Beyond the lyrical and visual content, some critics viewed Prince's incorporation of "white rock forms" in to his music as an attempt to cross over and an alienation of his "black roots."[54]

Although initially a supporter of Prince, Nelson George, one of the most notable Black music critics of the period, accused Prince of running from his Blackness.[55] In comparing Prince to funk pioneer George Clinton, British rock journalist Dave Hill elaborated on this argument:

> Black consciousness emerged in the sixties as a defence against the belittling, dominating consciousness of the white society. But while Prince's idealism was intense, and inspired by dreams of liberty which were no less vivid, his "uptown" scenario comprises a rainbow coalition of diverse individuals whose minds had shed all shackles of class, race, and sex. For Prince to define himself as "black" would be a restriction rather than a display of strength and pride. As such, it was a more escapist formulation than that of Clinton. But it would also enable him to conquer markets Clinton's embrace of his own blackness caused him to be excluded from.[56]

I believe that both George and Hill miss the mark in their respective analyses. Prince never ran from his Blackness, but rather, as Twin Cities music critic Steve Perry said, "He simply refused to submit to any kind of stylistic boundaries."[57] Moreover, Hill's erroneous assertion that Black consciousness surfaced in the 1960s neglects well over a century of American history replete with African American heroes and sheroes whose spirit Prince commonly embodied, whether consciously or not.

In a 1985 television interview on MTV, Prince responded directly to the accusations that he abandoned his "Blackness," insisting that he never left his roots and that his music was as funky as ever. He went on to say:

> . . . I was brought up in a black and white world. Yes, black and white, night and day, rich or poor. I listened to all kinds of music when I was young . . . and I always said that one day I would play all kinds of music and not be judged for the color of my skin but the quality of my work.[58]

In appropriating a theme here from one of Dr. Martin Luther King Jr.'s most famous speeches, Prince intuitively brings attention to some of the parallels his career shared with that of Dr. King's. As Dr. King was deeply influenced by scores of thinkers both Black and white, Prince was inspired by Black and white artists alike. Likewise, both men elicited support from people of all social and racial backgrounds. And finally, each was labeled a sellout (and sometimes worse) by some African American critics.

For Prince, it was never a matter of selling out. Instead, in Prince's world it was simply about combining all the genres that influenced him both as a kid and as he grew older. As for the criticisms leveled at Prince by George, Hill, and others, it was George Clinton himself who famously posed the question, "Who says a funk band can't play rock?"[59] Moreover, it was a generation of Black blues artists that planted the seeds of rock and roll.

The significance of Clinton's question is that it helps highlight the enduring history of racism and commercialism in the popular music industry. The legendary Bo Diddley was once quoted as saying, "When we sang for black people they called it rhythm and blues. When we sang the same songs for white people, they called it rock and roll. The audience was all that changed, not the music."[60] Michael Bane's classic 1982 text *White Boy Singin' the Blues: The Black Roots of White Rock*, chronicles the racist history of rock and roll, illustrating how performers such as Elvis Presley, The Beatles, and The Rolling Stones reaped all the credit and rewards, while the true pioneers of rock and roll like Fats Domino, Chuck Berry, and Little Richard were left out in the cold, a phenomenon that Bane refers to as "bulldozing the niggers."[61]

The historic issue of the white appropriation of Black music is one that has been discussed and written about over and over again.[62] It is interesting to note, and certainly to their credit, that a number of the top white acts from the 1960s to the present have stated that their primary musical influences and heroes came from jazz, blues, rhythm and blues, early rock and roll, and Motown.

Nonetheless, a number of Black artists, including Prince, have suffered through the accusations of selling out and not performing "authentically Black" music. Michael Eric Dyson vigorously challenges this characterization, arguing that one can trace the musical roots of artists such as Prince, Lenny Kravitz, Terrence Trent D'Arby, Living Colour, Fishbone, Bad Brains, and Tony Lemans, back to Black musical and cultural influences such as James Brown, Jimi Hendrix, Sly Stone, George Clinton, and Howlin' Wolf, just to name a few.[63] This acutely highlights the fact that the music of such artists is no less authentic than that of any other Black musical act. Vernon Reid, guitarist for the rock group Living Colour once said that "It's not odd that Black people play rock and roll—what's really odd is that people think it's odd."[64]

Journalist Greg Tate adds that his prophecy on the reemergence of Black rock was indeed coming true and bluntly stated that "Prince done stormed the white castle and come back handing the brothers and the sisters the keys to the rock and roll kingdom."[65] Considering all of this, the criticism leveled at Prince for deserting his Black musical roots is both misguided and uninformed. Furthermore, and just as important, I suggest that a close examination of the lyrical, visual, and representational content of Prince's work (including music, films, videos, live performances, and public statements) also demonstrate that Prince is anything but of guilty of "running from his Blackness."

Of great significance in Prince's career has been his ability to transgress rigid cultural and socially constructed boundaries, and thus, not allow himself to be narrowly and solely defined in terms of existing social categories. In essence, he has taken on the role of "border crosser," a term popularized by cultural studies expert D. Emily Hicks.[66] As Dyson contends, ". . . the goal should not be to transcend race, but to transcend the bias meanings associated with race."[67] I argue that Prince does this, and although he may idealize a world without socially constructed concepts such as race, his artistry clearly illustrates that he is aware of his Blackness, and understands the significant of "race" and its consequences in both American and global society.

MOVIE STAR—PRINCE AND THE REVOLUTION
ON THE SILVER SCREEN

In the summer of 1984, Prince was vaulted into superstardom with the release of the film *Purple Rain* and its award-winning soundtrack. Although Prince is not credited with the writing or directing of the film, the impetus for *Purple Rain* was his conception and contained what are said to be semiautobiographical tones. Accordingly, his substantial input and influence on the project go without saying. Set in Prince's hometown of Minneapolis, *Purple Rain* is a story that centers on the rivalry between "The Kid" (played by Prince; leader of the band The Revolution) and Morris Day (frontman for The Time), and their battle for musical supremacy at the local club First Avenue, as well as for the affections of the lovely singer Apollonia. While the outstanding musical performances inject ample excitement and are considerably responsible for the success of the film, *Purple Rain* is also a story that follows The Kid's personal and emotional struggles, which include family troubles, the relationship with his band, and his own shortcomings. The Kid's quest for personal and spiritual growth, expressed through both his music and actions, ultimately give the movie much deeper meaning.

Critically acclaimed, *Purple Rain* was called by many the greatest rock and roll picture of all time. One half of the famous duo Siskel and Ebert, film critic Roger Ebert called *Purple Rain* "One of the best combinations of music and drama I've ever seen."[68] And his television partner Gene Siskel, who also gave the film four stars, wrote that *Purple Rain* "is a compelling story as well as stylish musical entertainment. Prince is a charismatic presence."[69]

Among African American critics, noted film and music columnist Armond White stated that "Prince is as incendiary an icon as has ever existed on film," with "the genuine musicianship, singing and performance style to match all the musical legends."[70] The significance of such praise is the fact that all of *Purple Rain*'s stars are Black (with the exception of Apollonia Kotero, who is of Mexican descent). Nelson George, who vacillated between harsh criticism and great admiration for Prince during the 1980s, referred to *Purple Rain* as a forerunner in the new Black film movement that emerged during the decade led by directors such as Spike Lee, Robert Townsend, and others.[71] *Purple Rain* garnered a number of accomplishments, not the least of which was that (until recently) it proved to be the most financially successful motion picture of all time that did not contain a primary white actor or actress.[72] Moreover, the film was credited with successfully developing what were perceived as realistic and genuine human relationships.[73]

Greg Tate applauded *Purple Rain* and believes that the relationship between The Kid and his father evokes images, although tragic, that speak to the real obstacles that can occur in the lives of a Black father and son. Tate writes that *Purple Rain* "is certainly truer to the humanity and milieu of its black principles . . . than I've come to expect outside of independent black cinema."[74] He adds that to the film's credit "are Morris Day and Jerome Benton's Black vaudeville routines on and off stage, which make you wonder how much coldblooded coon bidness could be going on in the snowy white heartland."[75] Armond White also picks up on the use of black humor and the political edge that it provides when he writes that Day and Benton "resurrect and refine an ethnic performing style (a Cab Calloway–Lester Young hipsterism) that signifies social changes as much as it amuses."[76] The unconventional quality and power of this motion picture as it relates to race, is that the existence of race in *Purple Rain* is acknowledged as natural, unapologetic, and never having to be used to qualify the film. White best expresses this notion when he explains:

> *Purple Rain* doesn't avoid the white world; it is included without self-impeding awareness and recalls Lorraine Hansberry's "I don't go around thinking about being black twenty-four hours a day" as much as it fulfils Prince's utopian manifesto. The Black characters here are liberated from the hegemony of white movie creativity responsible for the depiction of Black characters as strange and different—not because of their social oppression, but out of the *Invisible Man* conventions in which Blacks don't really belong in the picture, so if they appear at all it is with diminished character and for unstated purposes. After *Purple Rain*, one can imagine movies where race adds to the characterization rather than defines it . . . Isolated yet ambitious, Prince has vaulted over the morass in which black people interested the movie image usually flounder, stuck in limbo between character and stereotype.[77]

Without question, *Purple Rain* achieved success on its own terms. However, the critical response concerning the subject of race, when addressed toward Prince's next motion picture, 1986's *Under the Cherry Moon*, was much less friendly, with Prince champion Armond White leading the onslaught of criticism.

Released in the summer of 1986, *Under the Cherry Moon*, written and directed by Prince, was widely disparaged not only for being what many critics thought was a poor film, but for what Black and white critics alike saw as problematic racial politics and representations. In fact, White accuses Prince of some "Uncle Tomism."[78] Others leveled similar charges and added that *Under the Cherry Moon* was simply a case of Prince's ego having finally run amok.[79]

The film is the story of two gigolos, or "bad boys" if you will, that set off from their native Miami for the south of France. Settling in the Riviera's resort city of Nice, Christopher Tracy (Prince) and Tricky (Jerome Benton) spend their time seducing beautiful and wealthy French women while absconding with their riches. Along the way, the young Mary Sharon, daughter of Isaac Sharon, the richest and most powerful man on the Cote d'Azur, comes to their attention. As Tricky notes that Isaac is worth about a billion dollars, Christopher sarcastically retorts, "Yeah, and I bet he kicked a billion asses to get it too."[80]

Christopher and Tricky initially pique Mary's interest when they crash her twenty-first birthday party with the intention of getting their hands on her birthday present: a fifty million dollar trust fund. Much to the dismay of her family, particularly Isaac, Mary and Christopher quickly develop an intense romance. And eventually, Christopher is no longer interested in the money as he has found his soul mate in Mary. This ultimately leads to a battle for Mary's affections between Christopher and her father, ending in Christopher's death at the hands of Isaac's henchman. In a June 1986 radio interview with deejay The Electrifying Mojo on Detroit's WHYT, Prince stated that there was an important message to the film and hoped audiences would recognize it when they left the theatre.[81] Many critics, however, Black and white alike, ridiculed and in some cases outright dismissed Prince's "true love" fantasy. To many, it seemed as if *Under the Cherry Moon* was nothing more than two Black "tricksters" chasing white women and their money, thus making fools of themselves and disrespecting their own Blackness.[82]

To the contrary, I argue that these critics overlooked the cleverness of what Prince was trying to do, and in doing so missed the larger point the film was hoping to convey. I don't view *Under the Cherry Moon* as suffering from troublesome racial politics; rather I see it as a shrewd critique of the historical legacy of racism, colonialism, and classism throughout both Europe and America, and their enduring prevalence at the end of the twentieth century.

Consider the setting for the film and the way that *Under the Cherry Moon* is constructed from start to finish. For centuries France has been seen as one of the so-called "liberal" models of Western civilization. Yet in *Under the Cherry Moon*, a visual examination of Isaac's estate presents the aura of an antebellum plantation or aristocracy, replete with its share of Black servants. And upon an analysis of the character Isaac Sharon, a number of labels come to mind, among which are racist, fascist, imperialist, nativist, xenophobe, elitist, and aristocrat. So when Christopher

Tracy and Tricky (read trickster) step onto the scene, Isaac disdains them because they are Black, American, carefree, and of a lower class. He calls them bums, whores, and even refers to Christopher as "boy."

Although the use of the word "boy" comes real close, there are no explicit racial epithets used in the film. Still, in my judgment, the implicit nature of these racial overtones makes them more subversive. Christopher and Tricky represent more than gigolos or con artists. To the racist minds of Mary's parents they are "bad niggers," tricksters even, who have come for their daughter, underscoring one the most historically significant and evocative fears of white parents: their child becoming involved in an interracial relationship and in particular, a romance with a Black man. You can clearly see the concern in the eyes of Mary's mother and the contempt in the eyes in Isaac, the first time they encounter Christopher. These scenes bring to mind Fanon's opening line from "The Fact of Blackness" (from *White Skin, Black Masks*), when, upon recognizing the presence of someone Black, a white person thinks, "'Dirty nigger!' or simply, 'Look, a negro.'"[83] This is the type of world that *Under the Cherry Moon* occupies. The payoff is the way that Christopher and Tricky resist these racial and cultural attitudes, and what they, particularly Christopher, come to learn in the process.

In one of the film's most unforgettable scenes, Mary, who initially has her own biases (she refers to Christopher as a peasant) attempts to "civilize" Christopher and Tricky by showing them "the finer side of life" at the exclusive restaurant La Bation. But Christopher's not having it and informs Tricky instead that "we are going to bring Mary Sharon down to our world." After Mary later says that "there's nothing in Miami but people who weren't born there, and drugs," Christopher snaps back that those people know more than Mary will ever "learn in her small, sheltered world." Then, on cue, Tricky pulls out a giant "jambox" from under the table as he and Christopher transform La Bation from a snobbish, high society eatery into a stirring dance club extraordinaire. The "pristine" Mary, who against her father's wishes, has struggled her entire life to have fun, finally comes down off of her perch and lets loose, dancing wildly across the floor while Christopher sings the funk workout "Girls and Boys."

This two-different-worlds motif, referring to both Black and white, rich and poor, and the divisions between them, is a major theme in the film, which may also explain Prince's impetus to shoot the film in Black and white. Another powerful scene is when Christopher challenges Isaac to try and stop him from seeing Mary, proclaiming "that you rich folks are always taking from people like me." Now that Christopher intends to turn the tables on Isaac, he adds he and Mary are in love and there is nothing Isaac can do to stop them.

Under the Cherry Moon also effectively employs the use of humor, which is both political and unapologetically Black. There are several examples of such comedy, perhaps the most memorable of which occurs when Christopher teaches Mary that the proper place to buy a Sam Cooke album is at the "wrecka stow." Regarding the comedic rapport between Christopher and Tricky, journalist Dave Hill writes:

> The hoodlum twosome's patter is stylized, badass, smartass black. They slap five; they imitate their mothers' down home indignation; they answer the phone by saying "What it is?" When Christopher juts his chin out and calls Mary a "cabbage head" in a memorably half-cock sparring tango scene, it is an insult delivered straight from the north side (Minneapolis) streets. Prince, who commandeered the direction of the film from an early stage, makes the most of the incongruity created by these culturally alien infiltrations into a formula-genre where blacks had previously only existed as freaks, menials, and Uncle Toms. The script is full of jokes which turn on the disrepute whites associate with black-American mores: in sexuality, musical taste, and most of all language. Quite a lot of the exchanges between Tricky and Christopher would be almost impenetrable to unhip whites, although these gags fell more like entourage in-jokes than "realism."[84]

Prince also injects a deep and defiant spiritual meaning into *Under the Cherry Moon*. Now that Christopher has found his true love, he is no longer interested in Mary's money and has learned to place the spiritual above the material (as the Prince track "♥ or $" plays in the background). He informs Tricky that "he's leavin' the business" (signifying their gigolo trade), noting that if two people really loved one another and their souls ultimately become one, then "the flesh is nothin'. We live in a parade." When Christopher is later killed by her father, Mary comes to the same realization, and in the end Christopher's death sets her free from Isaac's control.

In spite of the widespread condemnation of its racial politics and representations, *Under the Cherry Moon* stands up to and rebukes the racist, materialistic society that exists in both the film and real world. The film's closing credits feature a video performance of the song "Mountains," where Prince, further demonstrating this worldly awareness, proclaims:

> Once upon a time in a haystack of despair
> Happiness sometime hard to find

Africa divided, hijack in the air
It's enough to make you want to lose your mind.[85]

To his credit, not only does Prince maintain the qualities and experiences that keep him true to his Blackness, he also uncovers the essence of what makes all of us human, what makes us recognize our own soul and the humanity and souls of others.

As the calendar turned to 1987, Prince would continue to address racial, social, and political issues in his music. Released in the spring of 1987, the almost universally acclaimed double album *Sign ☉ The Times* tackles a myriad of critical subjects such as poverty, disease, guns, and death. And, the record's title track surveys the advent of AIDS, the proliferation of drugs, and escalating climate of violence. Here Prince sings:

At home there are seventeen-year-old boys
and their idea of fun
is being in a gang called the Disciples
High on crack and totin' a machine gun.[86]

In large part, "Sign ☉ The Times" is a stinging indictment of the deteriorating conditions in America and throughout the rest of the world. As author Timothy White puts it, this song "announces the slow boil of underclass rage . . . depicting the selfish, racist society that had precipitated it, asserting that governments are more comfortable spending money on corrupt defense contracts rather than black and poor people would reap what they sow."[87]

Prince followed *Sign ☉ The Times* with a concert film of the same name. Filmed at both The Ahoy in Rotterdam and at Prince's Paisley Park complex in the Minneapolis suburb of Chanhassen, the film was unanimously praised by fans and critics alike, with more than one writer calling it the best concert film ever.[88] In what was both a reference and a challenge to those who had previously denigrated Prince's sound, journalist Steve Perry called *Sign ☉ The Times* "the hardest shot of funk he'd ever delivered," adding that it was ill-conceived of anyone to accuse Prince of either running from his Black skin or Black musical heritage.[89] Yet this would only prove to be the tip of the iceberg relative to what Prince still had up his sleeves.

This iceberg metaphor refers to the legendary, unreleased and extensively bootlegged *Black Album* from late 1987. One of the most sought-after records ever on the black market, the album was officially released, apparently against Prince's wishes, by Warner Bros. in November 1994. The *Black Album* is an eight-song funk fest that was widely considered Prince's "Blackest" effort to date, musically and lyrically.⁹⁰ Originally titled *The Funk Bible*, it contains everything from the lascivious sounds of "Le Grind" and "Rock Hard in a Funky Place" to hard driving jams "Superfunkycalifrafisexy" and the instrumental "2 Nigs United 4 West Compton."

With tracks like "Bob George" and "Dead On It," the *Black Album* also delves into the genre of "gangsta rap" before the phrase had ever been coined. In "Dead On it," Prince employs the tradition of braggadocio when he raps:

> Negroes from Brooklyn play the bass pretty good
> But the ones from Minneapolis play it like it oughta should
> A nappy fro is better when U got a blue bonnet
> And the to and fro' is funky when the grease is dead on it.⁹¹

Shortly before its scheduled release in December 1987, Prince pulled the *Black Album* in favor of *Lovesexy*. Some have suggested that Prince abandoned the record because he preferred to put out the more positive message of *Lovesexy* as opposed to the angrier material of the *Black Album*.⁹²

However, there were also rumors that Prince and Warner Bros. clashed over the commercial viability of the record both in regard to its content and scheduled release right on the heels of the uber-successful *Sign ☮ The Times*.⁹³ Whatever the reason, part of the *Black Album*'s genius, whether intentional or not, was its "fall" into the black market enhancing its subversive and underground quality, or what Armond White calls its "rebel authenticity."⁹⁴ White adds that another aspect of the *Black Album*'s beauty is Prince's ability to accentuate the strength and eloquence of Black folk culture and its oral and musical traditions, or to use a common expression in the Black community, he is "down by law."⁹⁵

When *Lovesexy*, his most spiritual album to date, was released in May 1988, it also prepared the ground for the spectacular Lovesexy World Tour, which ultimately ran seventy-seven nights in forty-five cities throughout Europe, North America, and Japan. Prince staged the Lovesexy Tour as a means to address the ethical dilemma he struggled with in his decision to replace the *Black Album* with *Lovesexy*, as the first half of the show primarily features some of the darker, more libidinous material from his catalogue culminating in the belligerent fantasy "Bob George." Prince then pivots into *Lovesexy*'s reverent ballad "Anna Stesia" before storming through some of the album's other songs including the title track, "Eye No," "Glam Slam," and "I Wish U Heaven," along with standards such as "The Cross," "Let's Go Crazy," "When Doves Cry," "1999," and "Purple Rain."

In *Prince: A Music Portrait*, a 1989 documentary short by *Purple Rain* director Albert Magnoli, an anonymous fan dramatically describes the spectacle of the Lovesexy Tour following its legendary European finale at Westfallenhalle in Dortmund, West Germany:

> You leave a concert like this inspired. He's (Prince) actually got the nerve to say God is alive. How many people can say that, you know to 17,000 people, and yet, them all to say it back to him. It's great, you know it's positive. It tells you that there's a future to the world. He's got a message. He's got a reason for being up there.[96]

And in another documentary from that same era,[97] *The Prince of Paisley Park*, Mavis Staples references Prince's evolving spirituality in the lyrics to one of the first songs he ever wrote for her. Recorded in July 1988 at London's Olympic Studios—in between Wembley Arena dates on the Lovesexy Tour—"God Is Alive" boldly asserts:

> News is comin' like a hurricane
> Comin' down hard on those who live in vain
> Treatin' each other funky when u know we're all the same
> God is alive, this is not a game.[98]

Still, Prince made certain that he did not incorporate the spiritual tone on either the *Lovesexy* album, world tour, or other projects at the expense of his evolving social and political critique, particularly as it related to urban America.

On the B-side to the single "Glam Slam" ("Escape") and another of *Lovesexy*'s outtakes ("Welcome to the Rat Race"), Prince suggests that the world the younger generations have inherited from the older is a "rat race," teaching that it is "more hard to love than it is to hate."[99] In *Lovesexy*'s "Dance On," Prince mourns the death of so many "young brothers," while "Positivity" further examines society's despair by asking of those same young brothers:

> Who's to blame when he's got no place to go
> and all he's got is the sense to know
> is that a life of crime
> will help him beat you in the race.[100]

Similar themes of racial and economic disparity would continue to permeate Prince's later output, including through the medium of music videos.

In the spring of 1992, Prince teamed up with filmmaker Spike Lee to produce a pair of videos for the single "Money Don't Matter 2 Night" from the multiplatinum album *Diamonds and Pearls*. The two collaborated again when Prince, among a number of other high-profile African American celebrities, helped finance Lee's Academy Award–nominated biopic *Malcolm X*, and later contributed the soundtrack to Lee's 1996 film *Girl 6*. One of the two videos for "Money Don't Matter 2 Night" dramatizes the day-to-day life of a Black family in which both parents have been recently laid off. The father mocks the president's rhetoric about economic recovery, cynically inquiring, "Where are the jobs?"[101] As Prince sings of "users" and "snakes in every color, every nationality, and size," the likes of President George Bush, Army general and Persian Gulf war architect Norman Schwarzkopf, and Donald Trump appear on the screen in sharp contrast to the video's other images of people suffering from war, poverty, disease, starvation, and homelessness.

Then, just four months after the Los Angeles rebellion in April and May 1992, Prince released the single and video for "My Name Is Prince." The video summons multiple images of fire, violence, and the police, while people are being beaten on the streets. Prince appears with a large police badge across his chest, a microphone shaped like a gun, and a police style hat featuring a mask of gold chains that cover his face. One might infer that while the police forces project themselves as protective institutions, Prince's wardrobe in the video, and in particular his mask, symbolizes the police's attempt to conceal their true identity as an occupying force in nonwhite and poor white communities. This would become a recurring motif in Prince's future undertakings.

When Prince established a new band in 1990, which he dubbed the "New Power Generation," he added the "Game Boyz" to the mix, which consisted of rapper Tony Mosely and dancers Kirk Johnson and Damon Dickson. Prince first discovered the three childhood friends performing in the restroom at First Avenue during the filming of *Purple Rain* and featured them as extras in the movie. With the Game Boyz now in the fold, Prince and Mosely composed lyrics that deeply explored matters such as Black-on-Black violence, police brutality, and the pervasiveness of racism, which resulted in an abundance of new material.[102]

Several new songs appeared on the New Power Generation's 1993 *Gold Nigga* album, which was released independently by Prince's NPG Records. The albums only single "2gether," calls for Black unity and resistance to police violence, while the funky "Deuce and A Quarter" admonishes the systematic criminalization of Black people and the racist, corporate structure that perpetuates and benefits from it. In this song, Mosely raps in part that:

> See, the system wasn't made 4 me or U
> And as a matter of fact it wasn't made 4 a poor white who
> Gets their weekly hit
> Or should I say that weekly check.[103]

Also from this record is the comical, yet defiantly antiracist "Black Mother-fuckers in the House," which became a crowd favorite when played during Prince and the New Power Generation's Act 1 and Act 2 tours.[104]

Always looking to help a fellow artist, Prince began writing songs with analogous social and political themes for the likes of the young Tevin Campbell and legend Mavis Staples. On "Uncle Sam," from Campbell's 1993 album *I'm Ready*, Prince disputes some of the "alleged fruits" from the modern civil rights movement, arguing that the social and economic conditions of many Black Americans have steadily declined in recent years. From the perspective of the disenfranchised, Prince's lyrics claim that what they see today are "uncivilized rights with unenforced laws."[105] In "Paris 1798430," also written by Prince for Campbell, Prince preaches:

> Ebony American heart torn in two
> Watching his soul disappear with no trace or clue
> A brother got lost livin' 4 the city takin' dope from the man
> Ain't nowhere to run when it's from Uncle Sam.[106]

And while *Time Waits for No One*, Mavis Staples first release on Prince's Paisley Park label, was comprised of more traditional soul and gospel refrains, 1993's *The Voice* was a social justice juggernaut, which harkens back to her 1960s roots.

"The Undertaker," "Melody Cool," the title track, and a cover of Prince's 1988 "Positivity," all help to adroitly fashion the pro–civil rights proclivities of *The Voice*, but it is the salient "You Will Be Moved," that kicks the proverbial doors down. Staples, with the help of the Twin Cities gospel quartet The Steeles, roars through Prince's lyrics proclaiming:

> When the streets overflow with angry souls
> That's when you'll see the truth
> When the pain that you've inflicted comes back on your door 2 roost
> That's when you'll see the future, but you won't see you.[107]

So again, despite the previous criticism leveled against Prince to the contrary, he is steadfast in his racial and political critique of post–civil rights America, sounding the alarm in deference to resistance, not escapism. Then, of course, beyond Prince's social justice vision, have been his controversial sexual politics, especially his views on the nature and "morality" of sexuality.

DMSR—PRINCE, AMERICA, AND WESTERN SEXUALITY

Since the 1970s, there have been a multitude of philosophical studies designed to document American and Western conceptions of sexuality through a new lens. Much of this research argues that the dominant ideas and morality around sexuality are, in truth, socially constructed and systematized by political, economic, and cultural forces (Schur 1988; Peiss and Simmons 1989).[108] Furthermore, the social construction of sexuality and related mores has significant implications in respect to power relations and the categories of race, sex, and class.[109]

Perhaps the most groundbreaking work in this particular arena was provided by French philosopher Michel Foucault. Foucault's three-volume study on *The History of Sexuality* reinvented how some scholars think about sex and its relationship to the Western world. In order for the practice of sexuality to come under authoritarian rule, it had to be given its own discourse, language, or as Foucault writes, "it had to be put into words."[110] As such, the establishment of this hegemonic sexual discourse empowers those who have articulated and dictated it. Put another way, this social and political design manufactures the sciences that interpret sexuality and legitimizes the powers that govern it.[111] Thus, if one were to transgress the sexual and moral codes of a society (which may delineate with whom, how, where, and for what purpose one engages in sexual behavior), they may become subject to state discipline and ostracization. Still, aside from his achievement with *The History of Sexuality*, Foucault failed to provide an adequate examination of the relationship between race and sexuality in the West.[112]

Throughout America's history, nonwhite peoples have been socially constructed by the dominant group (that is, white men of influence and power) as bestial, uncivilized, and amoral.[113] It was suggested by the ruling class that Blacks, for example, were naturally instinctual (characterizing the body) and intellectually inferior (characterizing the mind), and therefore oversexualized by white society.[114] This delineation of Blacks as sexually amoral enabled the "culture makers," as historian Ronald Takaki calls them, to publicly hold them responsible for such diseases as syphilis and later AIDS.[115] Moreover, these systematic labels perpetuate the myths that Black men are inclined to sexual violence and Black women as sexually promiscuous and unchaste.[116]

A literary example of such stereotypes is found in Richard Wright's 1940 classic *Native Son*. Although Wright's protagonist Bigger Thomas accidentally kills Mary Dalton (a white woman), he is charged, convicted, and executed for both murder and rape even though he is innocent of both. Bigger's illegal and gruesome disposal of Mary's body was a horrific crime and cannot be overlooked. Nonetheless, the fact that Bigger took this course of action demonstrates the reality that, whether guilty of the crimes of rape and murder or not, he would surely die at the hands of the state if he were suspected in the least. The example of Bigger is what postcolonial scholar Abdul R. JanMohammed calls the discourse of "racialized sexuality."[117] The sexualized Black body struck fear into the minds of whites, thus provoking America's culture makers to attempt to control both Black and white sexuality.[118]

The objective here was to maintain white society's existence as a "virtuous people," resisting the pleasures of the body, which they characterized as a vice.[119] Foucault explains that the view of the body as taboo and something to be detested is in great contrast to the teachings of centuries past. Prior to the era of modernity, wisdom elicited strategies designed to make humans love and desire the body.[120]

The clash between the authoritarian repression of sex, and the perception of sex as natural and sensual, is illustrated in the sexual and racial symbolism of Herman Melville's 1851 masterpiece *Moby Dick*. According to Afro-Trinidadian historian and Melville scholar C. L. R. James, Captain Ahab is the typification of the white totalitarian master, while his vessel, the *Pequod*, is representative of nineteenth-century America.[121] The structure of the *Pequod* is thematic of the "white master race," where the ship's white crewmembers are portrayed as possessing superior mental capacity and the nonwhite crew are describes as savages who provide the brawn for the ship.[122] In essence, *Moby Dick* is a story of the Western man in relationship to nature and his obsessive desire to control and ultimately conquer it. This is represented by Ahab chasing the great whale through the sea in an attempt to harness it and kill it.

As for the principal sexual metaphor in the novel, sociologist Anthony Lemelle notes that Ahab represents Western man and the whale is symbolic of the male phallus.[123] Western man's desire to regulate sexuality is antithetical to human's innate longing for sexual expression. The whale, when it is not dominated, has the "mobility" to move about freely and in concert with the sea, which represents the female sexual organ (provided that she is an equal and willing participant), hence the title *Moby Dick* (changed from its original title *Mocha Dick*).[124]

The music of Prince embodies this free expression of sex. In describing the rise of secular song during the late nineteenth and twentieth centuries, historian Lawrence Levine writes that, "Black song depicted sex freely as a natural and expected part of life."[125] As such, much of Black music and culture has existed "outside the mainstream of middle class white morality."[126] Prince is an extension of this Black cultural tradition, exhibiting an affirmation, love, and uninhibited expression of sexuality through his work. Prince's first two albums, *For You* (1978) and the eponymous *Prince* (1979), were replete with sexual innuendos and double entendre, but nowhere near as brazen or controversial as Prince would soon become.

With *Dirty Mind* (1980) and *Controversy* (1981), Prince explored ground that had rarely if ever been walked on in popular music, singing about topics such as oral sex ("Head"), incest ("Sister"), and masturbation ("Jack U Off"). In addition to explicit lyrics and hypersexual themes, the images Prince conveyed through his style of dress and stage performance also shocked and offended many critics as he often appeared in underwear, a trench coat, and heeled boots.

Notwithstanding the sensibilities of some, Prince's music and charismatic live performances received a great deal of acclaim from both fans and journalists.[127] One critic wrote that *Dirty Mind* was a "record of Rabelaisian achievement, ditheringly obsessed with the body but full of sentiments that please and provoke the mind."[128] Another referred to the same record as musical miscegenation revealing Prince as a "rebel, sexual politician, and utopian visionary."[129] And Prince biographer Dave Hill asserts:

> *Dirty Mind* was nothing if not the flaunting of a particular style, and it the face of suffocating expectations. It is not simply that it could be ruder, but that it could not be more personal in its rudeness. It could not be more dismissive of the rock-business assumption that black artists were only viable when they dealt in traditional black music forms. It could not be more at odds with the full-blown, divisive Puritanism of the American power-structure, just at the moment when it is undergoing a fierce, white-hot revival, with Ronald Reagan its presidential standard-bearer.[130]

Notwithstanding Hill's praise and poignant social commentary, several other writers were far less kind in their assessment. For example, Nelson George, author of *The Death of Rhythm and Blues*, argued that Prince's music and live performances displayed a "disgusting immaturity."[131] Noted jazz and cultural critic Stanley Crouch offered that Prince represents "demonic vulgarity,"[132] while renowned Harvard psychiatrist Alvin Poussaint calls Prince sexually obsessed and exhibiting a "mysterious satanic, messianic quality."[133] There are also examples of Prince's behavior beyond his music that led to such derision. On a poster that accompanied the 1981 album *Controversy*, Prince, while in the shower, takes on a sensual pose wearing only a pair of bikini briefs as a crucifix hangs on the wall behind him. In one interview, Prince stated, "I feel so very close to God when I'm aroused. Never closer."[134] And, in response to his 1988 Lovesexy World Tour, a whirlwind experience of sexuality and salvation, one critic said that Prince "could be as dirty as a pornographer and as evangelistic as a preacher, all in the same show."[135]

The explicit nature and incorporation of sexual themes mixed freely with religious ones would also earn Prince the attention of the Parents Music Resource Center (PMRC) and numerous religious organizations. In December of 1984, the Zion Christian Center in the Minneapolis's twin city of St. Paul, held a demonstration to coincide with the Purple Rain Tour's five-night stand at the St. Paul Civic Center Arena, where they burned Prince albums outside the venue. One of the group's leaders theorized that the God Prince worships must be his genitals.[136] Nevertheless, none of these attacks fazed Prince.

Even prior to the release of *Dirty Mind*, Warner Bros. suggested to Prince that his forthcoming material would bring him under attack from organizations such as the NAACP.[137] But this advice left Prince unmoved. Instead, he challenged his critics by asserting that his lyrics represent everyday reality, adding that they are directed toward both his generation and teenagers in an effort to examine issues that others wish to disregard.[138] In response to claims that his material was "controversial," Prince commented: "I don't particularly think its controversial. I mean, when a girl can get birth control pills at age twelve, then I know she knows just about as much as I do, or at least will be there in a short time. I think people are pretty blind to it. Pretty blind to life, and taking for granted what really goes on."[139] While touring Europe for the first time in 1981, Prince told a Dutch journalist that the fact that so many people "lose their cool" behind the matter of sex is enough of a reason for him to keep writing about it.[140]

Throughout his career, Prince has consciously and consistently challenged American conventions with regard to sex, equating it with liberation, defying its racial taboos, and endowing it with a revolutionary quality. Among the most visceral manifestations of this philosophy is heard in the 1981 single "Sexuality," where Prince declares:

Come on everybody, yeah, this is your life
I'm talkin' 'bout a revolution, we gotta organize
We don't need no segregation, we don't need no race
New age revelation, I think we got a case.[141]

A year later, Prince's funk anthem "DMSR" from the breakout album
1999 expresses Prince's thoughts about pleasure as he chants, "I don't care
to win awards / All I wanna do is dance, play music, sex, romance/ Try my
best to never get bored / If you feel alright let me hear you scream."[142] In
the construction of American sexual thought and behaviors, pleasures of
the body have been considered taboo, perverse, and harmful.[143] Yet Prince
thoroughly and unequivocally rejects this notion, insisting that pleasure is
something to be revered, pursued, and in indulged in.

Prince's lyrics and visual imagery also confirm that he believes sexuality is
inextricably linked to the spiritual and psychological realms. In other words,
he views the sacred and the sexual as two sides of the same coin, another
blatant rebuff of the dominant Western model. In addition to an array of
sensuous ballads and raunchy uptempo funk, Prince probes the relationship
between the soul, mind, and body in songs like "Scandalous" and "Sexy MF,"
as well as in his film *Under the Cherry Moon*, and during the entire *Lovesexy*
album and subsequent world tour. Then there are other Prince songs such
as "Let's Pretend We're Married," "Horny Toad," "Erotic City," "Gett Off,"
and "Come," which religious cultural conservatives ("the moral majority")
would shout down as simply nasty.

Explicit sexuality and four-letter words would not be the only taboos
that Prince would deconstruct. Between 1978 and 1986, Prince's band
suffered a few defections, while at the same time incurring a few welcome additions, and still remained both multiracial and multigendered.
Eventually dubbed The Revolution, the band's makeup was significant as
Prince ultimately employed two women, Lisa and Wendy, not as vocalists but rather as musicians with equal footing. Prince got the idea for a
cross-cultural, cross-gendered lineup from one of his idols Sly Stone as
well as his mentor Pepé Willie, whose band 94 East featured not only the
teenage Prince but Bobby "Z" Rivkin, who would later become Prince's
own drummer in The Revolution.

Another critical aspect of Prince's sexuality that flies in the face of
the repressive sexual codes of the West is his lyrical and visual display of
androgyny. Psychoanalyst June Singer's research has illustrated that among
peoples throughout the world, androgynous principles have long been a
part of their routine life. Among cultural groups in native North America,

South America, Africa, India, and East Asia, social and religious rituals frequently display a natural, androgynous balance.[144] In addition to these societies, there are some Western cultures that transcend the cultural rigidity and prescriptive gender roles and codes that exist in America and most other western societies, which portray androgynous traits in a negative light. In the United States, writes men's studies scholar Clyde W. Franklin, "black male youth, like their white counterparts, learn to value masculine traits as well as their expressions. They, too, learn to devalue certain traits associated with femininity."[145] Prince, on the other hand, resisted this temptation, noting that it was attractive for himself to employ feminine characteristics such as empathy and emotion.[146]

Prince employs androgyny through his music and visual art in several ways, some of which can be seen through examining two of his films, *Purple Rain* and its sequel *Graffiti Bridge*. In *Purple Rain*, for instance, Prince's (The Kid's) mother and father closely resemble his own masculine and feminine sides. The Kid is extremely sensitive as is his mother, but also takes on the traits of his temperamental, abusive father. The Kid refuses to play the music composed by the two females in his band, Lisa and Wendy, and, similar to his father's treatment of his mother, he ultimately hits his girlfriend Apollonia. When his father attempts suicide, The Kid struggles over thoughts of taking his life as well. Yet he wisely resists this impulse and in essence, his father's apparent death represents the killing off of the "dominant male role" in himself. In the end, The Kid both mends his relationship with Apollonia and incorporates the music of Lisa and Wendy into The Revolution.

Released six years later, *Graffiti Bridge* and its androgynous themes are to be understood in its relationship to *Purple Rain*. It is not until *Graffiti Bridge* that we discover The Kid's father did in fact die in *Purple Rain*. As times are hard for The Kid, he struggles not to revert back to the ways of his father, writing imaginary letters to him and expressing his fear that he is "cursed to make the same mistakes you did."[147] He contemplates picking up the gun in a desk drawer, but again he resists and attempts to chart a course toward spiritual evolution.

One of the most heavily examined and celebrated examples of androgyny in Prince's music comes from the 1987 track, "If I Was Your Girlfriend," where Prince sings to his woman:

> Baby, can I dress you
> I mean, help you pick out your clothes before we go out?
> Listen girl, I ain't sayin you're helpless
> But sometime, sometime those are the things that bein' in love's about.[148]

Prince plays with this theme again in 1990's "We Can Funk," where he tells the current object of his affection "I will be your little baby / I can be your big strong man / I can be your girl or boy / I can be your toy."[149] Authors Jeff Hearn and Antonio Melechi observe that in songwriting such as this, Prince "polymorphously explores a field of undifferentiated desires."[150] Later, in 1992's "Arrogance," Prince implies that he is "man enough" to realize that he is both masculine and feminine.

While Prince exemplifies feminine qualities in those two songs, among others, the *Black Album*'s "Bob George" is a piercing critique of the socially constructed role on Black masculinity. In "Bob George," Prince's character personifies the image of a flamboyantly vindictive misogynist who curses and ultimately kills his woman. Many have speculated that the etymology of the song's title is a slight to Bob Cavallo, one of Prince's managers, and critic Nelson George. Regardless, and whether intentional or not, the use of two male names inflates the notion of masculinity and serves to critique both the hypermasculine characteristics of the song and the violent imagery associated with it. While performing this character, Prince also skillfully employs the use of self-deprecating humor. Inquiring as to what his unfaithful woman's lover does for a living, his response is priceless: "Manage rock stars? Who? Prince. Ain't that a bitch. That skinny motherfucker with the high voice."[151]

Prince also utilizes the visual mediums of music video and live performance to blur the line between gender norms. For example, in the video for 1989's "Scandalous," Prince appears against a black backdrop, wearing a bright red jumpsuit and fluently dancing in a manner that would be difficult to categorize as either masculine or feminine. Moreover, the careful lighting in this video reveals only one side of his face, symbolizing the duality of Black and white, male and female, a strategy he would soon use in *Graffiti Bridge*. Another instance of Prince's androgynous inclinations in music video comes from 1985's "Raspberry Beret." The first time we see Prince following the enormous success of the Purple Rain Tour, he flaunts a rather feminine, feathery hairdo that invariably had many women running to their stylists asking them to "Do my hair like Prince's."[152]

Prince continues to freely champion, parade, and toy with traditional feminine and androgynous characteristics through his songwriting, dress, and stage performance, and to feel completely comfortable in doing so. Prince's use of such paradigms further demonstrates his desire to reject social, cultural, and politically imposed behavioral codes at all costs. And as he continues to flout racial, sexual, and class conventions, he also calls attention to what he sees as the social deterioration of not only America but the larger global society as well.

THE FUTURE—IF THERE'S LIFE AFTER, WE WILL SEE

From early on in his career, perhaps as a nod to being brought up in the Seventh-Day Adventist faith, Prince made occasional reference to the apocalypse. Songs like "Ronnie Talk to Russia," "1999," "The Dance Electric," and "7," explored visions of the end times; however, Prince would also allude to his dread of a possible dystopian society which in his eyes has already begun to take hold. On his critically acclaimed soundtrack to the 1989 motion picture *Batman*, Prince opens with a sobering track titled "The Future," where he forewarns of an onslaught against the poor, the persistence of structural racism, and the resurrection of a more overt racism:

> Systematic overthrow of the underclass
> Hollywood conjures images of the past
> New world needs spirituality that will last
> I've seen the future and it will be . . . I've seen the future and it works.[153]

Some suggest that the paranoia and cynicism Prince expresses here in the face of an increasingly violent and authoritarian climate, is a highly rational position in an American society where the core values are lying, cheating, stealing, and sometimes murder.[154]

Nonetheless, Prince demands us to oppose such a world, and among the most notable examples of this is the film *Graffiti Bridge*. Released by Warner Bros. in November 1990, the much-anticipated sequel to *Purple Rain* was instantly met with scorn from both journalists and moviegoers alike. Film critics widely considered it poorly acted, written, and directed, while the general public found it a little too cosmic, too spiritual, and too difficult to follow. Notwithstanding such pervasive disapproval, *Graffiti Bridge*, in my estimation, offers a sagacious, subversive, and revolutionary message that defies the political and spiritual corruption that permeates society.

As in *Purple Rain*, this film pits "The Kid" (played by Prince) against Morris Day, frontman of The Time. Billy Sparks, owner of First Avenue (the historic venue featured in *Purple Rain*) has passed on and left half of a new club, Glam Slam, to The Kid and the other half to Morris. Yet fifty percent of the Glam Slam is not good enough for Morris. Disgusted by The Kid's music, which he refers to as "spiritual noise," Morris, who has 100 percent ownership in the club Pandemonium, insists that there is not enough revenue being generated by the Glam Slam. As such, he seeks to overtake The Kid while shaking down two other clubs (Clinton House, Melody Cool) in an attempt to gain complete control of the Seven Corners district of Minneapolis.

Prince, who wrote and directed the film, explicitly styles the imagery that composes the cityscape of *Graffiti Bridge*. Morris's own club, Pandemonium, is synonymous with chaos, mayhem, and destruction. In one scene, The Kid, when referring to Pandemonium says, "On the outside, it's very nice. It's the inside I got a problem with."[155] Inside, instead of an ordinary stage, The Time plays on a stage that resembles a skillet and encircled by a ring of fire as female dancers perform in cages high above the crowd. Morris is a materialistic, narcissistic, and morally vacant individual driven by his appetites for power, sex, and wealth. By contrast, The Kid represents a social, spiritual, and community-minded person who, while interested in promoting love and peace, is vehemently prepared to fight for his beliefs.

Before taking the stage to perform the song "Elephants and Flowers," The Kid applies "war paint" to his face, foreshadowing his spiritual war against Morris and the ideals he espouses. In the song's chorus, The Kid unabashedly sings:

> Love the one who is love
> The one who gives us the power
> The one who made everything
> Elephants and flowers.[156]

During this performance, he also dons a black-and-white checkered top and pants with one black leg and one white leg, emblematic of the duality of all things and the interconnectedness of opposites (akin to yin and yang). The Kid, who tells Morris that he needs to change his ways, also programs the message board above the Glam Slam marquee to project phrases such as "No one man will be ruler."[157]

When the character Aura, a mysterious, seemingly angelic figure enters the picture, The Kid and Morris (as they did with Apollonia in *Purple Rain*) become instantly smitten and start to battle one another for her affections. Aura, who arrives on the scene to help The Kid resist his worst instincts while keeping him on a positive spiritual path, also hopes to rescue Morris from his massive ego and avaricious ways. At one point in the movie, she recites the warning, "Seven corners, two souls fight. One wants money, one wants light. Without peace, without love, nothing's ever gonna turn out right."[158] This characterizes the ultimate conflict in *Graffiti Bridge*; the spiritual versus the material, or even the communal versus the individual.

This theme is brought home during one of the film's final scenes when, after the death of Aura, Morris is shown standing alone. By contrast, The Kid is surrounded by the people of Seven Corners performing, "Still Would Stand All Time," where he sings:

No one man will be ruler
Therefore love must rule us all
Dishonesty, anger, fear, jealousy and greed will fall
Love can save us all.[159]

In the end, The Kid brings Morris around to his way of thinking. Or, in other words, he successfully bridges the separation between two warring factions. So, in spite of its less than favorable critical and commercial responses, *Graffiti Bridge* takes a poignant and unfaltering stand in the face of an increasingly individualistic, ravenous, predatory, and violent world.

Prince would further advance the philosophy he sets forth in *Graffiti Bridge* on his 1992 single, "My Name Is Prince." Where he declares:

My name is Prince, I don't want to be king
Cause I've seen the top and it's just a dream
Big cars and women and fancy clothes
Will save your face, but it won't save your soul.[160]

At the edge of the twenty-first century, Prince continued to call out America's intellectually dishonest, morally bankrupt, and spiritually deficient "overlords" that were advancing the government further and further to the right. The policy implications of this political shift suggest a rising neglect of our inner cities and the probable reduction or elimination of social programs for those already impoverished by the violence of the racist/corporatist state.

Yet again, in spite of his distrust of the state, and while reminding us that, "In America, we're just not as free as we think," Prince rises above the nihilism of others and sounds the call for resistance.[161] Channeling the despair and rage of urban America, the lyrics to the Prince and Rosie Gaines–penned "The Voice," advises that the April 1992 uprising in South Central Los Angeles might have only been a dress rehearsal, declaring:

The nightsticks are still singin'
Four-part harmony on brother's back
Justice is doomed when we don't start no SH
And there's still some IT in all of that.[162]

Here, unlike Melville, who Takaki calls the "critic of despair,"[163] Prince embodies a defiant, postmodern spirituality refusing to accept the tyranny of the emerging police state.

EXODUS—THIS IS THE DAWNING OF
A NEW SPIRITUAL REVOLUTION

The transition from modernity to postmodernity, according to political scientist Floyd W. Hayes III, argues that:

> The absolutist sensibility of European Enlightenment is in question— its belief in the supremacy of rationalism; its search for certain truth; its faith in the power of science, the scientific method, and technology; its worship of a dualistic, hierarchical, and oppositional conception of social reality; and its belief in the superiority of Western culture and civilization and the inferiority of all other.[164]

Through his lyrics, imagery, and public commentary Prince has modeled this postmodern ideal, challenging conventional wisdom and crossing cultural boundaries through the integration of varied musical genres, mixed with his social and political philosophies. Through such qualities, Prince has come to represent a cultural symbol within the rise of postmodern thought.[165] In the song "Dance On" from 1988's *Lovesexy*, he proclaims: "It's time for new education, former rules don't apply / We need a power structure that breeds production, instead of jacks who vandalize." Prince also sees himself as part of the "New Power Generation" (the name he gave his band in 1990), and in the song of the same title, he announces to the power elite:

> We are the new power generation
> We want to change the world
> The only thing that's in our way is you
> Your old fashioned music, your old ideas, sick and tired of you telling
> us what to do.[166]

Yet it would not solely be Prince's music and lyrics that would typify the postmodern movement, but also one of his most controversial and misunderstood public actions as well.

On June 7, 1993, Prince's thirty-fifth birthday, he announced to the world that he was officially changing his name to the iconic symbol that combines the male and female gender signs: ♀. This symbol had long been part of his Prince's iconography, but actually deciding to make it his name sparked immediate backlash, ridicule, and speculation.[167] Some suggested that it was his attempt to legally free himself from his "oppressive" contract with

Warner Bros., à la George Clinton more than two decades before when his bands recorded under both Funkadelic and Parliament.[168] This proposition has merit in that ⚥ (or The Artist Formerly Known as Prince, as some have taken to calling him) would shortly thereafter dissolve Paisley Park Records, his Warner Bros. associated label, creating the independent NPG Records. And in 1994, NPG Records partnered with the Bellmark label to release "The Most Beautiful Girl in the World," under the name of ⚥. Although Warner Brothers didn't appear to object to this project or NPG's subsequent compilation album *1-800-New-Funk*, ⚥ was still under contract to the label and Warner executives expected him to live up to it.

One of the principal elements of the dispute between the artist and the label was ⚥'s prolific nature. With the exceptions of 1983 and 1993, Prince had released an album of new material every year since his career began in 1978. Not only did ⚥ now want to maintain that pace, he wanted the artistic freedom to put out even more music. Warner Bros., who from a business perspective didn't want to oversaturate the market, which they believed would invariably reduce ⚥'s record sales, was not willing to budge. For Prince's part, he did not seem to care if releasing one album on top of the other would decrease his sales potential.

During the summer of 1994, in a trade advertisement promoting the album *Come*, which would be their next-to-last official release under the name of Prince, Warner Bros. poked fun at ⚥, stating that they did not care what he called himself, they "just wanted to make a $ and have a good time."[169] ⚥ responded in kind with his own ad for *1-800-New-Funk* noting that at NPG, "We just want to bring u ⚥, so u can have a good time."[170] For ⚥, who had consistently taken unprofitable turns for the sake of his artistry, the issue was never money but rather the music and his fans, positioning him outside the capitalist aspirations of many other artists.

Warner Bros. did not relent and in November 1994 further capitalized ⚥'s talent (against his wishes) by issuing the previously shelved *Black Album*, which would mark their final "Prince" album. ⚥ viewed this as a particularly flagrant action considering the two albums that he wanted Warner to release, *The Gold Experience* and the New Power Generation's *Exodus*. In a 1995 press release, ⚥ lamented the fact that since Warner Bros. owned the rights to all his master recordings, it was exceedingly difficult for him to control his own musical destiny.[171] In retaliation for the *Black Album* and Warner Bros. not agreeing to put out his other work, ⚥ performed on *The Late Show with David Letterman* with the word "slave" written across the side of his face. Moreover, he chose the song "Dolphin," which intimates that all of us are subject to the racist, corporate elite and must demand our freedom. If he "came back a dolphin," Prince says:

> U can cut off all my fins
> but 2 your ways I will not bend
> I'll die before I let you tell me how 2 swim.[172]

Following that television appearance, ♀ continued to show up in public with "slave" on his cheek to the bewilderment and admonition of many. Still, ♀ remained undeterred and was informing Warner Bros. in particular, and the music industry in general, that he was prepared to fight them all the way.

As part of ♀'s desire to put out as much music as possible, he coined the term "polyvinyl acetate," which in other words means that the drugs he, his band, and his fans are down with are funk, rock, and soul, and lots of it. And, in an effort to more efficiently place his music in the hands of his fans, ♀ started to sell unreleased material out of his New Power Generation retail store in the Uptown district of Minneapolis. Considering the shameless greed and oppressive structure of the recording industry, ♀'s contention was that artists must develop alternatives to the customs and practices of the past.[173] While on tour in London in March 1995, ♀ stated in an interview:

The important thing is that my fans hear this music, whether It be through duplicating cassettes, or if we press up 10,000 CDs after the show and charge $5 each, just to cover costs you know? Even if we do what Pearl Jam does— just turn up at radio stations and play the people our music. That's what these shows are about, communicating with the fans. I go to a club and I see fans dancing to my records. They wave to me, I wave back and realize this is why I make music. Not for record companies.[174]

For their part, many of ♀'s fans responded favorably to this proposed model and at a show later that same month in Amsterdam, the audience broke out into a chant of "Fuck Warner Bros." ♀ then asked the crowd if he could bring back some executives from Warner Bros. so that they could repeat those sentiments, adding "Now that would be some funny shit."[175]

After an arduous battle that had been waged for more than two years, Warner Bros. conceded some and agreed to release *The Gold Experience* in September 1995. However, they would soon go back on their promise to release *Exodus* early that next year. So, unable to reconcile his differences with the label, ♀ decided that was the last straw and informed Warner Bros. of his desire to terminate his current contract and thusly, their nearly nineteen-year relationship.[176] In a December 1995 press release issued through Paisley Park, ♀ announced his plans to provide the final three albums, per his remaining contractual agreement, to the label with material from his legendary "vault" (of unreleased recordings) to be aptly titled *The Vault—Volumes I, II, and III*.[177]

This was a pivotal maneuver by ♀, who, if Warner Bros. agreed to his conditions, would be finally free to break from their control and move forward with his much anticipated four-CD set *Emancipation*. Warner Bros., no doubt looking to rid themselves of the headache ♀ had caused them, acquiesced and allowed him to leave the label under his own terms. While critics and fans alike now deliberated the notion that Prince's name change had actually worked in his quest for artistic freedom, ♀ left hints that there was more to it than that.

When he was initially asked how to speak the symbol in words, ♀ remarked that there was no pronunciation for it. From 1984's *Purple Rain* through 1994's *Come*, the credits to Prince's albums and films always contained the phrase, "May u live 2 see the dawn." However, with the "The Beautiful Experience," ♀'s first official release following the name change came the message, "Welcome 2 the dawn." For ♀, this signifies the dawning of a new spiritual revolution, a postmodern awakening if you will. In the epilogue to his 1994 book *The Sacrifice of Victor*, ♀ cryptically wrote that his name had been "regenerated as ♀." Adding that "For in the dawn, all will require no speakable name. To differentiate the ineffable one that shall remain."[178]

In ♀ 's world, names were not important, but "peace, love and understanding are.[179] Rock journalist Alan di Perna states that "knowingly or otherwise, ♀ allied himself with those postmodern intellectuals who believe that language is inherently deceitful—a tool of oppression wielded by those in power.[180] This premise is similar to what sociologist C. Wright Mills identified as "situated actions and vocabularies of motive."[181] Regardless of whether or not ♀ was conversant with postmodern literature or not, "Hello," the B-side to his 1985 single "Pop Life," demonstrates a seeming mistrust for words. Here he comments that "Isn't life cruel enough without cruel words? You see words are like shoes, they're just something to stand on."[182] He continues:

> I wish you could be in my shoes, but they're probably so high you'd all off and die. For you words are definitely not shoes. They're weapons and tools of destruction and your time is boring unless you're putting something down. What would life be if we believed what we read and a smile is just hiding a frown.[183]

And while ♀ may have evolved, unwittingly or not, into a postmodern icon, he no doubt also sharpened his social and political critique along numerous fronts, as evidenced by *The Gold Experience*, *Exodus*, and 1996's *Chaos and Disorder*. Through songs like "Bambi," "The Beautiful Ones," "Anotherloverholenyohead," "If I Was Your Girlfriend," or "The Ballad of Dorothy Parker," among many others, ⚥ has often explored the intricate and perplexing dynamics of the male/female relationship. Yet *The Gold Experience*'s lead track "Pussy Control," represents his first attempt at an unmistakably feminist theme.

Chided by *Rolling Stone*'s Carol Cooper as "gutter feminism,"[184] this track champions the strength, liberation, and independence of women, while rebuking the blatant culture of misogyny that currently permeates much of American music, video, and film. ⚥ explores this matter in a verse of the unreleased "Days of Wild," when he shouts:

> Hooker, bitch, and ho, I don't think so
> I only knew one I never told her though
> I thought about many times (Diss me?)
> That's the kind of shit that make you check your mind.[185]

On tracks like "Count the Days" from *Exodus*, and *The Gold Experience*'s "Gold" and "We March," ⚥ further expanded his take on America's economic disparities and the ongoing struggle for racial equity. In "Gold" he refers to an "ocean of despair" and notes that:

> There are people livin' there
> They're unhappy, each and every day
> But hell is not a fashion,
> So whatcha tryin' to say.[186]

"We March" asks "If this is the same avenue my ancestors fought to liberate / how come I can't buy a piece of it even if my credit's straight," while the chorus warns "Next time we march, we're kickin' down the door / Next time we march, all is what we're marchin' for."[187] On the *Exodus* track "Return of the Bump Squad," ⚥ revisits the subject of police violence, intimating that sooner or later such violence will be repaid in kind:

> Bow down motherfucker, surrender your rod
> Nothin' can save u unless His name is God
> U better get your house in order, it's gettin' late
> The return of the bump squad is comin' your way.[188]

And in that album's final track, "The Exodus has Begun," ♀ chastises America's political and economic elite, questioning "How can we call ourselves equal, when they're wages outweigh the time that they keep? . . . [They] offer us pennies, when its millions and millions that they reap."[189]

In July 1996, when the first of the three albums (newly titled *Chaos and Disorder*) due to Warner Bros. was released, the title track picks up where 1989's "The Future" left off, bemoaning the deteriorating state of the world:

> I'm just a no name reporter
> I wish I had nothing 2 say
> Lookin' through my new camcorder
> Trying 2 find a crime that pays.[190]

And, in "The Same December," also from *Chaos and Disorder*, ♀ ponders race again, stating there:

> Once was this ball with a line straight down the middle
> One side was black and the other one white
> And they both understood so little
> That they spent their whole lives trying 2 tell each other what time
> it was.[191]

Here, ♀ employs a metaphor to once again address what W. E. B. Du Bois called the greatest "problem of the twentieth century" in his 1903 classic *The Souls of Black Folk*.[192]

WELCOME TO THE DAWN

In February 1996, five months before *Chaos and Disorder*, ♀ established a website called The Dawn. It was a play on the maxim "May You Live 2 See the Dawn," which accompanied the liner notes of many of his recordings and all of his films dating back to *Purple Rain*. With the release of *The Gold Experience* in September 1995, that famous phrase morphed into "Welcome 2 the Dawn," and it was clear that the new website further represented ♀'s artistic evolution.

Among the first items posted on www.thedawn.com was a "Message from The Artist," in which ♀ wrote:

The first step I have taken toward the ultimate goal of emancipation from the chains that bind me to Warner Bros. was to change my name from PrincXe to ♀ . Prince is the name that my mother gave me at birth. Warner Bros. took the name, trademarked it, and used it as the main marketing tool to promote all of the music that I wrote. The company owns the name Prince and all related music marketed under Prince. I became merely a pawn used to produce more money for Warner Bros.[193]

In this letter to fans, ♀ once again noted that he was "prepared to deliver" three final albums (originally to be titled *The Vault: Volumes I, II,* and *III*) under the name Prince in order to fulfill his contract to Warner Bros., the first of which turned out to be *Chaos and Disorder*. However, in October of that year, just a few months after *Chaos and Disorder* dropped, an extraordinary announcement was made. Although Prince would still owe Warner Bros. a pair of albums, ♀ would soon be releasing a new triple album titled *Emancipation* on EMI Records.

The three-disc set—with each CD containing twelve songs and an exact running time of sixty minutes—was released on November 19, 1996, to considerable fanfare and a robust marketing strategy that would feature two major tours and a number of television interviews with ♀, including appearances on *The Today Show, The Chris Rock Show,* and *The Oprah Winfrey Show*, among others. These public appearances, quite a lot by ♀'s standards, were intended to celebrate his newfound artistic freedom and to continue to bring attention to the inequitable nature of the music industry. But they weren't without controversy, not to mention solemnity. It was rumored that ♀'s wife Mayte had recently given birth to their first child, who suffered from a rare genetic disorder and soon died. (The couple's son was born October 16, 1996, with Pfeiffer's Syndrome type II and was removed from life support a week later on October 23, 1996.) Devastated, ♀, who remained intensely private in spite of numerous television visits during this time, deflected the inquiries into the death of their child, instead suggested that everything was okay.

Perhaps the biggest event related to the release of *Emancipation*, at least in the eyes of ♀, was a television concert simulcast live around the world on MTV, VH1, BET, and hundreds of radio stations on November 12, 1996. ♀ closed the performance with the title track to the new album, the chorus of which reasserts his independence from Warner Bros.:

Emancipation—Free 2 do what I wanna

Emancipation—See U in the purple rain
Emancipation—Free 2 do what I wanna
Emancipation—Break the chain, Break the chain.[194]

Emancipation, which was actually ⚥'s third official release in 1996 (along with *Chaos and Disorder* and the soundtrack to the Spike Lee film *Girl 6*) quickly achieved double platinum status and received highly favorable reviews in *Rolling Stone, Spin*, the *Village Voice*, and many other outlets. In addition to several compositions that were inspired by ⚥ and Mayte's nuptials and the expectations of their first child, *Emancipation* also contained a multiple tracks that further explored ⚥'s quest for freedom including "White Mansion," "Slave," "Style," "Da, Da, Da," and "Face Down," where he chastises his critics who would:

Let him go down as a washed up singer, ain't that a bitch
Thinkin' all along that he wanted to be rich
Never respected the root of all evil and he still don't to this day
Bury him face down, let the motherfuckers kiss his ass, okay.[195]

So, immediately after his break from Warner Bros., ⚥ remained pretty much as controversial as he had ever been. More significantly however, just over nineteen years after signing his first recording contract that yielded eighteen studio albums, a greatest hits package, and four major motion pictures, ⚥ would continue to display his extraordinary talent as a composer, producer, arranger, multi-instrumentalist, and live performer. Furthermore, beyond his immense gifts, the first two decades of ⚥'s illustrious career was rooted in his rebel spirit and the racial, sexual, social, political, and spiritual messages he presented through his artistry.

Since the very beginning, Prince (and later ⚥) had been a rule breaker, achieving success on his own terms and fiercely opposing conventional notions of what are considered appropriate models of thought and behavior. By rejecting categorization of any kind, ⚥ symbolized a polymorphous being—a "border crosser" that recognized and promoted the spiritual unity in "apparent opposites." In addition to his voluminous musical catalogue, ⚥'s position as a social critic and cultural icon made an indelible impact on American popular music and the larger culture, transcending musical genres as well as race, gender, class, and nation. As Neal Karlen, a fellow Minneapolitan and renowned rock journalist told us in his 1990 *Rolling Stone* interview with Prince, as long as he is here, Prince/ ⚥ was "going to cause much ruckus."[196]

Notes

1. Amilcar Cabral, *Return to the Source* (New York: Monthly Review, 1973).

2. "Message from The Artist," November 1996, https://www.thedawn.com.

3. Frantz Fanon, *The Wretched of the Earth* (New York: Grove Press, 1963).

4. Dave Hill, *Prince: A Pop Life* (New York: Harmony, 1989).

5. Ariel Swartley, "This Prince Is No Pretender," *Real Paper*, March 1, 1980.

6. John Bream, *Prince: Inside the Purple Reign* (New York: Collier McMillan, 1984); Steven Ivory, *Prince* (New York: Perigee, 1985).

7. Steve Perry, "Ain't No Mountain High Enough: The Politics of Crossover," in *Facing the Music*, edited by Simon Frith (New York: Pantheon, 1988); Kurt Loder, *Bat Chain Puller* (New York: St. Martin's, 1990); Nelson George, *Buppies, B-Boys, Baps, and Bohos: Notes on Post-Soul Black Culture* (New York: Harper Collins, 1992).

8. Neal Karlen, "Prince Talks," *Rolling Stone*, September 12, 1985, 24–30.

9. Olmeca, *Prince* (New York: Proteus, 1984), 33.

10. Prince and The New Power Generation, "My Name Is Prince," track 1 on ⚥, Paisley Park/Warner Bros. Records, compact disc, 1992.

11. Ronald T. Takaki, *Iron Cages: Race and Culture in Nineteenth Century America* (Seattle: University of Washington Press, 1979).

12. Antonio Gramsci, *Prison Notebooks* (New York: International, 1971), 12.

13. Gramsci, *Prison Notebooks*.

14. Stuart Hall, "What Is This 'Black' in Black Popular Culture," in *Black Popular Culture*, ed. Gina Dent (Seattle: Bay Press, 1992), 21–36.

15. Fanon, *The Wretched of the Earth*, 168.

16. Takaki, *Iron Cages*.

17. Takaki, *Iron Cages*; David E. Stannard, *American Civilization* (New York: Oxford University Press, 1992).

18. David T. Goldberg, *Racist Culture* (Oxford: Blackwell, 1993).

19. Gramsci, *Prison Notebooks*, 123.

20. Fanon, *The Wretched of the Earth*, 173.

21. Cabral, *Return to the Source*, 41.

22. Fanon, *The Wretched of the Earth*, 179.

23. Stuart Hall, "Gramsci's Relevance for the Study of Race and Ethnicity," *Journal of Communication Inquiry* 10, no. 2 (June 1986): 5–27; Paul Gilroy, *Small Acts: Thoughts on the Politics of Black Cultures* (London: Serpent's Tail, 1993); Anthony J. Lemelle, *Black Culture: A War of Position in the Struggle for Emancipatory Democracy* (Chicago: Red Feather Institute, 1993).

24. Clarence Lusane, "Rap, Race, and Politics," *Race and Class* 35, no. 1 (July 1993): 41–56; Peter Okeafor, "Rap Music and the Politics of Urban Resistance in Late Capitalism," unpublished manuscript, Department of Sociology, Purdue University, 1994; Tricia Rose, *Black Noise: Rap Music and Black Culture in Contemporary America* (Hanover: Wesleyan University Press, 1994).

25. Anthony J. Lemelle, "Betcha Cain't Reason with 'Em: Bad Black Boys in America," in *Black Male Adolescents: Parenting and Education in Community Context*, edited by Benjamin P. Bowser (Lanham: University Press of America, 1991), 91–114.

26. Anthony J. Lemelle, "Killing the Author of Life, or Decimating 'Bad Niggers,'" *Journal of Black Studies* 19, no. 2 (December 1988): 216–31.

27. Lawrence L. Levine, *Black Culture and Black Consciousness* (New York: Oxford University Press, 1977); Charles P. Henry, "The Political Role of the Bad Nigger," *Journal of Black Studies* 11, no. 4 (June 1981): 461–82; Lemelle, "Killing the Author of Life."

28. Todd Gitlin, *The Whole World Is Watching: Mass Media in the Making and Unmaking of the New Left* (Berkeley: University of California Press, 1980).

29. Eugene D. Genovese, *The Political Economy of Slavery: Studies in the Economy and Society of the Slave South* (Middletown: Wesleyan University Press, 1989).

30. Fanon, *The Wretched of the Earth.*

31. Steve Sutherland, "Someday Your Prince Will Come," *Melody Maker*, June 6, 1981.

32. Arlene Schneider, *The Twin Cities New Age Directory* (Minneapolis: Schneider, 1984).

33. Prince, "Uptown," track 5 on *Dirty Mind*, Warner Bros. Records, compact disc, 1980.

34. Prince, "Uptown."

35. Barney Hoskyns, *Prince: Imp of the Perverse* (London: Virgin, 1988).

36. Prince, "Sexuality," track 2 on *Controversy*, Warner Bros. Records, compact disc, 1981.

37. Prince, "Sexuality."

38. Prince, "Let's Pretend We're Married," track 4 on *1999*, Warner Bros. Records, compact disc, 1982.

39. Prince, "Lady Cab Driver," track 9 on *1999*, Warner Bros. Records, compact disc, 1982.

40. Prince, "Lady Cab Driver."

41. Prince, "New Power Generation," track 2 on *Graffiti Bridge*, Paisley Park/Warner Bros. Records, compact disc, 1990.

42. Prince, director, *Graffiti Bridge* (Los Angeles: Warner Bros. Pictures, 1990).

43. Prince, "Annie Christian," track 7 on *Controversy*, Warner Bros. Records, compact disc, 1981.

44. Cornel West, *Prophetic Reflections: Notes on Race and Power in America* (Monroe: Common Courage, 1993); Floyd W. Hayes III, "From DuBois' Double Consciousness to Wright's Double Vision: Fragmented Blackness in the Age of Nihilism," presented at the annual conference of the Middle Atlantic Writers Association, Baltimore, Maryland, October 22, 1994.

45. Prince and The Revolution, "America," track 6 on *Around the World in a Day*, Paisley Park/Warner Bros. Records, compact disc, 1985.

46. Bream, *Inside the Purple Reign.*

47. Prince and the New Power Generation, "The Sacrifice of Victor," track 18 on ♀, Paisley Park/Warner Bros. Records, compact disc, 1992.

48. Prince, "Lady Cab Driver."

49. Prince and the New Power Generation, "Live 4 Love," track on *Diamonds and Pearls*, Paisley Park/Warner Bros. Records, compact disc, 1991.

50. Prince and the New Power Generation, "Money Don't Matter 2 Night," track 10 on *Diamonds and Pearls*, Paisley Park/Warner Bros. Records, compact disc, 1991.

51. Prince, "Party Up," track 8 on *Dirty Mind*, Warner Bros. Records, compact disc, 1980.

52. Prince, "Controversy," track 1 on *Controversy*, Warner Bros. Records, compact disc, 1981.

53. Dan Peters and Steve Peters, *Why Knock Rock?* (Minneapolis: Bethany House, 1984); Simon Reynolds, *Blissed Out: The Raptures of Rock* (London: Serpent's Tail, 1990).

54. Nelson George, *The Death of Rhythm and Blues* (New York: Pantheon, 1988); Perry, "Ain't No Mountain High Enough"; Hill, *A Pop Life*.

55. George, *The Death of Rhythm and Blues*.

56. Hill, *A Pop Life*.

57. Perry, "Ain't No Mountain High Enough: The Politics of Crossover."

58. Prince, "The MTV Interview," interview by Steve Fargnoli, MTV, November 13, 1985.

59. Funkadelic, "Who Says a Funk Band Can't Play Rock?!" track 3 on *One Nation Under a Groove*, Warner Bros. Records, compact disc, 1978.

60. Marc Eliot, *Rockonomics: The Money Behind the Music* (New York: Citadel, 1989), vii.

61. Michael Bane, *White Boy Singin' the Blues: The Black Roots of White Rock* (New York: Da Capo, 1982), 205.

62. Greg Tate, *Flyboy in the Buttermilk: Essays on Contemporary America* (New York: Fireside, 1992).

63. Michael Eric Dyson, *Between God and Gangsta Rap* (New York: Oxford University Press, 1996).

64. Merritt Malloy, ed., *The Great Rock 'N' Roll Quote Book* (New York: St. Martin's Griffin, 1995), 108.

65. Tate, *Flyboy in the Buttermilk*, 53.

66. Emily D. Hicks, *Border Writing: The Multidimensional Text* (Minneapolis: University of Minnesota Press, 1991).

67. Dyson, *Between God and Gangsta Rap*, 29.

68. *At the Movies*, "The Best of 1984," Gene Siskel and Roger Ebert (January 19, 1985; Chicago: Tribune Entertainment), television program.

69. Gene Siskel, "Prince Conquers in Purple Rain," *Chicago Tribune*, July 27, 1984, 11.

70. Timothy White, *Rock Lives: Profiles and Interviews* (New York: Henry Holt, 1984), 20.

71. George, *Buppies, B-Boys, Baps, and Bohos*.

72. White, *Rock Lives*.

73. Siskel, "Prince Conquers in Purple Rain"; Tate, *Flyboy in the Buttermilk*; Armond White, *The Resistance: Ten Years of Pop Culture that Shook the World* (Woodstock: The Overlook Press).

74. Tate, *Flyboy in the Buttermilk*, 55.

75. Tate, *Flyboy in the Buttermilk*, 55.

76. White, *The Resistance*, 11.

77. White, *The Resistance*, 12.

78. White, *The Resistance*, 53.

79. Bart Bull, "Black Narcissus," *Spin*, July 1986, 45–67.

80. Prince, dir., *Under the Cherry Moon* (Los Angeles: Warner Bros. Pictures, 1986).

81. Prince, interview by Charles Johnson (aka The Electrifying Mojo), WHYT (96.3 FM), Detroit, June 7, 1986, radio broadcast.

82. George, *The Death of Rhythm and Blues*; Hill, *A Pop Life*; White, *The Resistance*.

83. Frantz Fanon, *Black Skin, White Masks* (New York: Grove Weidenfeld, 1967), 109.

84. Hill, *A Pop Life*, 179.

85. Prince and The Revolution, "Mountains," track 8 on *Parade*, Paisley Park/Warner Bros. Records, compact disc, 1986.

86. Prince, "Sign O' The Times," track 1 on *Sign O' The Times*, Paisley Park/Warner Bros. Records, compact disc, 1987.

87. White, *Rock Lives*, 773.

88. Anthony DeCurtis, "Sign O' The Times: Prince Bounces Back with Bold Concert Movie," *Rolling Stone*, December 3, 1987, 16; Per Nilsen, *Prince: A Documentary* (London: Omnibus Press, 1993).

89. Perry, "Ain't No Mountain High Enough," 85.

90. White, *The Resistance*; Per Nilsen and David J. Magdziarz, "Ain't That a Bitch: The Story of the *Black Album*," *Uptown* 17 (1994), 6–13.

91. Prince, "Dead on It," track 3 on *The Black Album*, Warner Bros. Records, compact disc, 1994.

92. Hoskyns, *Imp of the Perverse*; Hill, *A Pop Life*.

93. Geoff Brown, *The Complete Guide to the Music of Prince* (London: Omnibus Press, 1995).

94. White, *The Resistance*.

95. White, *The Resistance*.

96. Albert Magnoli, dir., *Prince: A Music Portrait* (Los Angeles: Cinemax, 1989).

97. Bob Portway, dir., *The Prince of Paisley Park* (Los Angeles: Omnibus, 1991).

98. Portway, *The Prince of Paisley Park*.

99. Prince, "Escape" Free Yo' Mind from This Rat Race," B-side to "Glam Slam," Paisley Park/Warner Bros. Records, cassette tape, 1988.

100. Prince, "Positivity," track 9 on *Lovesexy*, Paisley Park/Warner Bros. Records, compact disc, 1988.

101. Spike Lee, dir., "Money Don't Matter 2 Night" (Minneapolis: Paisley Park/Warner Bros. Records, 1992).

102. John Duffy, *Prince an Illustrated Biography* (London: Omnibus Press, 1992).

103. The New Power Generation, "Deuce and a Quarter," track 5 on *Gold Nigga*, NPG Records, compact disc, 1993.

104. Antonio Garfias, "Prince and the New Power Generation: Act One," unpublished manuscript, Program in Drama and Theatre Arts, Purdue University, 1993.

105. Tevin Campbell, "Uncle Sam," track 7 on *I'm Ready*, Qwest/Warner Bros. Records, compact disc, 1993.

106. Tevin Campbell, "Paris 1798430," track 9 on *I'm Ready*, Qwest/Warner Bros. Records, compact disc, 1993.

107. Mavis Staples, "You Will Be Moved," track 4 on *The Voice*, Paisley Park/Warner Bros. Records, compact disc, 1993.

108. Edwin M. Schur, *The Americanization of Sex* (Philadelphia: Temple University Press, 1988); Kathy Peiss and Christina Simmons, *Passion and Power: Sexuality in History* (Philadelphia: Temple University Press, 1989).

109. Abdul R. JanMohammed, "Sexuality on the Racial Border: Foucault, Wright and the Articulation or Racialized Sexuality," in *Discourses of Sexuality*, edited by Donna C. Stanton (Ann Arbor: University of Michigan Press), 94–116.

110. Michel Foucault, *The History of Sexuality* (New York: Random House, 1978), 32.

111. Lynn Hunt, "Foucault's Subject in *The History of Sexuality*," in *Discourses of Sexuality*, edited by Donna C. Stanton (Ann Arbor: University of Michigan Press), 78–93.

112. Ann Laura Stoler, *Race and the Education of Desire: Foucault's History of Sexuality and the Colonial Order of Things* (Durham: Duke University Press, 1995).

113. Takaki, *Iron Cages*; Stannard, *American Civilization*.

114. Takaki, *Iron Cages*.

115. Peiss and Simmons, *Passion and Power*.

116. Angela Davis, *Women, Race, and Class* (New York: Vintage, 1983).

117. JanMohammed, "Sexuality on the Racial Border."

118. Calvin C. Hernton, *Sex and Racism in America* (New York: Grove Weidenfeld, 1965); Fanon, *Black Skin, White Masks*; JanMohammed, "Sexuality on the Racial Border."

119. Takaki, *Iron Cages*.

120. Foucault, *The History of Sexuality*.

121. C. L. R. James, *Mariners, Renegades and Castaways* (Detroit: Bewick/Ed, 1978); Takaki, *Iron Cages*.

122. C. L. R. James, *American Civilization* (Oxford: Blackwell, 1973); Takaki, *Iron Cages*.

123. Anthony J. Lemelle, Lecture in Black America (Sociology 514), Stone Hall, Purdue University, January 15, 1993.

124. Lemelle, Lecture (Sociology 514).

125. Levine, *Black Culture and Black Consciousness*.

126. Charles P. Henry, *Culture and African American Politics* (Bloomington: Indiana University Press, 1990).

127. Bill Adler, "Will the Little Girls Understand?" *Rolling Stone*, February 19, 1981, 55–57.

128. Ken Tucker, "Love and Lust in Minneapolis," *Rolling Stone*, February 19, 1981, 23–26.

129. Bull, "Black Narcissus," 46.

130. Hill, *A Pop Life*, 84.

131. George, *The Death of Rhythm and Blues*.

132. Stanley Crouch, *Notes of a Hanging Judge* (New York: Oxford).

133. Alvin F. Poussaint, "An Analytical Look at the Prince Phenomemon," *Ebony*, June 1985, 170.

134. Steve Turner, *Hungry for Heaven: Rock 'n' Roll and the Search for Redemption* (Downers Grove: Inter Varsity Press), 194.

135. Turner, *Hungry for Heaven*, 194.

136. Hill, *A Pop Life*.

137. Hoskyns, *Imp of the Perverse*.

138. Barbara Graustark, "Strange Tales from Andre's Basement," in *The Rock Musician*, edited by Tony Scherman (New York: St. Martin's, 1994).

139. Graustark, "Strange Tales from Andre's Basement," 127.

140. Prince, interview with Mick Boskamp, Sonesta Hotel, Amsterdam, May 29, 1981, compact disc.

141. Prince, "Sexuality."

142. Prince, "DMSR," track 5 on *1999*, Warner Bros. Records, compact disc, 1982.

143. Foucault, *The History of Sexuality*; Takaki, *Iron Cages*.

144. June Singer, *Androgyny* (New York: Anchor Press, 1976).

145. Clyde W. Franklin II, *The Changing Definition of Masculinity* (New York: Plenum, 1984).

146. Graustark, "Strange Tales from Andre's Basement."

147. Prince, *Graffiti Bridge*.

148. Prince, "If I Was Your Girlfriend," track 2, Disc 2 on *Sign O' The Times*, Paisley Park/Warner Bros. Records, compact disc, 1987.

149. Prince, "We Can Funk," track 7 on *Graffiti Bridge*, Paisley Park/Warner Bros. Records, compact disc, 1990.

150. Jeff Hearn and Antonio Melechi, "The Transatlantic Gaze: Masculinities, Youth, and the American Imagination," in *Men, Masculinity, and the Media*, edited by Steve Craig (Newbury Park: Sage, 1991), 228.

151. Prince, "Bob George," track 5 on *The Black Album*, Warner Bros. Records, compact disc, 1994.

152. Okeafor, "Rap Music and the Politics of Urban Resistance in Late Capitalism."

153. Prince, "The Future," track 1 on *Batman*, Warner Bros. Records, compact disc, 1989.

154. Anthony J. Lemelle, *Black Male Deviance* (Westport: Praeger, 1995); Hayes, "From Du Bois' Double Consciousness to Wright's Double Vision."

155. Prince, *Graffiti Bridge*.

156. Prince, *Graffiti Bridge*.

157. Prince, *Graffiti Bridge*.

158. Prince, *Graffiti Bridge*.

159. Prince, *Graffiti Bridge*.

160. Randee St. Nicholas, dir., "My Name Is Prince" (Minneapolis: Paisley Park/Warner Bros. Records, 1992).

161. Prince, "Chaos and Disorder," *New Power Generation*, Summer 1994.

162. Mavis Staples, "The Voice," track 7 on *The Voice*, Paisley Park/Warner Bros. Records, compact disc, 1993.

163. Takaki, *Iron Cages*.

164. Hayes, "From Du Bois' Double Consciousness to Wright's Double Vision," 21.

165. George Lipsitz, *Dangerous Crossroads: Popular Music, Postmodernism, and the Poetics of Place* (London: Verso, 1994); Dominic Strinati, *An Introduction into the Theories of Popular Culture* (London: Routledge).

166. Prince, "New Power Generation," track 2 on *Graffiti Bridge*, Paisley Park/Warner Bros. Records, compact disc, 1990.

167. Alan di Perna, "The Guitarist Formerly Known as Prince," *Guitar World*, November 1994, 50–65.

168. Rickey Vincent, *Funk: The Music, The People, and the Rhythm of the One* (New York: St. Martin's Griffin, 1996).

169. Warner Bros. Records, trade advertisement, 1994.

170. NPG Records, trade advertisement, 1994.

171. "Welcome 2 the Dawn: U have just accessed the ♀ experience," press release, Paisley Park Enterprises, December 22, 1995.

172. Prince, "Dolphin," track 8 on *The Gold Experience*, NPG/Warner Bros. Records, compact disc, 1995.

173. Julie Baumgold, "Glitter Slave," *Esquire Gentleman*, June 1995, 100–105.

174. Per Nilsen, ed., "Music Has to Be Free: ♀ in Conversation," *Uptown* 18 (1995), 6–7.

175. Prince and the New Power Generation, "The Ultimate Live Experience Tour," after show concert performance, The Paradiso, Amsterdam, March 26, 1995, compact disc.

176. Paisley Park Enterprises, "Welcome 2 the Dawn."

177. Paisley Park Enterprises, "Welcome 2 the Dawn."

178. Prince, (presents) *The Sacrifice of Victor* (Chanhassen: Paisley Park Enterprises, 1994).

179. Prince, *Neo Manifesto: Audentes Fortuna Juvat* (Chanhassen: Paisley Park Enterprises, 1994).

180. Di Perna, "The Guitarist Formerly Known as Prince," 54.

181. C. Wright Mills, "Situated Actions and Vocabularies of Motive," *American Sociological Review* 5, no. 5 (February 1940), 904–13.

182. Prince, "Hello ," B-Side to "Pop Life," Paisley Park/Warner Bros. Records, vinyl record, 1985.

183. Prince, "Hello."

184. Carol Cooper, "Gold Experience (album review)," *Rolling Stone*, November 2, 1995.

185. Prince, dir., *The Beautiful Experience* (Minneapolis: Paisley Park Pictures/Sky One, 1994).

186. Prince, "Gold," track 18 on *The Gold Experience*, NPG/Warner Bros. Records, compact disc, 1995.

187. Prince, "We March," track 5 on *The Gold Experience*, NPG/Warner Bros. Records, compact disc, 1995.

188. The New Power Generation, "Return of the Bump Squad," track 12 on *Exodus*, NPG Records, compact disc, 1995.

189. The New Power Generation, "The Exodus Has Begun," track 20 on *Exodus*, NPG Records, compact disc, 1995.

190. Prince, "Chaos and Disorder," track 1 on *Chaos and Disorder*, Warner Bros. Records, compact disc, 1996.

191. Prince, "The Same December," track 4 on *Chaos and Disorder*, Warner Bros. Records, compact disc, 1996.

192. W. E. B. Du Bois, *The Souls of Black Folk* (New York: Signet Classics, 1994).

193. "Message from The Artist," https://www.thedawn.com.

194. Prince, "Emancipation," live performance, Paisley Park Studios, Chanhassen, November 12, 1996, MTV television broadcast.

195. Prince, "Face Down," track 4, Disc 3 on *Emancipation*, NPG/EMI Records, compact disc, 1996.

196. Neal Karlen, "Prince Talks," *Rolling Stone*, October 18, 1990, 58–60.

Chapter 7

THE PRINCE OF GOTHAM

Prince's Multifaceted Batman Project

LAUREL WESTRUP AND PAUL N. REINSCH

In 1989, and not for the first time, Warner Bros. hoped that Prince would take a break. Between *For You* (released April 1978), and *Lovesexy* (released May 1988), he had released an album a year through the label and shepherded a range of other artists, their songs, and albums into the marketplace. As Duane Tudhal meticulously reveals, in 1983 and 1984 alone Prince created albums for The Time, Apollonia 6, Sheila E., and The Family while also creating his own *Purple Rain* album and numerous songs later released (or not released) under his own name.[1] Warner Bros. was confounded by his prolificacy (the conflict between Prince and the label over when and how much of his music to release would famously result in his "symbol" period). They didn't expect him to release another album until December 1989 at the earliest, and Michael Ostin, an artists & repertoire executive at WB, remarked, "All parties had decided that it didn't make sense for Prince to put out 'a Prince record' for some time."[2] While Prince did not officially release a "Prince record," he instead embarked on what would become a colossal multimedia project alongside Tim Burton's franchise-launching *Batman* (1989). Rather than creating a few songs for the film, as he was commissioned to do, Prince created his own Batman universe in the form of a nine-track album (*Batman: Motion Picture Soundtrack*), five singles (with remixes and B-sides), three music videos, and, although released a few years later and not officially part of the Batman project, a comic book called *Prince: Alter Ego* that interfaces with the earlier Batman work.

Though the *Batman* album was a success, some writers frame it as a cash grab by both WB and Prince, and others set it against Danny Elfman's orchestral score (which the film features more prominently). Perhaps more troubling is the continued neglect of the work by scholars of Batman media and scholars of Prince's music. This might be partially justified because copyright concerns kept Prince from releasing the *Batman* material on subsequent compilations—and within discographies it is replaced with "Scandalous," a song from the album and film. But Prince's Batman project warranted more and careful consideration. It is not merely work "inspired by" a film, or an album that Prince hastily completed as a way to escape WB's desire to curb his production. Rather, it is a complex multimedia work that critically interfaces with the Batman myth as well as Prince's other audiovisual work.

This chapter offers a close analysis of the materials that comprise Prince's Batman project and explores the ways the artist intervenes in Batman discourse. The Batman texts reveal Prince's ongoing concerns with the fluidity of race and gender, and yet these texts are different from Prince's previous work in that here he primarily plays with characters whose history and copyrights he does not control. Prince inhabits the perspectives of all of the film's famous comic book characters, alternately voicing Batman, Bruce Wayne, the Joker, and Vicki Vale. In the process, he not only confounds gender and racial distinctions, but also thoughtfully intervenes in the discourse around these established yet necessarily somewhat mutable (as they span media forms and decades of different artistic personnel) characters. To this end, he also creates a new character, "Gemini," who appears on the album and in the videos for "Batdance" and "Partyman" and is featured in the *Prince: Alter Ego* comic. In his earliest incarnation, Gemini is half Joker, half Batman, and entirely Prince. By performing the original Batman characters and adding his own to the mix, Prince demonstrates his ability to transform an existing commercial property while remaining true to his larger oeuvre.

THE PURPLE PRINCE MEETS THE DARK KNIGHT

Prince's Batman odyssey began in childhood, when Neal Hefti's famous theme song from the sixties show was, he claims, one of the first things he learned to play on piano.[3] But the project started to take shape in January 1989, when he flew to London at the behest of Tim Burton and Jack Nicholson (who plays the Joker in the film), both Prince fans, to watch some footage of *Batman*. Burton had already been using previously released Prince songs ("1999" and "Baby I'm a Star") as scratch tracks in a couple of scenes, and the director reportedly listened to Prince's music as he drove to the set each day.[4] By all accounts, Prince was riveted by his sneak peek at the film. After viewing forty or so minutes of the screening, he was overheard saying, "I can hear music. I hear the music in these scenes."[5] If he needed additional incentive, Warner Bros. ultimately paid him around $1 million dollars to participate in the project.[6] As he would do years later when in a prolonged contractual dispute with WB, Prince identified cinema as an outlet for his ceaseless musical production and creativity.[7]

Given the high price tag for his services, one might assume that Prince was expected to provide music for the whole film, but his music was actually only meant to augment the more substantial scoring duties of Danny Elfman, the rock musician–turned–film composer who had already worked with Burton on *Pee-Wee's Big Adventure* (1985) and *Beetlejuice* (1988). Elfman was apparently not fond of the decision to bring Prince onto the project. Years later, he told London's *The Telegraph* that the score was the most difficult of his career and that he had initially walked off the project when Prince was hired, only coming back into the fold after Burton talked him into it.[8] These negotiations may explain in part why only six of the nine songs Prince produced for the *Batman* album are heard in the film and why, of those, only three figure prominently: "Partyman" in the scene where the Joker "improves" the Flugelheim Gallery, "Trust" when the Joker embarks on his deadly parade in Gotham City, and "Scandalous" over the film's final credits.[9] As K. J. Donnelly points out, "There are narrative, aesthetic, and financial concerns which compete and together determine how music that mixes songs and score finally appears."[10] These concerns appear to have been especially complex when it comes to *Batman*, because Burton was not only trying to balance songs with a more traditional score, but his own vision of the Batman universe with the myriad versions of the property that had come before. Elfman's score did ultimately warrant its own release, albeit a couple months after the film and Prince's *Batman*.[11]

Both Burton's soundtrack and Prince's *Batman* did well commercially, but the Prince album was far more successful. In fact, as Dennis Hunt of the *Los Angeles Times* reported in July 1989, "Prince's 'Batman'—one of the fastest-rising sound tracks ever—is a smash of Gargantuan proportions, soaring high over its competitors on the Billboard magazine pop album chart. 'Batman' bounded up to No. 1 in just three weeks."[12] The *Washington Post*'s Richard Harrington remarked that "when the 'Batdance' single and the 'Batman' soundtrack recently stood atop their respective charts, and 'Batman' was the top-grossing film in the country, it was only the second time that this particular dollar triple had been achieved in the same week (the other time was with the Beatles' 'Help!' in 1965)."[13] *USA Today*'s Edna Gundersen, who wrote a slew of articles on Prince's Batman project, reported that a survey of record store owners "showed that record sales in June were down almost 25 percent compared to the same period last year. *Batman*'s June 23 release sparked instant sales jumps, with some retailers declaring it the biggest new release in memory."[14] The success of the album was good news for Prince, who hadn't had a no. 1 album since 1985's *Around the World in a Day*, and for WB, which had found the perfect synergy between a WB artist and a WB movie. However, despite the *Batman* album's success, or perhaps because of it, critics gave the album mixed reviews.

Some critics thought that Prince's songs did not serve the film as effectively as Elfman's compositions. Harrington opined that Elfman's score was "remarkable" and "much more central to and in tune with the dark-hued film than Prince's party-tracks."[15] Kim Newman of *Monthly Film Bulletin* felt similarly: "Prince's songs, which interrupt an outstandingly old-fashioned score by Danny Elfman . . . only get gratuitously in the way during two scenes."[16] *Newsday* reviewer Wayne Robins (1989) appreciated the Prince album overall, but thought that it failed to connect meaningfully with Batman. He calls the album "superficially appealing but emotionally limited."[17] He cites "The Future," with its more serious references to the exploitation of the underclass and moral turpitude, as one place where the album goes deeper, but ultimately concludes that "if this is what Batman sits around thinking about at home in Gotham City, then I'm Robin." Chuck Campbell of the *Palm Beach Post* defends the album only on the basis that "*Batman* is more a concept record than a literal sound track,"[18] thus expressing a conservative understanding of soundtrack albums. Writing in 2012, Steven Hyden of *The A. V. Club* exhibits a more expansive sense of what soundtrack albums can do: "Prince's *Batman* is more of a commentary on the film and its themes than a functional part of the film. It sounds like what it is: a bunch of songs Prince wrote after seeing a movie he thought was kinda cool."[19] The separation between the film and album gives Prince some latitude to go beyond simply trying to match or score the film. Nonetheless, Campbell worried that "Batman fans may object to the campy and sometimes flip attitude of this record."[20] This comment about campiness recalls some of the earlier incarnations of *Batman* and connotations of the Batman property that Burton consciously tried to avoid in the film with an eye toward launching a franchise for WB. While not nearly as serious as Christopher Nolan's later *Dark Knight* cycle or the Ben Affleck offerings, Burton's *Batman* was not nearly as campy as the sixties TV series, which audiences of the 1989 film, the authors included, would have remembered from syndication if not from its initial run.

Nonetheless, the 1989 *Batman* film and album were undeniably commercial. Several contemporaneous commentators read the film and its album tie-in as prime examples of 1980s media industry synergy. Eileen Meehan, who provides the most extensive exploration of this synergy, argues that "To understand *Batman* . . . requires that our analyses of the text and intertext, and of fandom and other audiences, be supplemented by an economic analysis of corporate structure, market structures, and interpenetrating industries."[21] She points out that it is no accident that one of the most significant mergers in media industrial history—the merger of Warner Communications, Inc. (WCI) and Time, resulting in the giant Time-Warner company—happened the same year that the *Batman* film and albums were released. The amalgamation of "book publishing, cable channels, song publishing, cable systems, recorded music, television production, magazine/comics publishing, film production, television stations, and licensing [made] Time-Warner the predominant media conglomerate in the world."[22] It also allowed the mega company to leverage the Batman property across multiple outlets, which included releases of comics and a novelization of the film, Batman merchandise, the two soundtrack albums, and music videos, the last of which would run on MTV, a network that WCI partially owned in 1989.

As Meehan suggests, the multimedia enterprise of *Batman* was widely hyped across the pop cultural terrain, and this enterprise worked largely through cross-promotion of all elements of the franchise. If Prince didn't inherently have anything to do with the Batman property, his and the caped crusader's shared corporate parentage made them a dynamic duo. Steven Hyden puts it well: "Pairing [Prince] with a profitable film franchise was corporate double-dipping at its most ingenious."[23] What is more, Meehan points out that Prince's wide appeal, both in terms of his persona and his riot of musical styles, brought key demographics to *Batman* that might not otherwise have tuned in. She notes that Prince's audience, based on data from market researcher Evaluative Criteria, Inc., was largely white women in their late twenties and early thirties. The lead single and music video, "Batdance," screened regularly on MTV, which still primarily catered to a white audience at that time, and yet the song's use of what she characterizes as a "rap-funk" style ensured that it was played on Black-oriented radio stations. This crossover apparently worked: rappers were seen wearing Batman logo t-shirts on *Yo! MTV Raps* around this time.[24] Meehan sums up:

The decision to showcase Prince as a musical guest on the film's soundtrack promoted the film to an audience atypical of comic fans (white women); the style of Prince's musical performance promoted *Batman* in terms of black culture to black youth despite the minimal role of black actors . . . in the film. All this had the effect of widening the pool of potential ticket-buyers for *Batman*.[25]

WB's strategy was clear: incorporating Prince into the Batman enterprise would help broaden the appeal of the project. Given WB's $30 million investment in the film, Prince's involvement provided one means for the company to hedge its bets.

Some fans and critics saw through this strategy, rejecting the union of Prince and Batman for its crass commercialism and potential destabilization of the Batman property. Justin Wyatt dismisses the claims in the album's liner notes that the vocals are by the Joker or Vicki Vale, stating flatly that the songs "obviously are sung by Prince."[26] He reads the album, and its claims of multiple voices, as emphasizing Prince's "pop persona" and demonstrating a "strong economic motive based on multiplying possible points of connection with the film."[27] Stephen Prince quotes Wyatt's remarks and mourns the loss of a stable model of media production with a feature film comfortably at the center: "The effect of these ancillary promotions is to multiply different versions of a given film such that one can no longer reliably identify its singular or truest incarnation."[28] Here (Stephen) Prince suggests that audiences might regard the Prince album as the "singular or truest incarnation" of Batman rather than the Burton film his work was meant to support. While Prince the academic seems opposed to such a destabilization of the "official" *Batman*, Prince the artist saw an opportunity to remake the Batman universe in his own image(s) and voice(s).

BATMAN, THE JOKER, AND GEMINI: THE DISPERSAL OF DIFFERENCE

As Prince became involved with *Batman*, commentators began to speculate about which character he most resembled. Jon Peters, a producer on the film as well as the album, told *Rolling Stone* in 1989 that "In a way Prince is Batman. . . . He's a very dark character, and he's complex and kind of mysterious and explosive."[29] Meanwhile in the same article, WB Music President Gary LeMel stated, "The Joker wears purple clothes, the poisonous gas released by the Joker in the museum is purple, the Joker's gang's cars are purple. . . .

To me, Prince's involvement was fated."[30] For Prince's part, he apparently saw elements of both characters, as well as Vicki Vale and Bruce Wayne, in himself—something he made explicit in the Batman songs and music videos. Ultimately, he would also insert himself, as well as a new, hybrid character, Gemini, into the Batman world, or at least the *Batman* (film) world. We're not so much concerned here with mapping Prince's persona onto any of these characters per se; rather, we're more interested in how he uses the existing and new characters to comment on Batman's world and, by extension, the world in which we live.

Batman was already a notoriously complex character before Prince's involvement, especially if set against Superman, DC's other equally famous male hero. Beyond his lifestyle of brooding vigilante justice, which walks the line between good and evil, several scholars have also read Batman as gay or sexually ambiguous. In "Batman, Deviance and Camp," Andy Medhurst traces accusations that Batman is gay all the way back to Fredric Wertham's anti-comics crusade, *Seduction of the Innocent* (1954).[31] Wertham, in misguided and homophobic terms, asserts that Batman and Robin's Wayne Manor milieu is "like a wish dream of two homosexuals living together."[32] Medhurst points out that Wertham's work had the effect not only of calling Batman's sexuality into question, but also of ensuring a backlash among Batman fans against such a reading. He writes that fans who "rush to 'protect' Batman and Robin from Wertham" merely re-entrench the homophobia inherent in his critique.[33] Medhurst goes on to trace the way Batman's masculinity and sexuality have been renegotiated in each incarnation of the property. The frequent "bad object" of the Batman enterprise is the sixties TV show. Another scholar argues that despite the series' attempts to frame Batman and Robin as straight through heterosexual relationships with Batwoman and her niece Bat-Girl, "there is a remarkable sense of camp about many of these stories, some involving a weeping Robin and hysterical Batman and concluding with the two heroes walking out arm-in-arm."[34] While such a scene in no way assures us that Batman is or isn't gay, it does produce a nonnormative gender reading. Medhurst concludes that the 1989 *Batman* swings back toward a more normative reading of Batman's gender and sexuality: "The film strives and strains to make us forget the Adam West Batman," in part through the undeniably heterosexual relationship between Bruce Wayne and Vicki Vale.[35] Wayne, and Batman, triumph over various rivals, including the Joker, for Vale's affections.

While the Joker is more unambiguously evil than Batman, he too can be read as sexually ambiguous. Medhurst argues that some of the campy, queer elements of the sixties Batman have since been displaced onto the

Joker. He calls this "sly displacement . . . the cleverest method yet devised of preserving Bat-heterosexuality."[36] Insofar as the Joker and Batman are mirror images of one another, Medhurst reasons, the Joker's "badness" can partly be figured in terms of homosexuality. He reads the 1989 *Batman*'s Joker as campy in the same vein as Adam West's sixties Batman. The character's queer subtext is bolstered by the Joker's appearance in the *Arkham Asylum* graphic novel (which came out the same year as *Batman*) in which the Joker calls Batman "honey pie" and pinches his behind—Batman replies by calling him a "filthy degenerate."[37] The film is clearly not so explicit, especially since the Joker is represented as having heterosexual interests, however perverse, in Alicia Hunt (Jerry Hall) and Vicki Vale (Kim Basinger). Nonetheless, these subtexts did exist prior to Prince's intervention and would return to the foreground in the Joel Schumacher-directed *Batman Forever* (1995) and *Batman and Robin* (1997).[38]

While Medhurst makes a good case for the movement of Batman and the Joker between poles of sexuality and gender, he is emphatic that the two characters must remain on opposite sides of the same coin in order for their rivalry to work. This duality is, in some ways, what Prince most upends in his own Bat-works. Some commentators seemed to want to associate Prince most with the Joker, in part because of their shared love of purple and in part because Prince's songs are most prominently featured in the Joker's scenes of the film. As K. J. Donnelly points out, Prince's "Partyman" does not merely operate as score in the Flugelheim Gallery scene; rather, "Joker and his gang's actions directly reflect the rhythmic impetus of the song through their dancing . . . the song is articulating and creating the dynamics of the action in a way reminiscent of song sequences in film musicals."[39] The same is true later in the film, when Prince's "Trust" drives the momentum of the Joker's murderous parade.

However, while most fans and commentators may have missed it, there is also a more sustained integration of Prince's music into Wayne's scenes. In her study of the film's music, Janet K. Halfyard explores how Elfman's "Love Theme" subtly derives from Prince's "Scandalous." As she writes, "the motif is not the melody sung by Prince but the accompaniment, which repeats this motif as a steady ostinato under the more improvisatory vocal line."[40] Halfyard notes eight appearances of this cue within the film and ten within Elfman's composed score. She argues that it "represents Bruce Wayne's point of view and his thoughts and feelings about" Vicki Vale.[41] Though his work is often described as simply writing pop music for *Batman*, Prince—via Elfman—does provide score for the film; his work does not operate solely as diegetic music within the film.

This blurring of authorship further complicates attempts to analyze, and even label, Prince's efforts. As Donnelly suggestively puts it, the *Batman* album "comprises its own narrative of sorts."[42] Robins begins his review by assuring readers that the album "isn't just another movie score: It's a Prince album as much as *Lovesexy*, *Dirty Mind* and *Purple Rain*."[43] Within a single page, Halfyard suggests the album might be labeled a "coherent and self-contained song cycle," a "miniature version of Burton's film," or a "miniature rock-opera version."[44] Prince's Batman work might also productively be read as an adaptation of the film, in the sense defined by Linda Hutcheon. In her influential formulation, "an adaptation is a derivation that is not derivative—a work that is second without being secondary. It is its own palimpsestic thing."[45] The *Batman* album, songs, and music videos borrow and shape ideas from the film and operate as adjuncts, although not subordinates to the film text.

If we look at the *Batman* album as its own work, connected to the film but able to function autonomously, we find that Prince works across and against the dichotomies inherent in the Batman universe and that he cannot be reduced to an association with any single character. While the film itself devotes as much energy to the Joker as to the titular hero, Prince's album spreads out the audience's attention even more widely. Prince's desire to inhabit all of the characters in *Batman* is evident from the moment a listener peeks at the liner notes to the album. Each of the song titles is followed by a designation of one or more characters' authorship. For instance, the first track on the album, "The Future," is notated "lead vocal by Batman." On other tracks, Vicki, Bruce, and the Joker, respectively, take the lead. Some of the tracks involve more complicated arrangements of characters, though. The different sections of "The Arms of Orion" are credited to "Bruce," "Vicki," or "Duet." The raucous final track, "Batdance," reads like a screenplay and one with perhaps more interest than the one filmed to create *Batman*. Even the film samples (such as the Joker's "This town needs an enema") are listed as song lyrics and credited to the characters. Here are contributions from the standard characters (Batman, the Joker, Bruce, and Vicki) as well as the Choir, the Bat Dancers, the Joker's Gang, Prince, and a new character, Gemini.[46] Gemini's role in the song seems to be that of a provocateur, one who instigates the action—his frequent use of refrains throughout the last part of the song are "Don't stop dancin'!" and "Let's do it." His shouted "Get the Funk up!" in the first part of the song is the most noticeable audio performance of the character. "Get" goes a little high and takes on a whining quality before "funk up" turns into a much lower growl.

Despite the alternation between different characters on the album, though, Prince's authorship overarches them all. He puts his mark on the album in part through the lyrics themselves, which are written Prince's idiom: "2," "4," and "U." While some other artists are credited, particularly Sheena Easton for singing Vicki's part on "The Arms of Orion," and Prince's father, John L. Nelson, with whom he cowrote "Scandalous," the liner notes emphasize that "all other instruments and voices are arranged & performed by Prince," a slight variation on the credits included in all official Prince album releases. Furthermore, the interpellation of Hefti's TV theme within "Batdance" allows Prince to directly link his work to the most famous audio representation of the Batman universe, insisting on the very continuity between the 1989 film and the TV series that Warners and Burton were at pains to conceal. Through the Hefti reference, Prince gives voice to the Adam West Batman, however fleetingly. Since the characters on the album must speak through Prince (when not appearing as audio samples from the film), he has the power to manipulate them and sing them into sonic existence.

Commentators at the time read the multivocality of the album as a means for Prince to express competing facets of his own persona. Wyatt, as noted above, sees the album as a vehicle for Prince's "pop persona."[47] He makes this claim as though one could define a singular Prince "persona." Chris Willman also states that the characters all "sound suspiciously" like Prince and goes beyond this to claim that they can be mapped on the artist: "The Joker represents the id side demanding instant gratification in the more party-hearty dance songs ('Electric Chair,' 'Trust,' 'Partyman') while Batman and Vicki are the innocent but still suitably sex-crazed romantics of the ego."[48] Writing for the *Toronto Star*, Mitch Potter praises the album as marking the "shedding of emotional baggage from a string of meandering, erratic albums" and a container for Prince to "vent his many personal demons," without specifying what exactly those might be.[49] For Potter the album, whether created initially for consumer purposes or not, clearly has emotional value for the artist.

It is certainly true that Prince uses *Batman* to voice some of the contradictions in his own world. For instance, Prince continues to wrestle with balancing spirituality (he comes out of the Joker persona to sing as himself, "Who do ya trust if U can't trust God? / Who can U trust—who can ya? / Nobody" at the end of "Trust") and eroticism (As Batman in "Scandalous" he sings, "2 night why don't we just skip all the 4-play, mama / And just get down here on the floor"). But the album is not purely an outlet for Prince's "personal demons." Rather, he also makes a case for the fluidity of the Batman characters—a fluidity that incorporates their unique histories as well as his own. We see a continuity between Batman's and the Joker's concerns about "the future" throughout the album. "Batman" laments on "The Future" that "I've seen the future / And boy it's rough," and yet there's also a sort of indeterminacy: "I've seen the future and it will be."[50] It will be . . . what? Is this fatalism (what will be will be)? Or should we read an ellipsis there: I've seen the future and it will be . . . At the end of the song, a sample of the Joker comes in, on echo: "Think about the future . . . the future . . . the future . . ." The Joker's intrusion segues into "his" song, "Electric Chair," which is next on the album. This song also picks up on the theme of the future with the celebratory and yet fatalistic lines "If a man is considered guilty / 4 what goes on in his mind / Then gimme the electric chair / 4 all my future crimes." These two songs, which work initially to set up continuities and discontinuities between Batman and the Joker, are reprised in "Batdance," where two of the most prominent lines, "I've seen the future and it will be" and "Then gimme the electric chair," are now attributed to Gemini. The former is also pitched down and noticeably lower than the line as sung by "Batman" in the earlier song. This repetition marks a fluidity between the subjectivities of Batman, the Joker, and Gemini—perhaps even an intersubjectivity between them.

This fluidity between characters and their voicing is evident throughout the album. Vicki Vale, for instance, is voiced by three different people. Sheena Easton sings her on "The Arms of Orion" (opposite Prince's Bruce Wayne), Prince himself sings her on "Lemon Crush," and Kim Basinger (via a sample from the film) voices her on "Batdance."[51] Bruce and Batman, of course, both sing to Vicki, in a slippage between the superhero and the lonely, orphaned bachelor who has characterized the duality of the Batman character throughout its long public life. The album highlights the way in which a single voice can be multiplied and inflected across different characters and also the way a single person can take on multiple subjectivities and multiple voices.

VISUALIZING PRINCE'S BATMAN: THE MUSIC VIDEOS

If the *Batman* album is about multiplicity and indeterminacy, then the same can be said of the music videos, perhaps even more so. The album's liner notes hint at the identity of Gemini via an evocative final image of Prince, shot by Jeff Katz, with half his face in darkness, but Gemini was first introduced visually in the "Batdance" music video (see Fig. 1). As in the song, Gemini is essentially the central character in the music video. In the song, Gemini sings lines previously uttered by Batman and Joker, but in the music video, this duality is more explicit: Gemini's appearance is divided between attributes of Batman and the Joker. The left side of his face is painted white, the hair green, and the suit purple while the right

Fig. 1. In the "Batdance" music video, Gemini is half Batman, half Joker, and entirely Prince. Authors screengrab.

side of his face is left plain, his hair black, and his body adorned with half a Batman emblem and half a bat cape. However, the fact that he doesn't wear half a bat mask means that Gemini is still easily identifiable as Prince and thus as a Black man. Gemini opens up, however subtly, the possibility of a Black Batman. Of course, this revolutionary possibility is complicated by Gemini's Joker half, which refuses that possibility. As in the "Batdance" song, Prince has his own identity separate from Gemini in the video as well. He is arguably the true hero of the video—the genius musician at the helm of the keyboard (and sometimes the guitar) who keeps the party rockin', albeit in understated black attire and loose, straight locks.

The beginning of the video aligns Gemini with the Joker and Prince with Batman. After a shot of a screen in the shape of the bat signal filled with TV static, we enter the bat cave (signaled by several Batman figures in repose) to find Prince uneasily leaning on his keyboard. He looks up to see Gemini appear within the bat screen, against a purple backdrop. The worried Prince hits a switch, and the song begins with Gemini thrashing in silhouette to a sample of the Joker's/Jack Nicholson's sinister laughter. While Prince and Gemini remain loosely allied with Batman and the Joker, respectively, neither is wholly one nor the other, and Prince (the artist, not the character) continues to play with multivocality and indeterminacy. Gemini sometimes visibly sings/says other characters' lines, for instance, the Joker's "And where is the Batman?" and Prince takes Gemini's line "I've seen the future and it will be"—doubly confusing since this was originally Batman's line in "The Future." Prince is also on screen with the Batdancers for "Oh, we got the soul / Hey, we got the sho' nuff get off 2 make the devil go, go."

This mini-operetta also features the multiplication of Batman, the Joker, and Vicki Vale. Batman is represented by the Batdancers, who are notably played by men and women. The Joker is similarly multiplied through "Joker's gang." The two gangs ostensibly battle throughout the video, but only in the manner of *West Side Story*'s or "Beat It's" highly choreographed showdowns. For his part, Gemini alternates between dancing with the bats and dancing with the Jokers. He is most excited, however, when the Vickis come on. Unlike the bats and the Jokers, the Vickis all appear to be biological women. However, we can see variations among this multiplicity as well. One of the Vickis wears a shirt that says "All this and brains too"—a nod to the film's representation of Vicki as a woman who must constantly deflect sexual attention to get her journalistic work done (even as she provides a heterosexual foil for both Wayne and the bat). In "Batdance," Prince locates himself within the Batman universe, but he also remakes it in his own image, where gender indeterminacy, multivocality, heightened sexuality, and a constant negotiation between seriousness and frivolity are the norm. His Batman work is logically the product of the same artist whose song "Controversy" in 1981 is something of a manifesto of rejecting others' labels and even incorporates the Lord's Prayer. He bends the DC Comics and Warner property to his will, apparently with less overt support for this intervention than Kendrick Lamar enjoyed for his *Black Panther* soundtrack in 2018.[52]

Prince released two other music videos in support of the *Batman* album, but the "Scandalous" video doesn't explicitly engage with the album's iconography or its characters (it's hard to imagine Batman in a sleeveless red jumpsuit), so we'll focus on "Partyman." Prince created two versions of the "Partyman" video—one that matches the album version of the song and an "extended" version that is set to a longer mix (labeled as the "Partyman video mix" on the "Scandalous!" maxi-single release, which is also known as the *Scandalous Sex Suite*).[53] The two videos aren't substantially different. Both feature the Gemini character, who is remade again for this video. Presumably set in Gotham, the video takes up iconography that may reference Alicia's white mask in the Flugelheim scene of the *Batman* film and that certainly references Gemini's half-white face. Here, though, instead of Gemini's half-white face standing out, it has become the norm. All of the partygoers wear white masks over half their faces (see Fig. 2). These masks approximate the appearance of Gemini, his henchmen, and the band, all of whose faces are painted half-white. Gemini seems to have

Fig. 2. Gemini in "Partyman" no longer wears half-Batman symbols, but Gothamites duplicate his new look. Authors screengrabs.

become more Joker-esque, in that he no longer wears the half-bat attire, but his hair is still only half green. Unlike "Batdance," this song is attributed entirely to the Joker on the album, which may account for Gemini going further over to the dark side. Like the Joker's poisoning of Gotham in the film, Gemini poisons the partygoers, leaving them all dead (or at least incapacitated) by the end of the video.

In the video, Gemini becomes the king to Prince's, well, prince. The openings of the two versions of the "Partyman" video vary slightly, but both function to introduce the "new king in town," who is also, of course, "the funkiest man U've ever seen." In the extended version of the video, Prince's band plays a jazzy number while partygoers wonder aloud, "But where's the guest of honor?" In the shorter version, the party is more abruptly interrupted by the appearance of Gemini's henchmen, made recognizable by their purple suits. In both versions, the henchmen come with a decree, which they unfurl and then read: "All hail to the new king . . . Partyman," after which Gemini comes whistling in, in silhouette. He does some classic rock'n'roll moves to the beats of lightning sizzles, as the crowd mutters. Finally, he lands in a fierce pose that causes all the fires in the palatial room to flare and points to the band to start the party. It's a party fit for a king, and Gemini is seen carousing over the next several minutes with all manner of partygoers, including, in the extended version, a chimpanzee in a Batman shirt.[54] By remaking Gemini again in this video, Prince demonstrates that the character is not a fixed entity. Rather, he is a cipher through which Prince can play with the Batman world without being confined to its rules. Finally, the classic Batman characters are notable in their absence in both versions of the "Partyman" music video, leaving Gemini, not the Joker, the new king in town.

THE EXPANDED PRINCE-BATMAN UNIVERSE:
A COMIC BOOK AND EXTRA SONGS

"Partyman" was the last Prince music video to feature Gemini, but the character would reappear a few years later, albeit in a significantly modified form, in one of the most understudied works of Prince's career: the comic book *Prince: Alter Ego* (1991).[55] In *Alter Ego*, Gemini no longer appears divided in two, and he is no longer explicitly "played" by Prince. Rather, a different kind of mirroring dynamic emerges, one arguably more akin to the classic Batman-Joker opposition. *Alter Ego* Gemini is Prince's childhood friend-turned-nemesis—his dark rival for rock superiority (and for Prince's not-so-subtly named love interest, Muse). As one panel of the comic puts it, "Twin cities, twin men. Dark has the light, yin has its yang, and . . . Batman has his Joker." This description is telling for the way it resets Batman in Prince's own universe: the Twin Cities of Minneapolis-St. Paul. And while the Twin Cities may not be as rough as Gotham, Prince still must intervene, Batman-like, to foil Gemini's Joker-like scheme to foment violence and chaos through his anarchic guitar playing. As Prince pulls even with Gemini in a motorcycle chase, Gemini quips, "You really *do* think you're Batman, don't you?" These references work in some ways to extend the reach of the Batman property. After all, Piranha Music, which released the comic, was a DC imprint, and at least three of the artists who worked on the book—writer Dwayne McDuffie, penciller Denys Cowan, and inker Kent Williams—had worked on *Batman* comics previously.[56]

While the links between Prince's *Batman* and *Alter Ego* are unmistakable, *Alter Ego* not only resets the story in Minneapolis, but also refigures the conflict between the Batman and Joker characters in more musical terms. Music is the source of Prince and Gemini's initial friendship and also their ultimate enmity. Prince meets Gemini after Gemini hears him jamming in his basement, and they become fast friends: "Two kids jamming endlessly, united like brothers in an endless quest to unlock the secret power of music." But as they develop their superheroic musical powers, their goals diverge. Prince's power is "to move an audience's heart . . . to unite them under a groove . . . to create a sound as brilliant and warming as sunlight," while Gemini's sound "pulses with a desperate rage. His guitar lines tear into the soul of his audience, pushing them beyond the edge of reason . . ." Finally, they reach an artistic and philosophical impasse: "Each is convinced of the correctness of his vision. Prince believes the music must be used to nurture the human spirit; Gemini, to unleash the primal urges and free the rage within humanity." Gemini departs with the band on his aptly named Apocalypse World Tour, reaping destruction everywhere he goes. We see him a few panels later, on a TV screen, looking inebriated and out-of-control in MTV land. After some twists and turns that show Gemini temporarily institutionalized, he returns to the Twin Cities for a final showdown that plays out as a guitar battle. Spoiler alert: Prince's sweet sounds triumph over Gemini's deadly chords.

It is Prince's musical intuition that tells him his old rival has returned, and this musical sense seems to connect the two characters like an umbilical cord or an uncanny mutual awareness between twins. In the first few panels of the book, upon returning to Minneapolis from his own tour, Prince notices something amiss in the musical atmosphere. As we see him ride into town on his motorcycle, a caption tells us, "It's like hearing a favorite old single playing slightly off-speed. You know the song well enough that even a slight variation is . . . disturbing." Later, Prince determines that this musical disturbance is emanating from the Glam Slam, his home venue. As he nears and then enters the club, "He remembers the sound from his childhood. Now as then, composition and performance alike are brilliant, chaotic and powerfully disturbing." But before Prince has this revelation, he initially mistakes Gemini's music for his own: "The singer sounds like *him*, a *lot* like him. For that matter, so does the music." In the next panel, over a closeup of Prince with a single iconic curl on his forehead, the caption continues his revelation: "This is more than some clever mimic. It doesn't just *sound* like him. It *is* him." Here the comic raises questions about the slippage between the two characters, as did "Batdance" before it. In *Alter Ego*, Prince actually looks a bit more like the Gemini of "Batdance" and "Partyman"—he has curly hair in most panels, and he is characterized by purple accents in his lighting and clothing. Meanwhile, Gemini looks a bit more like the Prince of "Batdance"—he has straightened hair in most panels, and he wears a black vest and pants. But Gemini's appearance also varies more than Prince's throughout the comic. In some panels he is portrayed as a light-skinned Black man of similar stature to Prince. In other panels, he appears bigger, butcher, and Blacker than Prince. In yet other panels he takes on a monstrous greenish cast. More id than alter ego, Gemini might represent Prince's anxiety over his own pop powers.

Whether they are for good or for evil, though, these powers are explicitly Prince's. *Alter Ego* may take *Batman* as a template, but Prince is ultimately his own superhero and Gemini his own villain. The story is set not in the DC universe but in the Prince universe. As in the *Batman* album and surrounding texts, *Alter Ego* remixes references from Prince's repertoire. A marquee announces Gemini's Apocalypse World Tour band as "Power Generation," and later, after he has stolen the band back from Prince, a flyer calls them "The New Power Generation." When *Alter Ego* came out, the New Power Generation was Prince's actual band. He had christened them a year earlier in *Graffiti Bridge* (1990), a Prince-directed film that reprised another musical rivalry featuring another Prince alter ego (*Purple Rain*'s The Kid). The New Power Generation also played on Prince's 1991 album *Diamonds and Pearls*, an ad for which appears on the back cover of *Alter Ego*. In this way, *Alter Ego* provides continuity between the *Batman* project and Prince's larger oeuvre.

The B-sides that Prince and WB chose to include with the *Batman* singles function similarly to expand the Prince-Batman universe and to put the *Batman* project into conversation with Prince's larger body of work. Throughout his career, Prince used singles as a vehicle to release music that, for whatever reason, he could not find space for on albums. These releases, whether featuring a single added song or several, can also reveal new meanings in individual songs through a change of sonic context. The remixes include "The Purple Party Mix" of the "Batdance" track that includes a number of samples from Prince's back catalogue. B-sides include "Sex" on the "Scandalous!" maxi-single, which Greenman reads as a possible sequel to "Erotic City," one of Prince's finest B-sides. As he writes, "Like most sequels it fell short of the original, though a cover of the song made for a bright spot on the debut album of a Dutch band with the unlikely name of Lois Lane."[57] The song's stern lyrics are especially jarring coming just before the "Scandalous Sex Suite," which expands the track to more than nineteen minutes and three sections. Saxophone and guitar solos appear between snippets of conversation between Batman and Vale, here voiced by Kim Basinger. As noted above, the song's video (in its original version) drops the pretense that Prince sings as Batman, and this seduction skit does not demonstrate much interest in claiming that Batman is courting Vale; it sounds more like Prince and perhaps real-life girlfriend Basinger are documenting their affection for posterity.[58]

The song that is perhaps most striking for its appearance in the Batman singles is "Feel U Up." Credited to Prince on the single for "Partyman," the song was recorded and originally planned to be released on the *Camille* album and credited to Camille.[59] Prince's unreleased or unrealized projects are as fascinating as his official oeuvre, and no project invites more speculation and analysis than the *Camille* album. This is the case not because its proposed contents are unknown—they are well-established—but because of the nature of the album itself. Camille was an alter ego Prince created through manipulating the speed of the recordings. By pitch-shifting his voice, Prince created a distinctive, and feminine, voice. Simon Reynolds, in an article that doubles as obituary and analysis of the Camille song "If I Was Your Girlfriend," writes: "Prince's pitch-shifted, feminized vocal sound was the wholly logical, yet completely unexpected and surprising, extension of his compulsion to dissolve borderlines."[60] That song, along with "Housequake" and "Strange Relationship," appear on *Sign O' The Times*, the double album that carries components originally intended for the *Camille, Dream Factory*, and *Crystal Ball* releases. The Camille songs are sonically striking and were even more unique in the context of the mid-1980s. For Reynolds, "If I Was Your Girlfriend" demonstrates that "Prince posed himself as a human question mark, a mystery creature who could not be contained by conventional categories."[61]

Greenman makes a similar point in his volume, arguing that Camille's voice "interrogated and deconstructed the way that gender functioned in his songs. This pitch-shifted version of Prince hovered between male and female and, in the process, cracked open previously conventional issues of power, sexuality, ego, and id."[62] This description might almost double as a description of the Gemini character, although the author does not link the two creations. Prince kept the Camille songs but abandoned a sustained presentation of the character in the form of an album credited solely to "Camille." Gemini, created less than three years after the decision not to release *Camille*, can be read as a continuation of Prince's interest in putting on sonic masks. Greenman also importantly notes that Camille can be compared to George Clinton's characters, such as Sir Nose, featured on Parliament's records in the 1970s.[63] Clinton creates characters to offer audiences new ideas and new sonic experiences. From Spooky Electric to Camille, Prince also explores audio personae and ways to express new ideas and moods. Prince's Camille predates the advertised audio masks of Prince's *Batman*, but only by a few years, and also sits comfortably alongside them. In each case, Prince performs the act of performing.

CONCLUSION: PRINCE AS FILMMAKER

Ed: *Purple Rain*?
Shaun: No.
Ed: *Sign O' The Times*?
Shaun: Definitely not.
Ed: The *Batman* soundtrack?
Shaun: Throw it.[64]

When Prince's *Batman* is referenced in popular culture, it is typically in negative terms. In the above exchange from *Shaun of the Dead* (2004), the LP is deemed suitable for use as a weapon against zombies rather than music to be preserved. Similarly, early in *The LEGO Batman Movie* (2017) the Joker's use of Prince music is mentioned as evidence of his historic inability to defeat Batman. When the Joker says, "Well, tonight is going to be different! Tonight is my greatest plan yet, and trust me, Batman's never going to see it coming," Pilot Bill immediately responds, "Like the time with the parade and the Prince music?"[65] Both filmic references, though admittedly jokes, position the work as a failure: it is a lesser Prince offering and perhaps even a lesser Batman offering. Each film also flatters the audience by linking this Prince release and this Batman film to other texts that the audience is allowed to admire, such as *Purple Rain* and *The Dark Knight* (2008). Prince's Batman does, however, stand between *Purple Rain* and *The Dark Knight* in the sense that it is both his and not his, a Prince work and (a work commissioned for) a Hollywood blockbuster. When asked to write a few songs, Prince fundamentally transformed the Batman universe (even if his revisions did not endure for WB or DC). His work demonstrates his understanding of the multimedia landscape of the late twentieth century. And his decision to pressure the boundaries of "Batman" is no less laudable than the work of respected auteurs Tim Burton and Christopher Nolan.

There are hints of a budding discourse on Prince as a filmmaker. While almost certainly reviewing *Batman* and its accompanying music videos, media critic Matt Zoller Seitz (2016) tweeted some of his thoughts in the fall of 2016. Among them is this expression of desire: "I wish Prince had directed at least one Batman movie. His BATMAN-themed videos are more psychologically perceptive than any of the films."[66] Though forceful, the fact that this quote has made its way onto the album's *Wikipedia* entry indicates the paucity of the Prince/Batman discourse. And Seitz provides an answer to his own stated desire: why not regard the music videos as Batman films? Nothing actually prevents scholars from subjecting the videos to the same level of analysis that the film, and its numerous sequels, generated and continue to generate. And, even more importantly, Prince's Batman encompasses an album, singles, music videos, and a comic book. His Batman project evades even a broad definition of "movie" or "film." These materials contributed substantially to Prince's lifelong projects of exploring sexuality, spirituality, and multivocality while also bringing a perspective too often silenced—that of a Black man—to the world of franchised comic book properties.

More generally, Prince's audiovisual endeavors as a writer, director, and producer warrant more analysis. To label him a "filmmaker" is actually limiting, but it is a start. His work creating several music videos, the features *Purple Rain, Under the Cherry Moon* (1986), *Sign O' The Times* (1987), *Graffiti*

Bridge, and even the straight-to-video *3 Chains o' Gold* (1994), await serious scholarly attention. The fact that Prince did not live to complete his memoir, and that there will be no new Prince music (beyond old music released in drips from "the vault"), have been and will continue to be mourned. But the scholarship on Prince has certainly not exhausted the artist's oeuvre, particularly where his film and TV work is concerned. One option is to explore the thematic and aesthetic links between his music and "film" work. The assumption that a film is more significant than its soundtrack album cannot be assumed in the cases of Prince's works (including *Batman*). These complex audiovisual works can withstand auteur analysis better than many a contemporary "visionary" filmmaker's work. And though he was not likely to acquiesce to being labeled a "Black" filmmaker, locating Prince's output in the fraught history of African American media seems logical and perhaps necessary. Arguably, his interventions in the realm of cinema faced even greater obstacles than his music labor. As Sam Davies argues: "he stands in a lineage of Black filmmakers looking for an independent space within Hollywood. Like Melvin Van Peebles in the 1970s or Harry Belafonte with his company HarBel in the late 1950s, Prince wanted to graduate from starring to directing to controlling the means of production. The results may have been mixed but the scale of the ambition can only be admired."[67] Linking Prince's efforts to the history and study of Black audiovisual media, and independent filmmaking, holds significant promise for a deeper appreciation and understanding of an artist more powerful and elusive than any superhero.

Notes

1. Duane Tudahl, *Prince and the Purple Rain Era Studio Sessions: 1983 and 1984* (Lanham: Rowman & Littlefield, 2018).

2. Quoted in Michael Goldberg, "Prince Scores Batman Film," *Rolling Stone* 555 (June 29, 1989), 21.

3. Richard Harrington, "Prince, on Track with Batmusic," *Washington Post*, September 6, 1989. This is savvy marketing and also is quite plausible for a musician of his generation.

4. Goldberg, "Prince Scores Batman Film."

5. Quoted in Goldberg.

6. Harrington, "Prince, on Track with Batmusic."

7. Prince composed songs—that went unused—for James L. Brooks's *I'll Do Anything* (1994) and his work as performer and composer forms the music and soundtrack album for Spike Lee's *Girl 6* (1996). Though written for the former, "Don't Talk 2 Strangers" was used in the latter film.

8. Ian Freer, "Batman v Superman the Musical: Which Superhero Has the Best Theme Tunes?," *The Telegraph*, March 30, 2016. One of Elfman's next projects was scoring Warren

Beatty's *Dick Tracy* (1990), featuring Madonna, a film that pushed three soundtrack albums into the marketplace.

9. Scholars such as Justin Wyatt and Stephen Prince state that the film only includes three (presumably meaning these) of Prince's songs as evidence of the music's lack of importance. See Justin Wyatt, *High Concept: Movies and Marketing in Hollywood* (Austin: University of Texas Press, 1994), 49; and Stephen Prince, *A New Pot of Gold: Hollywood under the Electronic Rainbow, 1980–1989* (Berkeley: University of California Press, 2002), 136.

10. K. J. Donnelly, *Magical Musical Tour: Rock and Pop in Film Soundtracks* (New York: Bloomsbury, 2015), 105.

11. Its cover features an image from the film of Batman's plane silhouetted in front of the moon, while Prince's cover has the Batman symbol that was ubiquitous in 1989 on the film poster and merchandise, perhaps especially T-shirts.

12. Dennis Hunt, "Prince and Ex-Eagle Flying High," *Los Angeles Times*, July 21, 1989, sec. Morning Report: Pop LP Chart.

13. Harrington, "Prince, on Track with Batmusic."

14. Edna Gundersen, "Prince's Batting Record: A Big Hit Soundtrack," *USA Today*, July 17, 1989.

15. Harrington, "Prince, on Track with Batmusic."

16. Quoted in Donnelly, *Magical Musical Tour*, 109.

17. Wayne Robins, "Batmusic by Prince," *Newsday*, June 18, 1989.

18. Chuck Campbell, "Prince's 'Batman' Ingenious," *Palm Beach Post*, July 14, 1989.

19. Steven Hyden, "Prince's Batman Soundtrack Is Not the Embarrassment It's Reputed to Be," *The A.V. Club Music* (blog), accessed February 15, 2018. https://music .avclub.com/prince-s-batman-soundtrack-is-not-the-embarrassment-it-1798233864.

20. Campbell, "Prince's 'Batman.'"

21. Eileen R. Meehan, "'Holy Commodity Fetish, Batman!': The Political Economy of a Commercial Intertext," in *The Many Lives of the Batman: Critical Approaches to a Superhero and His Media*, edited by Roberta E. Pearson and William Uricchio (New York: Routledge, 1991), 49.

22. Meehan, "'Holy Commodity Fetish,'" 49.

23. Hyden, "Prince's Batman Soundtrack."

24. Meehan, "'Holy Commodity Fetish,'" 55.

25. Meehan, "'Holy Commodity Fetish,'" 55.

26. Wyatt, *High Concept*, 50.

27. Wyatt, *High Concept*, 51.

28. Prince, *A New Pot of Gold*, 136.

29. Quoted in Goldberg, "Prince Scores Batman Film."

30. Quoted in Goldberg, "Prince Scores Batman Film."

31. Andy Medhurst, "Batman, Deviance and Camp," in *The Many Lives of the Batman: Critical Approaches to a Superhero and His Media*, ed. Roberta E. Pearson and William Uricchio (New York: Routledge, 1991), 149–63.

32. Quoted in Medhurst, "Batman, Deviance and Camp," 151.

33. Medhurst, "Batman, Deviance and Camp," 152.

34. Will Brooker, "Batman: One Life, Many Faces," in *Adaptations: From Text to Screen, Screen to Text,* edited by Deborah Cartmell and Imelda Whelehan (London: Routledge, 1999), 189.

35. Medhurst, "Batman, Deviance and Camp," 161.

36. Medhurst, "Batman, Deviance and Camp," 160.

37. Medhurst, "Batman, Deviance and Camp," 160–61.

38. The cycle of needing to "normalize" Batman after he goes astray would continue with the Nolan films starting with *Batman Begins* (2005).

39. Donnelly, *Magical Musical Tour,* 111.

40. Janet K. Halfyard, *Danny Elfman's Batman: A Film Score Guide* (Lanham: Scarecrow Press, 2004), 68.

41. Halfyard, *Danny Elfman's Batman,* 69.

42. Donnelly, *Magical Musical Tour,* 108.

43. Robins, "Batmusic by Prince."

44. Halfyard, *Danny Elfman's Batman,* 66.

45. Linda Hutcheon, *A Theory of Adaptation,* 2nd ed. (New York: Routledge, 2012), 9.

46. Gemini was introduced in the "Batdance" single and music video, which came out before the album, but he was not identified as such until release of the album's liner notes.

47. Wyatt, *High Concept.*

48. Chris Willman, "Record Rack: Prince's Gotham City Batdance: Id and Ego," *Los Angeles Times,* June 18, 1989.

49. Mitch Potter, "Prince Back in Form with High-Funk Batmobility," *Toronto Star,* July 7, 1989.

50. Ben Greenman notes the resonance between Prince's lyrics and "Lincoln Steffens's famous assessment of the USSR, 'I've seen the future, and it works,'" though this assessment is beyond the scope of this chapter. Ben Greenman, *Dig If You Will the Picture: Funk, Sex, God, and Genius in the Music of Prince* (New York: Henry Holt, 2017), 149.

51. The unreleased Kim Basinger album *Hollywood Affair* is rumored to have involved Prince, but there is no real evidence supporting this position. That Easton appears here is not surprising given her work with Prince, including the earlier duet "U Got the Look," and recording songs created by Prince, such as the notorious (at least to the P.R.M.C.) "Sugar Walls."

52. There is far too little mention of Prince's earlier efforts in creating a commentary album for a superhero movie in the praise for the *Black Panther* album. See Phillips (2018) for one review that acknowledges Prince's work for *Batman.* Not surprisingly, the Lamar-curated *Black Panther* album was followed a week later by an album of Ludwig Göransson's score.

53. The song, and single, add the exclamation point to the title. As listed on the *Batman* album there is no punctuation.

54. This is most easily read as a not-so-sly dig at Michael Jackson's chimpanzee friend Bubbles. Two years earlier Prince had famously declined to sing "Bad" as a duet with Jackson (reportedly in part because of the song's opening line: "Your butt is mine"). The singers' rivalry went back at least to the onstage duel (by most accounts won by Jackson) in the presence of James Brown in 1983. See Rembert Browne, "Rembert Explains the '80s: James

Brown & 'Friends' at the Beverly Theater in 1983," *Grantland* (blog), October 25, 2012, https://grantland.com/hollywood-prospectus/rembert-explains-the-80s-james-brown-prince-michael-jacksonat-the-beverly-theater-in-1983/ and Dexter Thomas, "Prince, Michael Jackson, and James Brown on Stage Together Was a Moment We Didn't Deserve," *Los Angeles Times*, April 21, 2016, https://www.latimes.com/entertainment/music/posts/la-et-ms-prince-michael-jackson-james-brown-20160421-snap-htmlstory.html.

55. Dwayne McDuffie et al., *Prince: Alter Ego* (New York: Piranha Music, 1991).

56. McDuffie and Cowan would go on to co-found Milestone Media, a company whose mission was to increase minority representation in comics and animation.

57. Greenman, *Dig If You Will*, 78. Prince in fact recorded the song for the band and they added their voices to his music. See "Sex," Prince Vault, accessed January 10, 2021, http://www.princevault.com/index.php?title=Sex.

58. Basinger's moans can be heard on the song, leading to more than a few rumors about a Basinger-Prince tryst. Biographer Ronin Ro is a bit cagey about the relationship, focusing more on the duo's professional pairing at the time. Basinger worked with Prince on an early treatment of *Graffiti Bridge*, his next film, although she ultimately left the project. See Ronin Ro, *Prince: Inside the Music and the Masks* (New York: St. Martin's Press, 2011), 190–91.

59. Prince's choice of this name is typically read as a deliberate reference to Alexina Barbin, whose memoirs were published with an introduction by Michel Foucault in the early 1980s.

60. Simon Reynolds, "How Prince's Androgynous Genius Changed the Way We Think About Music and Gender," *Pitchfork*, April 22, 2016, https://pitchfork.com/features/article/9882-how-princes-androgynous-genius-changed-the-way-we-think-about-music-and-gender/.

61. Reynolds, "How Prince's Androgynous Genius Changed."

62. Greenman, *Dig If You Will*, 95.

63. Greenman, *Dig If You Will*, 95.

64. Edgar Wright, director, *Shaun of the Dead* (Universal Home Entertainment, 2004).

65. Chris McKay, director, *The LEGO Batman Movie* (Warner Bros., 2017).

66. Matt Zoller Seitz (@mattzollerseitz), "I wish Prince had directed," Twitter, October 8, 2016, 10:00 a.m. https://twitter.com/mattzollerseitz/status/784800642518945796.

67. Sam Davies, "Lock, Stock and Barrel," *Sight & Sound*, August 2016, 58.

Chapter 8

NOT IN VAIN

The Artistry of Denise Matthews

SAMUEL FITZPATRICK

Critics are usually dismissive of Prince's protégées. I've never read the derisive phrase "Prince protégée" as coming from a place of heartfelt admiration and respect.[1] Many (mostly) young women who worked with Prince were enveloped by his long shadow. Musically, they sounded too much like him. Physically, they looked too much like him. Often, he spoke through them and, more often, renamed them. I would argue that "Vanity" was, indeed, Prince's greatest creation. However, the persona, the character, the name, did not suit the spirit of Denise Matthews. She was different; she was special. She was not a typical "Prince protégée." Prince could not control her. He said as much during his somber 2016 "Piano & A Microphone" tour date in Melbourne, Australia: ". . . She and I would fight. She was very headstrong 'cause she knew she was the finest woman in the world. She never missed an opportunity to tell you that."[2] When Denise chose to play the role that Prince bestowed upon her, she did so flawlessly, and other artists inevitably took note.

In fact, "Vanity" was the prototype for Madonna. Without "Nasty Girl" (1982), there would be no "Like a Virgin" (1984).[3] Madonna's celebrated evocation of Marilyn Monroe's performance of the song "Diamonds Are a Girl's Best Friend" (performed for the 1953 film *Gentlemen Prefer Blondes*) in her 1984 visual for the track "Material Girl" greatly overshadowed the release of "Vanity's" debut solo album, *Wild Animal*, through the revered Motown record label. Interestingly, *Wild Animal* was released only two days before (November 10, 1984) *Like a Virgin* (November 12). Yet, while the latter propelled Madonna into the lofty heights of pop superstardom (so much so that she is placed alongside Prince and Michael Jackson as one of the leading icons of the 1980s), the former marked the beginning of a steady decline for "Vanity." Just as the prodigious and multitalented Dorothy Dandridge was denied the fame that Monroe achieved with relative ease, Denise could only go so far playing the character that was tailor-made for her. Note also that Dandridge and Matthews are best known for playing harlots (see Dandridge's breakthrough performance in *Carmen Jones* [1954], released only a year after *Gentlemen Prefer Blondes*). There remains much more to be said pertaining to this disgraceful history of diminishing Black femininity in favor of championing white womanhood, but that is outside the scope of this essay. Here, I assert that Denise reclaimed the "Vanity" persona during her residency at Motown and transformed the character into a vehicle for female empowerment that laid the foundation for contemporary artists such as Beyoncé, Mýa, and Rihanna.[4]

While Motown did provide Denise with many opportunities to extend her reach as a solo artist—her performance in the 1985 cult classic *The Last Dragon* was praised by some critics, who rightly noted that in the film ". . . [she] radiates a sweetness seldom seen in her other work"—the venerable, yet crumbling record label could not compete with the likes of Warner Bros., which was riding high after the groundbreaking success of Prince's 1984 *Purple Rain* album and film (another factor that undoubtedly contributed to Madonna's ascendency into the musical stratosphere).[5] Denise knew her worth and refused to settle for anything less than the complete fulfillment of her creative potential. When "Vanity" walked off the set of *Purple Rain*, abandoning the role that was originally written for her, she escaped Prince's orbit and never looked back. The simple fact that she did so, and was able to achieve some measure of success in the aftermath of her departure from Prince's camp, is noteworthy. At the time, she stated, "I needed one person to love me, and he needed more."[6] The "me" that she refers to here is Denise, the woman that Prince viewed as a reflection of himself.

Shortly after Prince announced his plan to utilize the ineffable "Love Symbol," which had appeared in many forms throughout his career, in place of his pronounceable birth name in 1993, the woman named Denise also had a revelation. In 1994, she nearly died after many years of abusing a drug that destroyed many Black lives during the 1980s and 1990s: crack cocaine. She reflected on this experience in her now out-of-print memoir *Blame It on Vanity: Hollywood, Hell, & Heaven*.[7] What followed was a swift conversion to Evangelical Christianity, which in many ways paralleled Prince's subsequent baptism into the religious doctrines of the Jehovah's Witnesses and a complete disavowal of the "Vanity" façade.

More recently, much has been made of the fact that Denise and Prince died in the same year, at the same age. Indeed, it is tempting to think of this as an astounding cosmic coincidence. Nonetheless, much has yet to be written regarding the ways in which this remarkable woman transcended the status of mere Prince protégée—or as she once comically referred to it in a filmed interview for *Ebony/Jet* magazines, the state of being ". . . a walking, talking, encyclopedia on Prince"—and paved the way for the numerous musicians and personalities that Prince mentored and promoted throughout his career. I'm bothered, but not surprised, by the fact that Denise has vanished—insomuch as she has once again been relegated to the status of the protégée "Vanity"—from the realm of public remembrance in the wake of Prince's shocking and untimely passing. It is apparent, even in the *Ebony/ Jet* interview mentioned above that was filmed in the midst of her departure from Prince's camp, that Denise struggled to reclaim her identity—"I just feel that . . . I should start talking about myself . . ." was her response to the question, "Have you ever done an interview when no one asked you about Prince?"—that she wanted to celebrate herself and that she longed to be admired and respected. I have a great amount of respect for Denise Matthews. I continue to think of her as the Prince tributes pile up one after the other; as neglectful think pieces reference her as a mere footnote in the career of a genius.[8] A prolonged, comprehensive critical analysis of Denise Matthews is long overdue. She is worthy of such treatment. This is a start.

"3 X 2 = 6"

Denise Matthews, the former model for Pearl Drops Toothpaste and Japanese Coca-Cola ads, stands on the *Soul Train* stage in a black dress and heels with her back turned to the audience.[9] On her left is Susan Moonsie, wearing pink, and on her right is Brenda Bennett, wearing green. There's something different about this January 1, 1983, *Soul Train* performance. Normally, the famous *Soul Train* dancers are too preoccupied with introducing television viewers to the latest and hippest dance moves to pay attention to the performance taking place on the stage. As the opening percussive riffs of "Nasty Girl" begin to play over the elaborate sound system (despite the fact that there are microphones on stage, the ladies will lip-sync to the record), the audience is riveted, barely moving. The three women shaking their hips and snapping along to the funky beat have put them in a trance. There are catcalls and shrieks of delight before the song begins. "Vanity" especially is working the crowd into a frenzy.

As the first verse of the song begins, the camera zooms in, capturing every move of the clear focal point of the group: the incredible, exotic beauty asking the crowd, ". . . Don't you believe in mystery? / Don't you wanna play my game?" She is a very carefully crafted mix of Diana Ross and Tina Turner; the leader of a group that has borrowed as many elements from Motown's the Supremes as they have from Rick James's the Mary Jane Girls.[10] Vanity 6 is edgier than the former and a bit more sophisticated than the latter. In any case, the *Soul Train* dancers and Don Cornelius are clearly smitten with them. The smooth, fairly conservative, host of the program cannot help but express his glee after reappearing on the stage to interview the group once the performance concludes: ". . . Come to me my darlings" is his giddy and, when examined through a contemporary lens, somewhat inappropriate response to the three ladies demurely walking over to greet him.[11] By now, of course, all eyes are on them, and the catcalls, whoops, and whistles continue unabated even as Cornelius begins his interview. "They bad ain't they?" Cornelius asks the raucous audience. As things begin to quiet down, the host points out the group's origins in Minneapolis, Minnesota, providing potentially naive television viewers with an immediate connection to Prince and his other side project the Time—who acted as the session players on Vanity 6's debut album—and receives some additional biographical information from "Vanity," Susan, and Brenda: "I'm from Canada," says "Vanity." "I'm from Minneapolis," says Susan. "I'm from Boston," says Brenda. The disparate locales seem to suit the three separate personalities of the women in the group. "Vanity" is aggressive female sexuality personified. Susan plays the slightly less naughty but still devastatingly sexy "Lolita" figure. Brenda is the tough, yet alluringly feminine counterpoint to both. Indeed, an intriguing mix.

Later in the show, they will perform their single "He's So Dull," penned by Revolution member Dez Dickerson, a rockabilly song that contains many elements of Prince's "Ronnie Talk to Russia" (*Controversy*, 1981) and showcases "Vanity's" signature acid-tongued vocals.[12] Along with "Nasty Girl," the track is another highlight of the group's eponymous debut album. Missing from the *Soul Train* showcase is "Drive Me Wild," a minimalist funk speak-sing number featuring Susan, which places her own playful brand of girlish naughtiness front and center. Nonetheless, considering the fact that both "Nasty Girl" and "He's So Dull" feature "Vanity's" vocals so prominently—although she does swap vocal duties with Susan and Brenda throughout the album—they were natural song selections to introduce the group to its primary audience: the enthusiastic consumers of Black soul, funk, and R&B. *Vanity 6*, the album, is also notable for its nod to the elements of electronic, dance, rock, and New Wave that sent Prince records like "1999" and "Little Red Corvette" to the top of the charts. The meticulously crafted allusions to these genres were added to the mix to increase Vanity 6's album's reach as Prince courted the bourgeoning MTV generation. However, the group owes a great debt to R&B predecessors and contemporaries such as the all-female band Klymaxx and the Mary Jane Girls.[13] While *Vanity 6* does incorporate the sound and style of these groups into their sonic repertoire, the album also dares to venture into uncharted musical territory on several tracks such as "Make-Up," "Bite the Beat," and "3 x 2 = 6." Arguably the funkiest and best-sounding "Prince protégée" project, *Vanity 6* (released August 11, 1982) was *1999*'s sonic counterpart (released later that year on October 27th) and the launching pad for Denise Matthews's career in music.

Vanity 6 is a forward-sounding project that suits Prince's own futuristic leanings on *1999*. If fans are often tempted to compare the group to Rick James's Mary Jane Girls, they are overlooking the steps that Prince took to differentiate his group's sound from the grooves being created by his funk rival. The album itself represents a very successful collaboration between Prince, the ladies of Vanity 6, and the Time, who worked together to lend the album its unique Minneapolis sound. The synth-heavy tracks on *Vanity 6* are sonically superior to the bass-laden songs on *Mary Jane Girls*. The sound is an ambiguous and sparse funk-rock tailor-made for the dance floor. "Nasty Girl" sets the tone for the album with its relentless drum-machine driven rhythmic workout. After a quick and thrilling guitar lick, the album introduces "Vanity," whose whispery staccato speak-singing drips with a type of sophisticated sensuality that is absent in Joanne "JoJo" McDuffie's long, languorous, and drawn-out vocals on the *Mary Jane Girls* track "All Night Long." "Nasty Girl" is brighter, more vibrant. Lyrically, the song does not so much serve as an unsatisfied woman's open invitation to a hot night of lovemaking, as it represents a liberated woman's challenge to a potential lover to meet her standards before the lovemaking can begin: "I'm lookin for a man to love me / Like I never been loved before / I'm lookin for a man that'll do it anywhere / Even on a limousine floor."

In this sense, certainly, *Vanity 6*'s lyrical content is far more progressive than that of *Mary Jane Girls*. The "Vanity" persona's mysterious nature is also more intriguing than the relatively straightforward recording-studio soul chanteuse that McDuffie offers on "All Night Long": "That's right, pleased to meet you / I still won't tell you my name / Don't you believe in mystery? / Don't you wanna play my game? . . ." Although "Vanity" does subject herself to the male gaze when she coyly inquires "Do you think I'm a nasty girl? . . ."

she is not defined by it. She is ". . . livin' in a fantasy" that springs from her own imagination; her ". . . own little nasty world." She stops the band when she doesn't like the groove and demands that they play something she can croon to. She will only accept "7 inches or more. . . ." She's assertive, dominant, and ultimately, unimpressed: "Is that it? / Mmm, wake me when you're done / I guess you'll be the only one having fun . . ." The song's final lyric, more than any other, implies that "Vanity" is not easily satisfied. She is the director of this particular sexual fantasy, and the male suitor must measure up and perform in order for it to be completely fulfilled.

The effectiveness and brilliance of "Vanity's" brief spoken reproach of the lover who is unable to maintain his stamina is due to Denise Matthews's immense flair for roleplay in the recording studio: ". . . Vanity? Nobody could talk like her," Prince noted in an interview with *Rolling Stone*'s Brian Hiatt while discussing the necessity of his collaboration with the ladies of Vanity 6 in bringing the project to life. Indeed, "Vanity's" gift for gab is an essential ingredient of several tracks on the album. In this regard, the second most notable song featuring her signature brand of speak-singing is side 2's "If a Girl Answers (Don't Hang Up)." Yet, Denise's ability to fully inhabit the character that Prince created for her is most remarkably displayed on "Nasty Girl." As he insinuates during Hiatt's revealing interview for *Rolling Stone*, although "Vanity" was primarily a product of Prince's imagination, he needed Denise's voice to breathe life into the character in the studio.

It is evident that Denise, the singer, is still developing her sound on tracks such as "Wet Dream" and "He's So Dull." and on this matter, fans who contend that the Mary Jane Girls' McDuffie is a stronger vocalist do offer a convincing argument. Denise takes a back seat to Susan on "Drive Me Wild," which is another example of the album's innovative utilization of speak-singing, synthesizers, whimsical sound effects, and the industrial Linn drum machine that would make Prince world-famous. "If a Girl Answers (Don't Hang Up)" is a comedic back and forth between Denise, Brenda, and Prince (playing a sharp-tongued girlfriend vying for the affections of a man named "Jimmy"). Interestingly, the track also highlights Brenda's talent for delivering a Sugar Hill Gang–inspired rap to settle the verbal sparring session between Denise and Prince. The return of the funk bass on this song also indicates the album's attempt to acknowledge the influence of Rick James's work with the Mary Jane Girls. "Make-Up," once again featuring Susan's speak-singing, sounds like it could belong on *1999* and certainly acts as a rapid leap forward from the nostalgic funk of "If a Girl Answers (Don't Hang Up)." The sonic twin of "He's So Dull," the rockabilly "Bite the Beat" places Brenda's sultry voice front and center, with Denise and Susan acting as backup vocalists.

The album's eighth and final track, the feminist anthem "3 x 2 = 6," serves as the project's final testament to Denise's attempts to develop her vocal chops. Like much of the album, the song seems to be designed for heavy rotation on both R&B and rock radio. Its sound is very similar to 1999's "Free." The track's allusion to Greta Garbo, a Hollywood Golden Age persona that influenced other eighties superstars such as Janet Jackson, in the lyrics, "When I'm older, I wanna be a movie star just like Greta Garbo / Then I could tell everybody what to do / Well, she was so cool, it was plain to see that she was in control / I bet she never played the part of anyone's fool . . . ," emphasizes both Prince's cinephilia and the "Vanity" persona's evocation of remarkable, strong-willed women from celebrated bygone eras. Madonna, who undoubtedly used *Vanity 6* as the blueprint for the construction of her own musical persona, would do the same later in 1984 when referencing Marilyn Monroe on the *Like a Virgin*'s opening track, "Material Girl."[14] Denise's last contribution to the album, and ultimately to the Prince camp, represents her continuing attempts to mold the "Vanity" character into something that suits her particular skill set. As her relationship with Prince began to crumble, Denise began contemplating how best to utilize the "Vanity" persona in the construction of her next solo project for Motown Records, which would offer her a long sought-after opportunity to branch out on her own, and to reclaim and revise the "Vanity" character according to her own terms.

"OOH, LOOK AT ME . . .": THE VIDEOS[15]

Nasty Girl

From left to right: Brenda, Denise, and Susan stand facing away from the camera in front of two black Doric columns and what appears to be frosted glass. The three ladies of Vanity 6 are fidgety, perhaps nervous, as they prepare to begin their choreography. Wearing blue, black, and red dresses that are classier than the typical Mary Jane Girls attire, but less conservative than the evening gowns often donned by the Supremes, their stilted poses signal that this is their first music video, a very early experiment in the genre that would eventually be transformed forever by Michael Jackson's "Thriller" short film. After a few counts, Denise emulates the performance technique often utilized by Diana Ross, Florence Ballard, and Mary Wilson: regimented, sequential motion coordinated by the lead singer. Much like Diana Ross,

Denise initiates the choreography, followed in turn by Susan (standing at rear right), and finally Brenda (standing at rear left).

Four more counts and then the ladies begin filing out of a black door, again in sequential order: Denise is the first to appear, followed by Brenda, and then Susan. The clumsiness of the editing is apparent; although Brenda initially leads the ladies through the door, by the time they emerge onto the primary performance space she is a few strides behind Denise. By now, the trio is a bit more confident, though clearly still not quite at ease with being in front of the camera. Denise's sultry gaze introduces "Vanity" for the first time. The character emerges fully formed from Denise's fervent facial expressions. She's not merely lip-synching; she's acting.

Drive Me Wild

Susan takes the lead in this video, which seems to be a visual metaphor for lost innocence (represented by the iconic teddy bear that Susan clutches while lying in bed, which appears and disappears during the opening sequence) and sexual fantasy—a cinematographic wet dream. This visual is another brilliant examination of the thin line that separates human consciousness from the dream world. Throughout the video, the viewer is challenged to identify what is real and what is merely a product of the imagination. Denise and Brenda materialize just moments after the video begins, appearing in a thick haze of studio mist, which is both a nod to Prince's aesthetic during this era and another symbol of the dream world. Slowly walking through Susan's bedroom door, entering the room in which she lies asleep, and hovering over her menacingly, the opening sequence also subtly touches on the nightmarish aspects of the dream state; invasion of personal space and violation of the body. Denise and Brenda force Susan out of bed and together the three vanish into the blinding white mist.

The trio enter a vintage vehicle (perhaps a Ford Thunderbird? Not sure which year), Denise first, followed by Susan (still wearing her peppermint-striped pajamas), and finally Brenda, who will sit on the driver's side and take the wheel. Just before she closes the door, she tosses the metaphorical Teddy on the black pavement, and then the three women take off. After a bit of driving through the thick white fog, Brenda suddenly stops the vehicle and the three ladies of Vanity 6 begin watching themselves perform the title track of the video in their stylized lingerie. As a whole, the video's visual quality, production, and editing—as well as the ladies' performances and the group's choreography—is superior to that displayed in the "Nasty Girl" visual. The three women seem much more comfortable being in front of the camera, which mostly lingers on Susan (who gives an outstanding performance) and Denise.

Midway through the video, the ladies are once again instantly transported to a fantastically surreal dance party. Prince's bodyguard Charles "Big Chick" Huntsberry makes a brief cameo, wearing a black T-shirt emblazoned with the checkered "Rude Boy" button that Prince wears on the cover of his 1981 album *Controversy* (Prince mastered the art of continuity and creating a shared universe long before Marvel Studios) and a bizarre fairy king costume. Revelers dance, skip, and generally make merry wearing masks (including one resembling former President Richard Nixon) and clown costumes (many of these visual references would later make up a large part of the *Purple Rain* film's aesthetic). There's even a belly dancer, a very early allusion to the art form that Mayte Garcia would contribute to Prince's ever-evolving oeuvre in the early and mid-nineties. Denise, Susan, and Brenda are once again wearing their dresses. While Susan dances with a gentleman dressed in quintessential New Wave attire, and Brenda fends off an overeager suitor, Denise dances with various revelers on the periphery of the camera's gaze.

As Susan lays her head on her beau's shoulder and closes her eyes, the scene once again shifts, providing a rapid review of the video's previous scenes, which also seems to represent the end of REM sleep and the gradual emergence of waking consciousness. Intriguingly, as this rapid visual sequence concludes and the camera once again gazes on Susan lying in her bed, the teddy bear that she seems to be holding in the beginning of the video has vanished. The last frames of the video invite the viewer to question whether she's lost her innocence (another allusion to the wet dream theme) or if she was ever truly innocent (was she really holding that teddy bear or was it just another element of the dream world?). An underrated classic, "Drive Me Wild" is a lasting testament of the brilliance of the Vanity 6 project.

He's So Dull

The climax of Vanity 6's experiment with the music video genre, "He's So Dull" is the most visually engaging of the three videos starring the group. Performing on a soundstage composed of enormous pink and purple squares, Denise, Susan, and Brenda dance along to the rockabilly track penned by original Revolution guitarist Dez Dickerson. While "Drive Me Wild" provided Susan with a chance at taking lead, in this visual, the camera is firmly fixed on Denise. Any traces of the performance anxiety that plagued the three women in the "Nasty Girl" video have long since vanished, and Denise particularly provides the camera with a brilliant performance that is tailor-made for an MTV audience. Her facial expressions, her seductive gaze, her attire (part dominatrix, part stage magician) are a perfect reflection of the "Vanity" character's essential qualities, which all emanate from an assertive and uncompromising female sexuality.

Her performance, of course, is also perfectly in sync with the track's lyrics, which express a woman's annoyance at the clumsy attempts of an awkward gentleman to win her affections. Near the end of the video, Brenda briefly steps out in front, which perhaps indicates another one of Prince's attempts to appeal to a mostly white MTV audience. However, this moment pales in comparison to what follows. In the final moments of the video, Denise cruelly toys with the milquetoast gentleman who serves as the subject of the track's lyrics. She grabs his stuff, tossing aside his science magazine, discarding his hat, plucking the glasses from his face, gives him a passionate kiss, and throws him down a stylized set of pink and purple stairs; humorously feigning shock as the actor tumbles to his doom. The last look that she gives the camera, as studio-produced wind wafts through her dark hair, can only be described as "sexy evil." The video's significance rests on the fact that it provides a final look at the Vanity 6 group in its short-lived prime; bathed in limelight and enjoying their newfound fame.

"7TH HEAVEN": REFLECTING ON THE SECOND ANNIVERSARY OF DENISE MATTHEWS' PASSING

"Innovator." "Groundbreaking." "Icon(oclast)." "Legend." "Genius." "Superstar." "Rest in peace." These words and phrases now seem to lack poignancy after the loss of so many loved and celebrated individuals. As writers rush to publish clever think pieces on the meaning of a person's life and career, and book-length analyses of their impact on popular culture, fashion, and our understanding of creativity, how often do we simply say "thank you?" Nothing more, nothing less. Thank you for stepping into the blinding limelight so that I could see someone like you succeed. Thank you for having the courage to bear the terrible, horrifying burden of celebrity so that the world could enjoy the fruits of your labor. Thank you for doing things that made you, and us, uncomfortable. Thank you for challenging us to look at you in order to look at ourselves. Thank you for suffering so that we could experience ecstasy. Thank you for sharing your pain; thank you for revealing your insecurities. Thank you for standing before the harsh gaze of fans and critics alike naked, bold, and beautiful; thank you for overcoming your shyness. Thank you for exorcising your demons; thank you for saying no, enough, for leaving the past behind when you felt it was time to move on and to grow. Thank you for coming to terms with the past in order to become a better human being. Thank you so much Denise Matthews. We wish u eternal bliss, peace, and rest in 7th Heaven.[16]

Notes

1. A Reuters article titled "Former Prince Protégé Ready for Her Solo Shot" comments on the various travails faced by former Prince protégé Támar, whose solo project was shelved after her brief tenure in Prince's camp during the *3121* era (2005–2006). Speaking on her effort to escape the music legend's shadow, Támar states, "I don't have anything negative to say, and I don't feel defeated . . . I'm pushing forward" (Reuters, "Former Prince Protégé Ready for Her Solo Shot," February 18, 2007, http://www.reuters.com/article/music-tamar-dc-idUSN1629467020070219).

2. Daniel Kreps, "Prince Pays Tribute to Vanity at Australia Concert," *Rolling Stone*, February 17, 2016, https://www.rollingstone.com/music/music-news/prince-pays-tribute-to-vanity-at-australia-concert-73997/.

3. Beyoncé and Mýa continue to reference Denise as a major influence on their artistry, and both have performed renditions of "Nasty Girl" while on tour.

4. Vanity 6, *Vanity 6*, Warner Bros. Records, 1982.

5. Madonna and Prince were labelmates at Warner Bros. Records at the time of *Like a Virgin*'s release in 1984.

6. Kory Grow, "Prince Collaborator Vanity Dead at 57," *Rolling Stone*. February 16, 2016, https://www.rollingstone.com/music/music-news/prince-collaborator-vanity-dead-at-57-224480/.

7. Marjon Carlos wrote a thoughtful, but far too brief, analysis of Denise's legacy in February 2016 for *Vogue* magazine that complements my argument concerning Denise's singular significance as an artist in her own right: "Prince has certainly amassed a number of muses over his lengthy career—Apollonia, Mayte, Sheila E.—all of whom left a singular impression as style and musical harbingers. But it was Vanity, née Denise Matthews, who passed away yesterday at 57, in whom he reportedly met his match." Marjon Carlos, "The memory of Prince Protégé Denise 'Vanity' Matthews Will Live On. *Vogue*, February 16, 2016, https://www.vogue.com/article/vanity-prince-last-dragon-rihanna-80s.

8. Denise Matthews, *Blame It on Vanity: Hollywood, Hell, & Heaven* (N.p.: Denise Matthews Pure Heart Ministry, 2004).

9. See note 13.

10. See Darold Zeb, "Vanity 6 (*Soul Train*) Nasty Girl," Daily Motion. https://www.dailymotion.com/video/x2zjn3i. Accessed April 13, 2024.

11. Cornelius makes this remark at 3:25 in the YouTube clip of the Vanity 6 *Soul Train* performance titled "Vanity 6- Nasty Girl (+Interview) (Soul Train 1982)."

12. See James Cameron, "He's so Dull," *YouTube*, April 25, 2013, https://www.youtube.com/watch?v=3c4hoImITAA.

13. Rick James adamantly claimed that Prince conceived his idea to create the group Vanity 6 after serving as the opening act on James's 1980 Fire It Up tour. Vanity 6 and the Mary Jane Girls embodied unbridled female sexuality and empowerment.

14. Ernest Hardy seems to support my argument. He writes, "Though the sexually empowered pop femmes of today are often deemed daughters of Madonna (and in most ways most are,) Vanity 6's eponymous debut album of unbridled, unapologetic female lust and sexual empowerment dropped a year before Madonna's debut, which was positively tame in comparison. And the trio rocked lingerie as stage-wear long before cone bras were a gleam in Madonna's (and Gaultier's) eyes." Ernest Hardy, "RIP: Denise 'Vanity' Matthews," *Crave*, 2016, http://www.craveonline.com/music/954825-denise-vanity -matthews-jan-4-1959-feb-15-2016#IOHHothyDXdt7L6y.99 (page removed).

15. These analyses of the Vanity 6 video projects are "close readings" of the visuals. This writer referred to YouTube to locate and examine the videos.

16. "7th Heaven" is the title of Denise's contribution (as "Vanity") to the soundtrack for the 1985 Motown Productions film *The Last Dragon*. The following reflection on the second anniversary of Denise Matthews's passing was originally written on February 15, 2017. The original title of this piece was "Thank You so Much . . ." and was derived from the lyrics of Prince's 1988 *Lovesexy* single "I Wish U Heaven." In part, the song's lyrics read: "For your every touch, I / Thank you so much . . ."

CONCLUSION

The authors in this volume have captured in bold relief Prince's vision, show-manship, and entrepreneurial spirit in a way that helps readers understand the depths of Prince's talent, work ethic, and creativity. Zada Johnson's take, for example, on the much maligned and box-office failure *Under the Cherry Moon* is courageous and unusually insightful, demonstrating an ability to contextualize this film in a way that allows her to unpack several important elements that others, to date, have not picked up on. Masculinity has been featured prominently in works written about Prince, be they popular magazine pieces or rigorous academic scholarship in refereed journals. The matter of masculinity has played out in his movies, performances, and music. Sherman White, Aaron J. Kimble, and Jerod Lockhart avoid the boilerplate angle of masculinity taken by others and instead choose to focus on the role of masculinity in the relationship between African American fathers and their sons in the United States. Using the movie *Purple Rain* as their lens, each man takes the reader on an autobiographical tour of their lives, taking special care to revisit certain memories and punctuate events that not only affected but defined their relationship with their fathers. Meanwhile Shannon Cochran shows how Prince and Sheila E.'s gender performativity can be used as an instructional pedagogical tool to enlighten and raise the consciousness of young college students.

While many works about Prince are nothing more than hagiographies, these writers do not hesitate to delve into, or dare I say challenge, some of Prince's personal preferences. "The Most Beautiful Girl in the World" affords Cassandra D. Chaney to do a deep dive into Prince's conception of beauty, which by the way parallels that of many Black men who, while they fashion themselves to be pro-Black, seem to prefer fair-skinned mates as opposed to darker-complexioned women. In many instances, Prince's women are not only not dark but are often not Black. Neither of the women Prince married were Black, nor were the women featured in his videos. The phrase "light, bright and damn near white" is appropriate here. This is not to say that Prince's taste in women left something to be desired, but his proclivity for exalting lighter-complexioned women over dark-complexioned women is not unrelated to a larger societal problem regarding race, both within the Black community and outside of it. At the same time however, Chaney argues that Prince challenged European beauty norms in a way that highlighted cross-cultural standards of beauty, and in turn affirms the race, age, and marital and parental status of women everywhere.

Tony Kiene, Laura Westrup, Paul Reinsch, and Samuel Fitzpatrick round out this book with extraordinary insights into Prince's highly successful Batman project and the genius of the three-woman group Vanity 6, featuring the seductive and alluring Denise Matthews, who had many men of a certain age salivating. Vanity 6 was just one of Prince's successful, if short-lived, successes whose imprint on American music and cultural is far-reaching. Then there is Kiene's analysis of the politico-sociological elements of both Prince's personal life and professional career from the time he hit the scene until he broke with Warner Bros.

About the Contributors

CASSANDRA D. CHANEY, PhD, is the J. Franklin Bayhi Endowed Professor in Human Development and Family Science, School of Social Work, College of Human Sciences and Education at Louisiana State University (LSU). Chaney is broadly interested in the experiences of African Americans in the United States. Under this umbrella, she examines the emotional closeness and intimacy narratives of African Americans in dating, cohabiting, and married relationships, with a particular interest in relationship formation, maintenance, and stability. She also explores how religiosity and spirituality support African Americans. Professor Chaney also examines the representation of African American couples and families (such as structural and functional dynamics) in popular forms of mass media (television shows, music videos, songs) as well as demonstrations of Black masculinity and femininity. She also examines Blacks' historical and contemporary relationship with law enforcement. Given the unique challenges of Black families, her research provides recommendations regarding how policy can better meet the needs of Black families who experience heightened rates of incarceration, unemployment, weakened family structures, and racism. Most important, her scholarship is rooted in a strengths-based perspective and is devoted to emphasizing the various ways that Black families remain resilient in the face of numerous challenges. Chaney has published one hundred manuscripts and book chapters and was coauthor with Ray V. Robertson of the book *Police Use of Excessive Force against African Americans: Historical Antecedents and Community Perceptions (Policing Perspectives and Challenges in the Twenty-First Century)* (2019). Chaney was a visiting professor at the University of Gondar (Gondar, Ethiopia) during 2019 and was appointed by LSU Interim President Tom Galligan to serve on Louisiana's Police Training and De-Escalation Task Force during 2020–2021. Chaney is currently writing a book on the narratives of African American couples in strong, stable, happy marriages.

SHANNON M. COCHRAN is professor in the Department of English and the Department of Interdisciplinary Studies, coordinator of the African American Studies and Women's and Gender Studies programs at Clayton State University, and coeditor (with Judson L. Jeffries and Molly Reinhoudt) of *Feel My Big Guitar: Prince and the Sound He Helped Create*, published by University Press of Mississippi. Included in her body of work on race, gender, and body politics is the intersectional examination of how representations in visual and narrative cultures impact the lived experiences of African American identities.

SAMUEL P. FITZPATRICK is the assistant professor of English in the School of Liberal Arts at Spalding University. He teaches courses covering American and African American literature, as well as composition, at the undergraduate level. Fitzpatrick specializes in "Post–Vietnam era" (post-1975) American and African American literature. Prior to Spalding, Fitzpatrick worked as a visiting assistant professor at the University of Iowa. Fitzpatrick holds a Doctor of Philosophy and a Master of Arts in English from the University of Iowa, and a Bachelor of Arts in English from the George Washington University.

JUDSON L. JEFFRIES, PhD, is professor of African American and African Studies at the Ohio State University. He is the founding editor-in-chief of *Spectrum: A Journal on Black Men*.

ZADA JOHNSON has a PhD in anthropology from the University of Chicago and is presently associate professor of Urban Community Studies at Northeastern Illinois University in Chicago. Johnson's research includes African diasporic performance traditions, urban culture, and popular culture. Her essays on the musical legacy of Prince have appeared in the *Journal of African American Studies*, the *Journal of Theology and Culture*, and *Theology and Prince*.

TONY KIENE holds a BA in African American Studies and sociology and an MA in American studies, both from Purdue University. He has spent the past twenty-six years in the Twin Cities entertainment and non-profit sectors, which includes time at Penumbra Theatre Company and the Minneapolis Urban League. Kiene currently pens two Prince-related columns—"Purple Music: Musings on the Minneapolis Sound," published in the *Minnesota Spokesman-Recorder*, and the PRN Alumni Foundation's "Alumni Spotlight: Stories from the Park." He is the coauthor of Pepé

Willie's memoir, *If You See Me: My Six-Decade Journey in Rock and Roll*, published in 2020 by Minnesota Historical Society Press.

AARON J. KIMBLE currently serves as a senior project manager for DeKalb County as well as a clinical therapy associate for both A Place for Me Counseling and WholeHeart Psychotherapy. Kimble serves as the chair for the Hotel/Motel, Multifamily and Tattoo Parlor Task Forces, where he uses this avenue to promote social justice through researching and writing policy for socioeconomic change. As a multifaceted clinician, Kimble focuses on assisting clients through holistic healing of the body, mind, and spirit. Kimble utilizes cognitive behavioral, psychodynamic, and emotionally focused therapies to assist individuals, couples, and families in achieving their mental health goals. Kimble specializes in treating clients with sexual and performance issues, grief, narcissism, LGBT+, and social justice concerns. Kimble earned a Bachelor of Arts in psychology from LSU, an MBA in Management from AIU-Atlanta, a PhD in Organizational Leadership from the Chicago School of Professional Psychology, and a Master of Arts in Counseling Therapy from Northwestern University. Kimble believes strongly in the personal mantra of working hard and playing hard.

JEROD LOCKHART is a 2017 graduate of the Chicago School of Professional Psychology with a PhD in organizational leadership. He has an MA in industrial/organizational psychology from Roosevelt University and a BS in psychology from Bradley University. The majority of his career involved being a staunch advocate for the over 600,000 Chicagoans with disabilities who live, visit, and work in Chicago. This role has allowed him to instruct over 20,000 municipal, social service, and private entities in Disability Awareness and Etiquette training. His current function is on accessibility leadership training and employee resource group development for the City of Chicago. In addition, his research interest involves employee reactions to voluntary self-identification forms for disability accommodation.

MOLLY REINHOUDT, PhD, is managing editor of *Research in African Literatures* and *Spectrum: A Journal on Black Men* in the Department of African American and African Studies at the Ohio State University.

PAUL N. REINSCH holds a PhD in critical studies from the School of Cinematic Arts at the University of Southern California. He is currently associate professor of practice in Screen/Stage Studies at Texas Tech University in the School of Theatre and Dance. He is coeditor of *The Soundtrack*

Album: Listening to Media and coeditor of *Python beyond Python: Critical Engagements with Culture*. Reinsch vividly remembers the first time he saw the "Little Red Corvette" video on MTV.

LAUREL WESTRUP received her PhD in cinema and media studies from UCLA, where she is now a continuing lecturer with Writing Programs and the Honors Program. She is coeditor with fellow Prince fan Paul N. Reinsch of *The Soundtrack Album: Listening to Media* and coeditor with David Laderman of *Sampling Media*. Her work on the intersections of popular music and media has also appeared in several journals and numerous collections.

SHERMAN M. WHITE has a PhD in organizational leadership from the Chicago School of Professional Psychology. His professional experience has been equally spent in leadership and management roles in the private sector and academia. His research interests focus on examining marginalized populations, specifically, the African American father-son relationship, race and gender in the workplace, cultural mistrusts, leadership, and class and work identity.

INDEX

www.ingramcontent.com/pod-product-compliance
Lightning Source LLC
Chambersburg PA
CBHW020354270326
41926CB00007B/433